Paola Antonelli
Anna Burckhardt
Paul Galloway

Never Alone

Video Games as Interactive Design

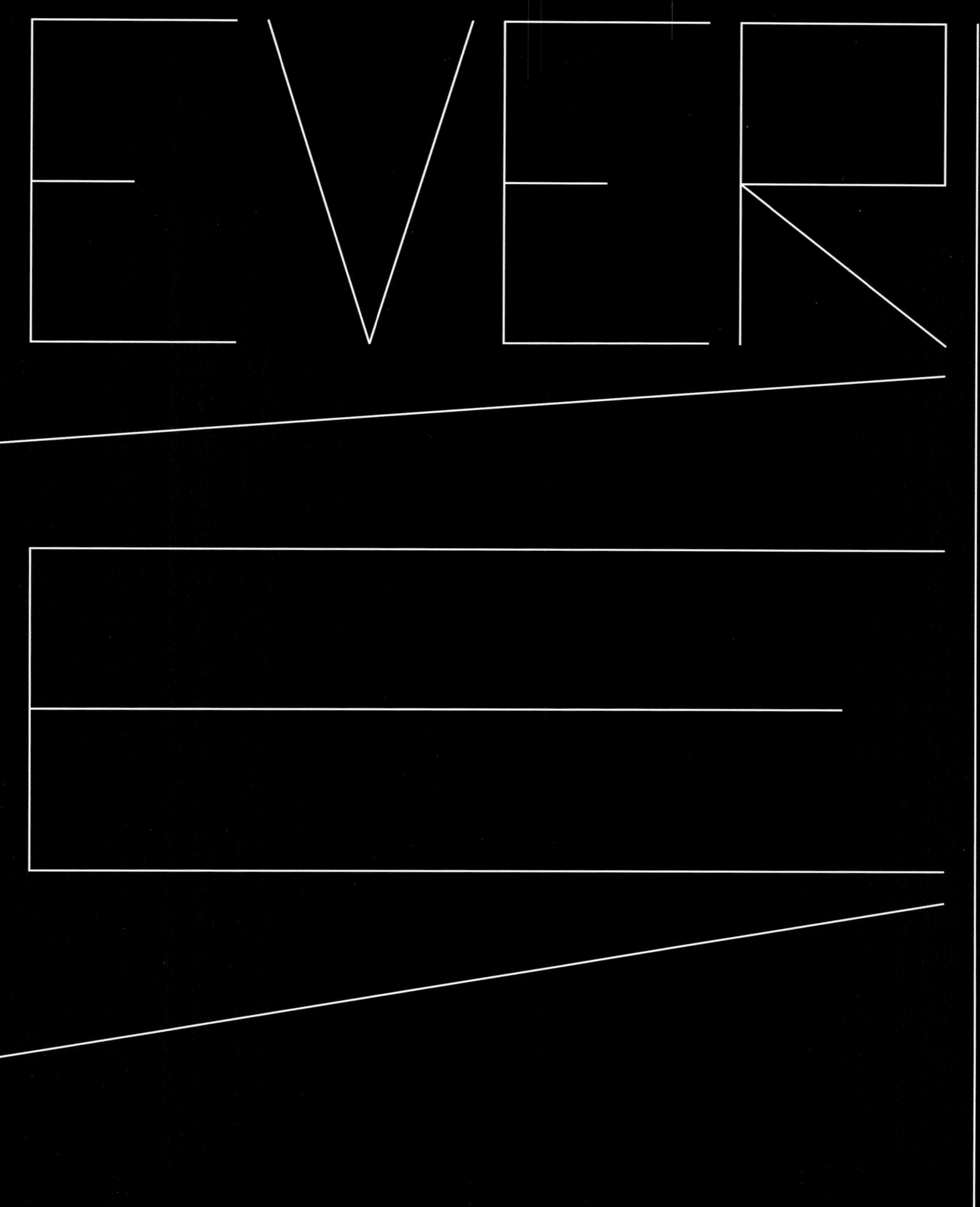

The Museum of Modern Art, New York

Allianz ⑪

Allianz is proud to sponsor *Never Alone: Video Games and Other Interactive Design* at The Museum of Modern Art. Our lives are increasingly mediated by electronic interfaces as we navigate, learn, and connect, and *Never Alone* brings MoMA's characteristic insight to a new dimension of this experience: video games, apps, and the devices through which we engage with them. As a study of the relationships among game designers, players, and machines, this exhibition provides a perceptive analysis of digital space and of human behavior within it. Fueled by a recent acquisition of fourteen video games, which complement the Museum's existing holdings and bring the total number in the collection to thirty-six games from 1972 to 2018, *Never Alone* positions video games as groundbreaking examples of interactive design.

Since 2016, Allianz has partnered with The Museum of Modern Art to make possible a series of Design and Innovation programs. Through the celebration of the work of visionary architects and the examination of design through new lenses, Allianz is committed to supporting a better, more sustainable, and more inclusive tomorrow. Our engagement with the art of today reflects this belief, and we are honored to support the work of architects, designers, and visionary thinkers who are pushing the boundaries of modern art.

About Allianz
The Allianz Group is one of the world's leading insurers and asset managers with more than 100 million retail and corporate customers in more than 70 countries. Allianz customers benefit from a broad range of personal and corporate insurance services, ranging from property, life, and health insurance to assistance services to credit insurance and global business insurance. Allianz is one of the world's largest investors, managing around 766 billion euros on behalf of its insurance customers. Furthermore, our asset managers PIMCO and Allianz Global Investors manage 1.7 trillion euros of third-party assets. Thanks to our systematic integration of ecological and social criteria in our business processes and investment decisions, we hold the leading position for insurers in the Dow Jones Sustainability Index.

ユニクロ UNIQLO

Since 2013, in pursuit of the idea of "Art For All," UNIQLO and MoMA have worked together to share art and design with the world through free-admission programs and exciting digital content. In the spirit of this partnership, UNIQLO is proud to support *Never Alone: Video Games and Other Interactive Design*.

As part of The Museum of Modern Art's collection, video games—including Tetris, Pac-Man, Katamari Damacy, and The Sims—are being recognized as transformative works of interactive design. A dedication to making good design accessible has been part of UNIQLO's DNA since its founding, and it is a privilege to join The Museum of Modern Art in presenting these groundbreaking expressions of contemporary design.

About UNIQLO and Fast Retailing
UNIQLO is a brand of Fast Retailing Co., Ltd., a Japanese retail holding company with global headquarters in Tokyo. Fast Retailing is one of the world's largest apparel retailers, and UNIQLO is Japan's leading specialty retailer.

UNIQLO continues to open large-scale stores in some of the world's most important cities and locations, as part of its ongoing efforts to solidify its status as a global brand. Today the company has more than 2,300 stores in 25 markets including Japan, North America, Europe, and Asia Pacific. In addition, UNIQLO established a social business in Bangladesh together with Grameen Bank in 2010, and today there are more than 15 Grameen-UNIQLO stores, mostly located in Dhaka.

Fast Retailing is committed to changing fashion, changing conventional wisdom, and changing the world. It is dedicated to creating new, unique clothing that enriches the lives of people everywhere.

Contents

8 **Foreword**
Glenn D. Lowry

12 **Never Alone**
Paola Antonelli
Anna Burckhardt
Paul Galloway

1
32 **The Input**
Paul Galloway

36 Magnavox Odyssey
38 Pong
40 Space Invaders
42 Asteroids
44 Pac-Man
46 NetHack
48 Tetris
50 Snake
52 Katamari Damacy
54 Canabalt
56 Monument Valley

2
60 **The Designer**
Anna Burckhardt

64 Tempest
66 Yars' Revenge
68 Another World
70 Myst
72 Portal
74 Dwarf Fortress
76 Passage
78 flOw
80 Flower
82 Journey
84 Papers, Please
86 Never Alone
88 This War of Mine
90 Inside
92 Everything Is Going to Be OK
96 Getting Over It with Bennett Foddy
98 Return of the Obra Dinn

3
102 **The Player**
Paul Galloway

106 Street Fighter II
110 SimCity 2000
114 The Sims
116 Vib-Ribbon
118 Eve Online
120 Minecraft
122 Biophilia
126 The Stanley Parable

130 Glossary
134 Index
136 Acknowledgments

144 Trustees of
The Museum of
Modern Art

Great video games embody the best of contemporary culture: visual daring, technological innovation, and social relevance; moreover, at their core, they are paragons of collaborative spirit. The discussion, often heated, about whether these games are art is characterized by the same tension that has accompanied the arrival of new forms of expression throughout art's history. The important question, however, is not whether we consider games to be art—or design—but how we will continue to evaluate and debate what we value as a society. As a laboratory for dialogue between the established and the experimental, the past and the present, The Museum of Modern Art has a long history of fostering exactly this kind of debate. The exhibition *Never Alone: Video Games and Other Interactive Design* examines the thirty-six video games in MoMA's collection as objects that encourage us to reconsider the imperatives of creativity in the world today. And to come to the conclusion that yes—video games belong in art museums.

The fields of design and architecture have been central to the story of modernism. At MoMA, since its founding more than ninety years ago, they have been presented as catalysts for new ways of thinking, from *Machine Art*, in 1934, which displayed industrial objects on pedestals to be admired for their formal qualities, to *Items: Is Fashion Modern?*, in 2017–18, which posited that what we put on our bodies both depends on and creates the cultural and social environments through which we move. Video games are compelling examples of design bringing together diverse disciplines—programming, illustration, economics, music, science, and drama, among others—to structure wholly new experiences.

The exhibition title was inspired by Never Alone (Kisima Inŋitchuŋa), an elegant game that follows Nuna, a young Iñupiaq girl, on her search for the source of an environmental calamity. The game brings her tribe's heritage and relationship with nature to the fore, suggesting design's potential to actively engage with some of the myriad problems in our increasingly unstable and unpredictable world. Late in 2019, few of us expected to spend the next year staring at a grid of our coworkers' faces on a computer screen—or the incalculable loss that would follow. But new forms of connection emerged from the months of the pandemic, in part through the ways in which interaction designers mediate the relationship between human and machine. The products of interaction design, whether Zoom video calls or Fortnite battles royal, served as social adhesive when so much threatened to pull us apart. Never Alone's lessons of wisdom and community demonstrate that even in the darkest of times we can find one another.

Organized by Paola Antonelli, joined by Paul Galloway and Anna Burckhardt, in MoMA's Department of Architecture and Design, this publication explores interactive design through the video games in the collection, while the exhibition broadened the view to include hardware, websites, and other interfaces. I am grateful to the organizers and to their many colleagues throughout MoMA who brought this ambitious effort to fruition in the midst of the challenges imposed by the Covid-19 pandemic. And on behalf of the staff and Trustees of the Museum, I would also like to thank Allianz, UNIQLO, and the Annual Exhibition Fund for their generous support of the exhibition.

Glenn D. Lowry
The David Rockefeller Director
The Museum of Modern Art, New York

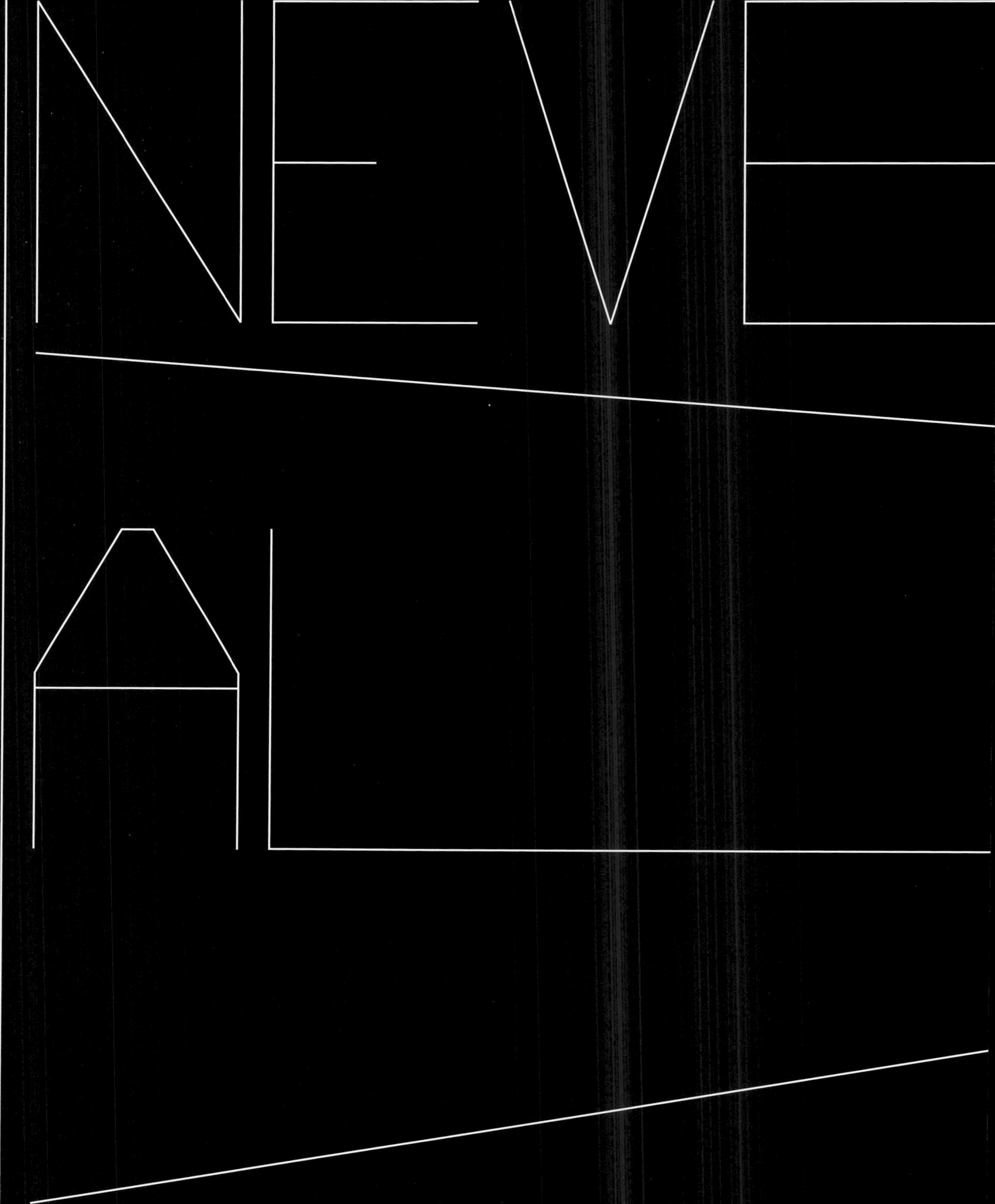

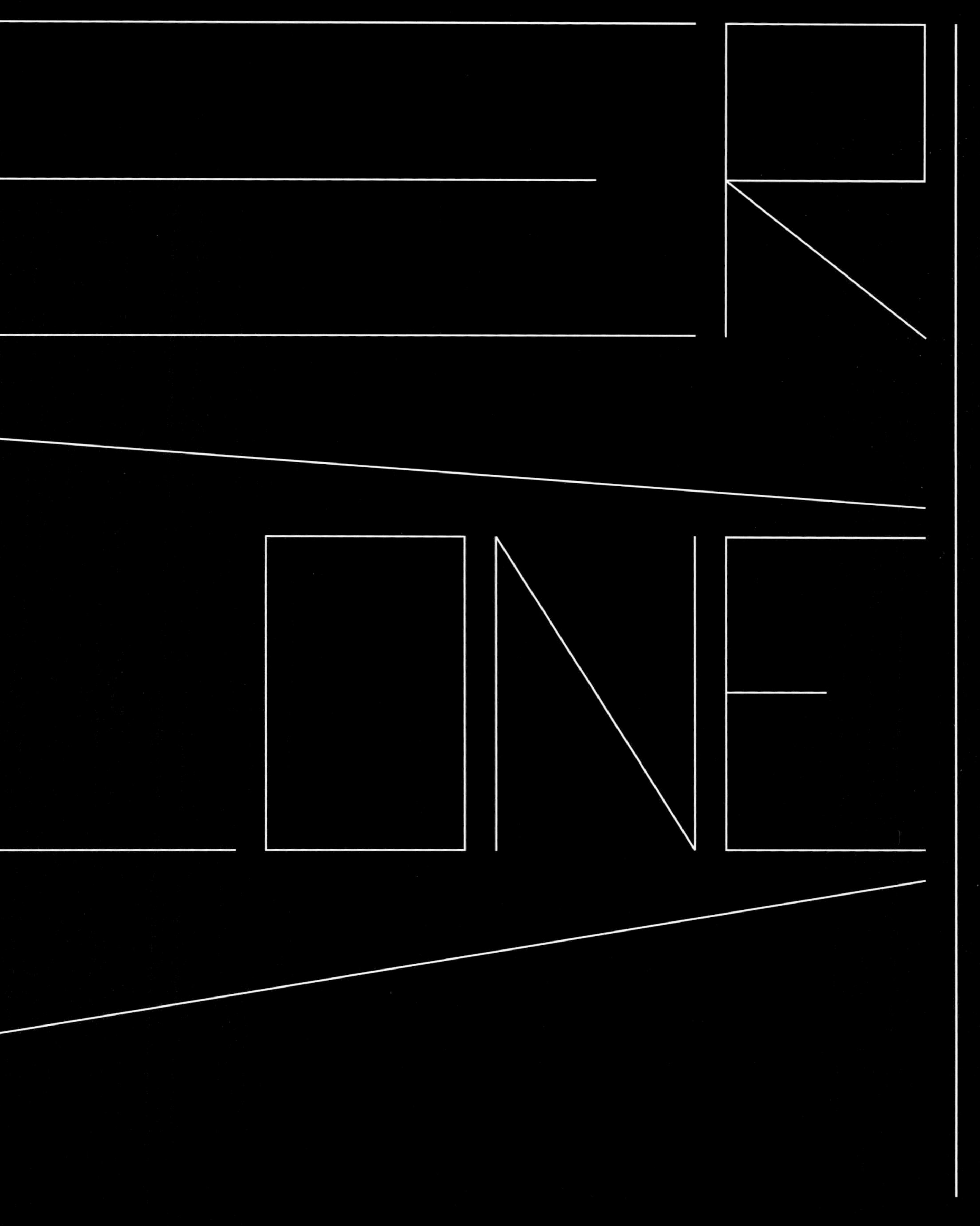

"I'm here live. I'm not a cat."

On February 9, 2021, during a livestream of the proceedings of Texas's 394th Judicial District Court, held over the video-call platform Zoom due to the Covid-19 pandemic, the attorney Rod Ponton found it necessary to clarify this matter as he struggled to disable a filter that had replaced his face with that of a kitten (fig. 1).[1] After a year of terrifying death totals and continuous societal disruption, this moment of levity struck a chord among the hundreds of millions of people around the world who had become accustomed to similar disruptions in group video calls: cameras left on by mistake, children barging into business meetings, and coworkers constantly having to call out "You're on mute." The YouTube video of this interface hiccup was widely shared over social media and in hundreds of memes, but its impact suggested something larger not only about the nature of the contemporary self (about where a person ends and an avatar begins) but also about the nature of social interaction in our time. Over the two years of on-and-off lockdown and isolation, many of us became keenly aware of how difficult it is to seamlessly exist with others, and how the friction that results from the imperfect tools we use to do so is as revealing as the benefits.

This is the territory of interactive design, which over the past forty years has become the primary facilitator of the dialogue between humans and devices, and, consequently, between humans as well. The focus on interaction itself is not new; designers have been thinking about the ways we relate to objects—how we use them, respond to them, cherish them—since the invention of the first tool millions of years ago. Today, the interfaces through which we communicate with computers, smartphones, and applications give us access to the networks and systems that drive contemporary transactions; successful interactive design translates and simplifies them so we are able to manage our lives without extensive technical training. Jon Kolko, in 2011, defined interactive design as "the creation of a dialogue between a person and a product, system, or service. This dialogue is both physical and emotional in nature and is manifested in the interplay between form, function, and technology as experienced over time."[2] Interactive design is not just for paying bills online and tracking shipments; video games, one of the most vital categories of interactive design, concerns itself with play—an act that billions of people engage in every day and that has become a dimension of interaction in its own right. In 2012, The Museum of Modern Art acknowledged the importance of this form of contemporary creativity

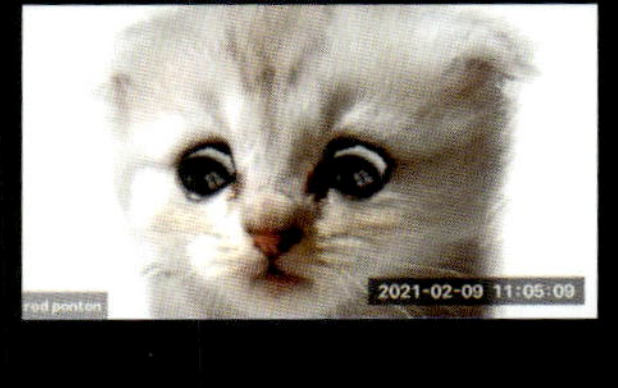

Fig. 1. "Kitten Zoom Filter Mishap," from a livestream of Texas's 394th Judicial District Court, February 9, 2021

1. "Kitten Zoom Filter Mishap," 394th District Court of Texas, livestreamed February 9, 2021, youtube.com/watch?v=KxIPG Pupdd8&t=1s. See also Daniel Victor, "'I'm Not a Cat,' Says Lawyer Having Zoom Difficulties," *New York Times*, February 9, 2021.

2. Jon Kolko, *Thoughts on Interaction Design* (Burlington, MA: Morgan Kaufmann, Burlington 2011), 15.

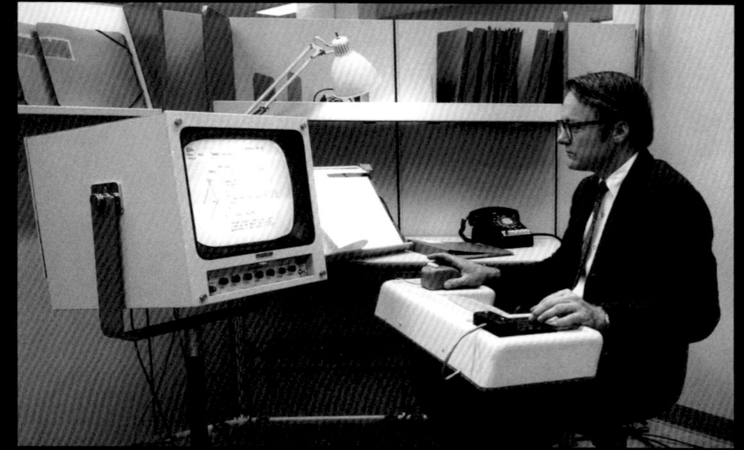

Fig. 2. Douglas Engelbart's mouse prototype demonstrated by the engineer Bill English, December 9, 1968

and production with the acquisition of fifteen video games (a number that has since grown to thirty-six).

The sophisticated exchanges and relations built into video games find us far from the early days of digital interaction, when only engineers and technicians with specific training were able to communicate with computers, through either code typed directly into them or aids such as tapes and punched cards. Interactive design evolved to make these powerful tools easier to use. Consider the mouse: in 1964, Douglas Engelbart, an engineer at the Stanford Research Institute, designed the prototype for a device, the size and shape of a bar of soap, that would "select objects on the screen, to tell the computer that you wanted to do something with them" (fig. 2).[3] The mouse required nothing more than basic hand-eye coordination to make computers more comfortable to operate, and its fundamental selection dynamic, the acts of pointing and clicking, continues to influence the design of digital interfaces to this day.

Even with a mouse, however, long columns of programming code remained impenetrable to anyone not trained to read and write it. As personal computers became more widely available in the 1980s, the need for more legible interfaces gave rise to revolutionary solutions. In 1981, for the Xerox Star computer, the scientists Alan Kay, Larry Tesler, and Dan Ingalls developed the first graphic user interface, or GUI, in which icons with real-life equivalents, such as documents, file folders, and a trash can, showed users how to organize physical office tasks within digital spaces. For the GUIs of Apple's Lisa (1983) and Macintosh (1984), which reprised the template set by Xerox, Jef Raskin and Steve Jobs hired the artist Susan Kare to illustrate these icons, and the results

3. Douglas C. Engelbart, interview by Bill Moggridge in Moggridge, *Designing Interactions* (Cambridge, MA: MIT Press 2006), 17.

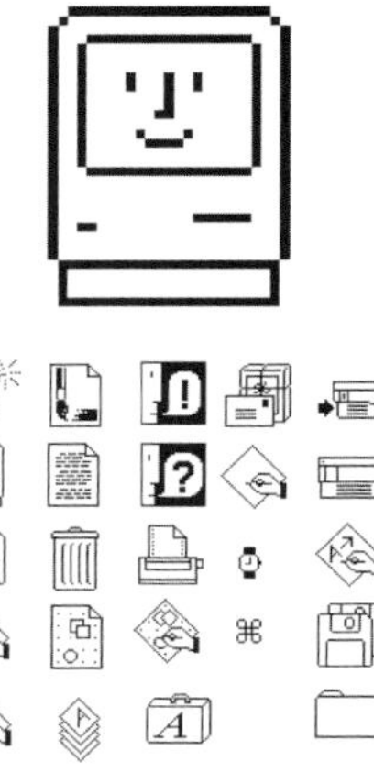

Fig. 3. Susan Kare. Icons for
Mac System 1. 1984

4. Gillian Crampton Smith,
"What Is Interactive Design?,"
foreword to Moggridge,
Designing Interactions, xiv.

5. Each book and its accompanying software focuses
on a different aspect of the
computer as a visual medium.
The Reactive Square (1994),
for example, translates sound
into motion graphics, with
ten squares that respond to
commands spoken into the
microphone, and in Flying
Letters (1995), the mouse activates a series of interactive
typographies.

are some of the most familiar pixel-based figures in the history of personal computing: the little smiling Mac, the maddening wristwatch, and the ominous lit cherry bomb, among others (fig. 3). And in 1993, Marc Andreessen led a team of programmers at the National Center for Supercomputing Applications (NCSA), at the University of Illinois Urbana–Champaign, to develop the graphical web browser Mosaic, which, by adding images, hyperlinks, and windows to text-only pages, opened the World Wide Web to people all over the world.

We need more than well-designed objects and interfaces to negotiate complex digital and computational systems, however. Interactive design also concerns itself with our behaviors in response to these systems, and with the shaping of stimuli to elicit specific responses. Many behaviors in the digital realm began as metaphors of physical life—such as the formal salutations of written correspondence adapted in email greetings—and then evolved into singular digital ones, such as the casual brevity of text messaging. Interactive design can be as spatial and nuanced as architecture, and as instinctively readable: "A chapel speaks a different architectural language than a supermarket," the interactive-design pioneer Gillian Crampton Smith wrote, "and everybody can read the difference."[4] The interfaces of TikTok and Tinder are easily distinguished from that of an ICU heart monitor, and just as carefully designed. Both the spending habits and impulsive responses of supermarket shoppers are influenced by more than the layout of products in aisles and on shelves and the packaging of those items: their actions are also shaped by the interface through which they pay—a human cashier; a self-service scan-and-bag station; or a system, such as the one introduced in 2018 for the Amazon Go convenience stores, that uses machine learning, sensors, and artificial intelligence to track the items customers put in their baskets and then automatically charge them as they leave.

Interfaces have become so integrated into our lives that they have also become the basis of marketing wars, such as the epic competition between Apple and Google—and their ecosystems of communication, information management, and entertainment—for our loyalty and our dollars. In these and other highly successful digital ecologies, the ubiquity of the platforms and the ease of using them belies an extraordinary amount of ongoing work behind the scenes. They are not finite objects but complex entities, and their design requires an architectural and choreographic approach, an aesthetic sense, a firm grasp of cognitive science, and a feeling for narrative.

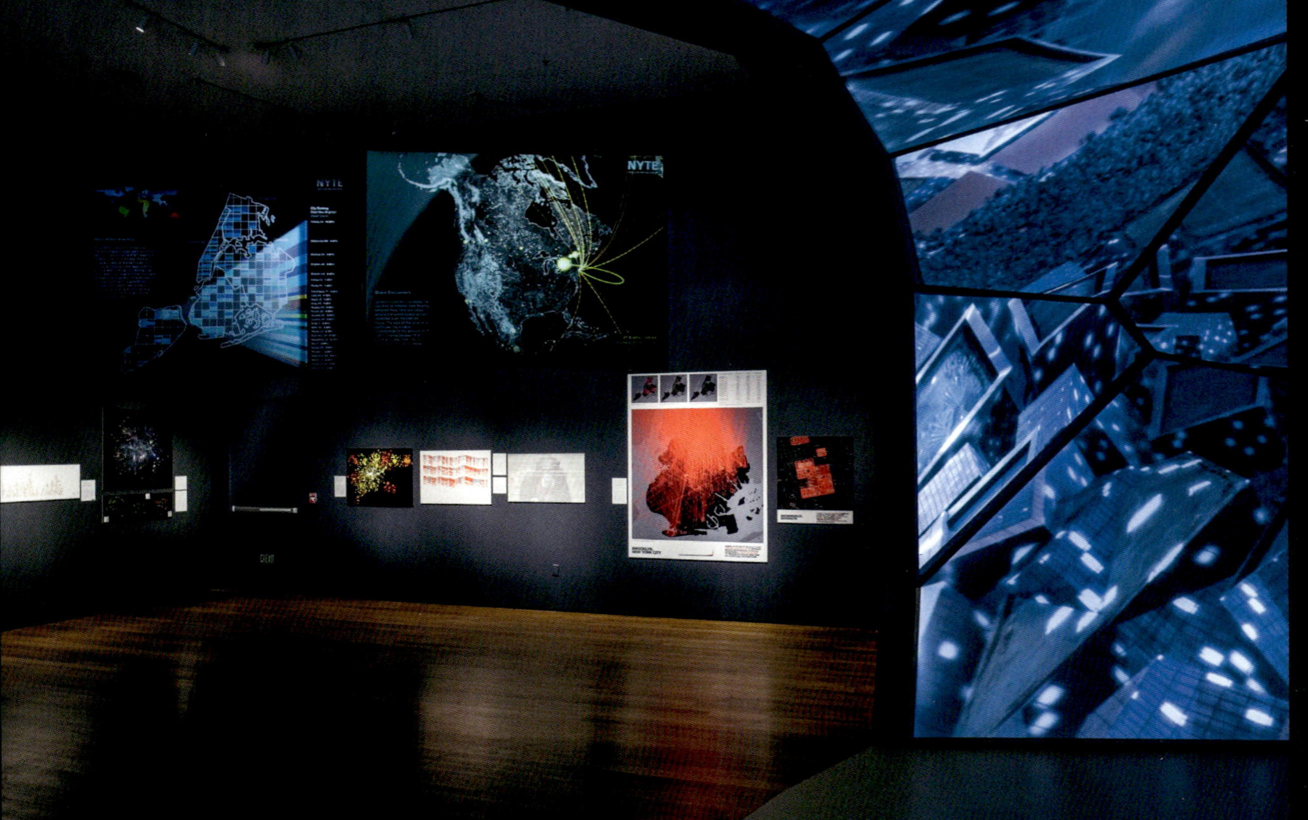

Fig. 4. *Design and the Elastic Mind*, The Museum of Modern Art, New York, February 24–May 12, 2008. Installation view

Interactive Design at The Museum of Modern Art

The Museum of Modern Art's first acquisition in interactive design, in 2006, was John Maeda's Reactive Books (1994–2006): five printed volumes, each with a CD-ROM of digital components.[5] The pace of acquisition since then has been slow and deliberate: these new types of artifacts present considerable challenges to traditional museum systems and protocols. Over the last sixteen years, however, the criteria and goals for the collection have been fine-tuned, in particular through the exhibitions *Design and the Elastic Mind*, in 2008 (fig. 4), and *Talk to Me: Design and the Communication between People and Objects*, in 2011,[6] and the collection has grown to include interfaces, apps, visualizations, icons, hardware, and video games.[7]

6. *Design and the Elastic Mind* (February 24–May 12, 2008) focused on the relationship between design and science, and *Talk to Me* (July 24–November 7, 2011) on the interaction between humans and objects.

7. On February 21, 2006, at the Symposium on the Future Development of MoMA's Graphic Design Collection, Paola Antonelli discussed the future of MoMA's visual-design collection with a team of experts in their fields: the graphic designers Tarek Atrissi, Michael Bierut, Matthew Carter, and Khoi Vinh; the new-media designer Hillman Curtis; the digital-media producer and designer Peter Girardi; the design writers Emily King and Rick Poynor; and the creative director Mikon van Gastel. The event produced, among other recommendations, new categories and checklists of possible works for acquisition.

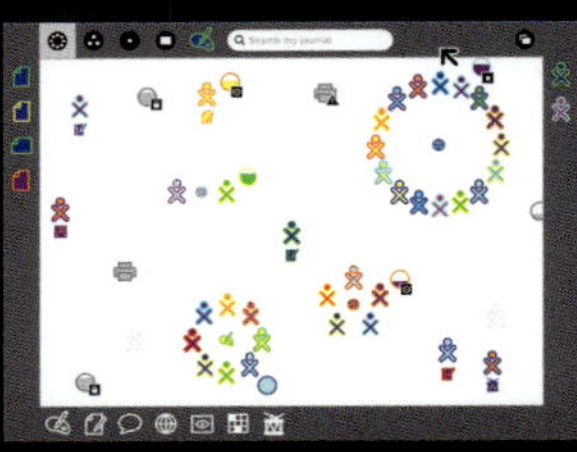

Fig. 5. Pentagram, Lisa Strausfeld, Christian Marc Schmidt, Takaaki Okada, Walter Bender, Eben Eliason, One Laptop per Child, Marco Pesenti Gritti, Christopher Blizzard, and Red Hat, Inc. Sugar interface for the XO Laptop. 2006–07. The Museum of Modern Art, New York. Gift of the designers

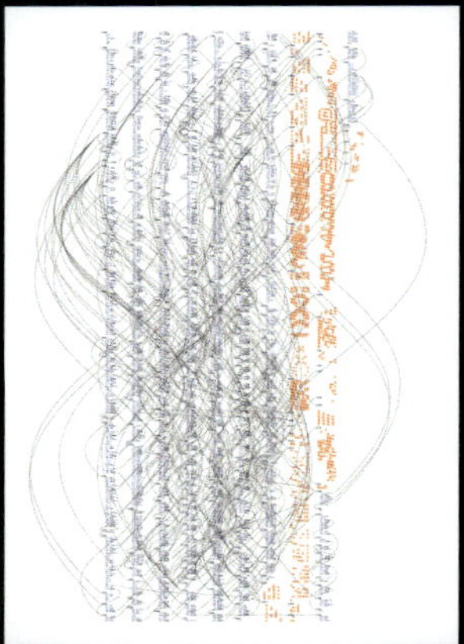

Fig. 6. Ben Fry. Distellamap (Pac-Man). 2004. The Museum of Modern Art, New York. Gift of the designer

Among the singular examples of interface design in MoMA's collection is Sugar (fig. 5), which was created for One Laptop per Child, an ambitious plan, launched in 2005, to produce and deliver inexpensive laptops to schools in the Global South. The interface privileged community and ease of use, with a feature that used bright, clear icons to show children the proximity of their friends at various school activities. The XO laptop (the OLPC hardware for which Sugar was created) was also designed with children in mind; it was lightweight, no bigger than a textbook, and had a handle for carrying. Developed on an open-source, Linux-based operating system and focused on sharing and collaboration, Sugar was an early example of the participatory ethos of Web 2.0, but the market is not always a meritocracy: the innovative, too-ahead-of-its-time interface—along with technical, geopolitical, and a host of other issues—contributed to the demise of the OLPC plan.[8]

Good visualization design renders the datasets of complex interactions as legible, comprehendible graphics, sometimes in familiar formats such as maps, pie charts, or graphs, and sometimes in entirely original forms. In Distellamap (Pac-Man), Ben Fry translated the code and data in a Pac-Man Atari 2600 cartridge into columns linked by slender curves, highlighting the commands within the game's mathematical construction that direct programming jumps from one location to another (fig. 6).[9] Rather than analyzing the code behind one of the most well-known video games of all time, Distellamap celebrates its fluidity with an equally elegant digital portrait.

Some interactive-design objects forced us to turn our idea of ownership inside out. As MoMA expanded its collecting practices to acquire living objects made of code, the curators discarded the assumption that any form of physical possession was necessary. In 2010, for example, we acquired the @ sign (fig. 7). As a symbol available in the public domain

8. Development specialists and journalists as well as the general public have criticized the One Laptop Per Child program for failing to consider the real needs and conditions of the countries it was targeting. In 2005 Marthe Dansokho, a Cameroonian woman, pointed out that "African women who do most of the work in the countryside don't have time to sit with their children and research what crops they should be planting. We know our land and wisdom is passed down through the generations. What is needed is clean water and real schools." Sylvia Smith, "The $100 Laptop: Is It a Wind-Up?," CNN online, December 1, 2005, edition.cnn.com/2005/WORLD/africa/12/01/laptop/. For a compendium of the problems that plagued the program, see Adi Robinson, "OLPC's $100 Laptop Was Going to Change the World—Then It All Went Wrong," The Verge online, April 16, 2018.

9. The Distellamap series is based on "columns of assembly language, most of it either math or conditional statements (if x is true, go to y). Each time there is a 'go to' instruction, a curve is drawn from that point to its destination. When a byte of data (as opposed to code) is found in the cartridge, it is shown as an orange row: a solid block for a '1' or a dot for a '0.'" Ben Fry, "Distellamap," 2004, benfry.com/distellamap/.

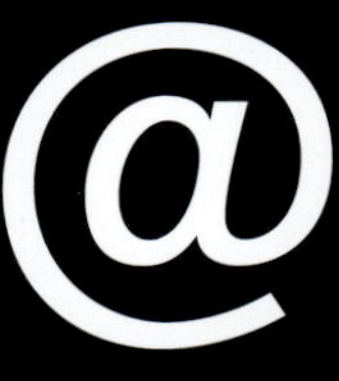

Fig. 7. Ray Tomlinson. @. 1971. The Museum of Modern Art, New York

Fig. 8. Shigetaka Kurita. Emoji. 1998–99. The Museum of Modern Art, New York. Gift of NTT DOCOMO, Inc.

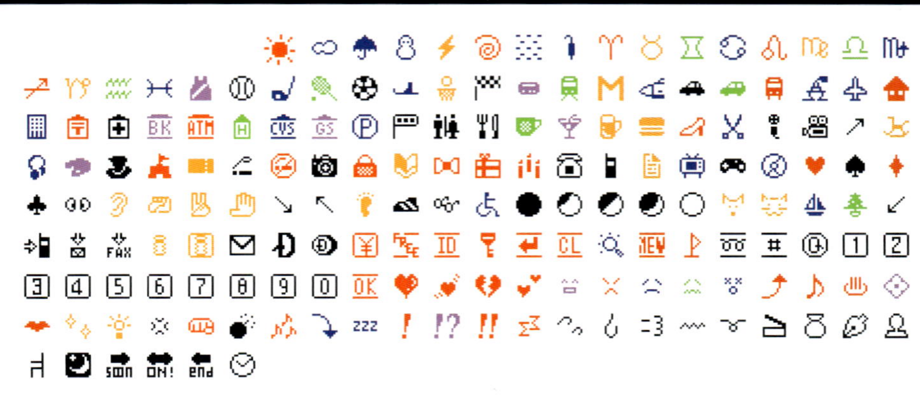

and on every keyboard and touchscreen, it cannot be owned, and its acquisition is essentially symbolic. By anointing it as part of our collection, however, we highlight its tremendous power as an act of design: as an interface-in-a-symbol, possibly more than a millennium old, the @ sign is the kernel of human-to-machine (and human-to-machine-to-human) communication.[10]

The Google Maps Pin, designed by Jens Eilstrup Rasmussen, is another powerful interactive icon, one that has introduced new connections and behaviors in a concise, evocative manner. Its upside-down teardrop shape, based on an old-fashioned object, has become a ubiquitous symbol for a corporeal location mapped in the digital world, a fitting illustration of the way in which our relationship to the physical world has changed since the advent of smartphones. And Shigetaka Kurita's set of 176 emoji (fig. 8), acquired by MoMA in 2016, is another staple of contemporary communication: these pioneering translingual symbols form the design basis for the more than 3,600 such icons in use today.[11]

10. One theory of the origin of the @ symbol is that it was used in medieval manuscripts as a ligature, fusing the two letters of the Latin preposition *ad* ("at," "to," or "toward") into a single stroke of the pen. It was used as an accounting abbreviation by merchants all over the Western world through the centuries; it appeared on the keyboard of the American Underwood typewriter in 1885 as the "commercial 'a,'" as an abbreviation of the word "at"

or as a stand-in for the phrase "at the rate of" in commercial invoices. It appeared on the original list of ASCII (American Standard Code for Information Interchange) characters in 1963, and in 1971 the electrical engineer Ray Tomlinson, looking for an underused key on his keyboard, chose @ for the world's first email address. See William F. Allman, "The Accidental History of the @ Symbol," *Smithsonian Magazine* online, September 2012.

11. Emoji (*e* meaning "picture" and *moji* meaning "character") were integral to the rise of text messaging in the early 2000s and have come to play a large role in electronic communication. NTT DOCOMO released Kurita's original emoji for its cell phones in 1999.

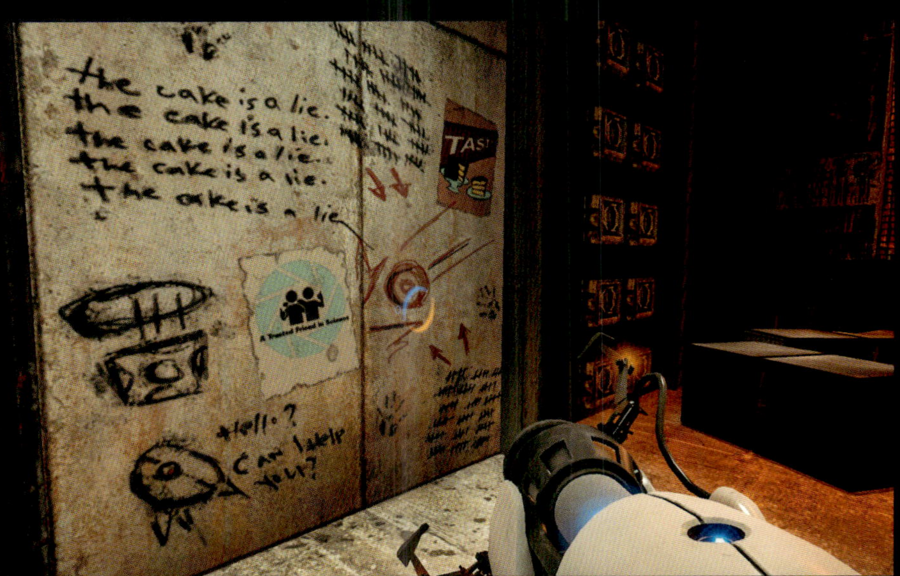

Fig. 9. Portal. 2005–07 (page 72)

Video Games as Interactive Design

Play is the guiding principle of video-game design. And while the inter-faces of smartphones and vending machines are governed by mundane considerations such as usability, consistency, and immediacy, the goals for video-game interfaces are reset and redefined from game to game. Like other forms of interactive design—including analog board games—video games usually have a predetermined set of rules, but the best games allow for chance, and for a player's autonomy.[12] A game like Portal (fig. 9 and page 72), for example, is programmed to obey laws of physics such as the conservation of mass, energy, and momentum, but players are given tools that allow them to violate those laws—either in ways the designers have anticipated or in ways they have not. The classic game model laid out by the theorist Jesper Juul balances the strictures of successful game interfaces with the flexibility required for play: "1) a rule-based formal system; 2) with variable and quantifiable outcomes; 3) where different outcomes are assigned different values; 4) where the player exerts effort in order to influence the outcome; 5) the player feels emotionally attached to the outcome; 6) and the conse-quences of the activity are optional and negotiable."[13] For Juul, these six features, although not constituting an exhaustive list, must be present for something to be a compelling game.

12. The rules define the game, and definitions of what consti-tutes a game and its features have varied throughout history. The cultural theorist Roger Caillois sorted games (and play) into four categories: agôn (com-petition), alea (chance), mimicry (simulation or make-believe), and ilinx (vertigo). Caillois, *Man, Play, and Games*, trans. Meyer Barash, reprint ed. (Paris: Gallimard, 1958; Urbana: University of Illinois Press, 2001), 12.

13. Jesper Juul, *Half-Real: Video Games between Real Rules and Fictional Worlds* (Cambridge, MA: MIT Press, 2005), 7–8.

The agency of the player is at the heart of Juul's model: the player's relationship to the complex system of interactions that constitutes a game, from pushing buttons or keys to select an avatar's next move to choosing to go through one door instead of another. The writers Katie Salen Tekinbaş and Eric Zimmerman argue that "to create instances of meaningful play, experience has to incorporate not just explicit interactivity, but meaningful choice."[14] Meaningful play emerges when a player chooses an action within a game's designed system, and the system responds in a way that moves the individual experience forward. Unlike a click on an app, which (ideally) results in one outcome, a video-game player's actions can have different results, depending on factors such as effort, strategy, and rewards—and how much the player invests in each.

As gamers make choice after choice, they become increasingly aware of the processes and stakes involved. Because pressing the correct combination of buttons at the right speed yields better results than haphazardly pushing random commands, players of Asteroids (1979, page 42) can easily understand the relationship between their physical actions—the movements of their body through the input—and progress in the game. Because choosing to navigate Journey (2012, page 82) alongside an anonymous companion, rather than alone, slows the pace of gameplay but heightens the game's emotional impact, players may rethink the idea of progress, and adjust their choices accordingly. In The Stanley Parable (2011, page 126), players can outright ignore the game's prompts and commands, tilting the stakes of interaction in favor of the player, and of freedom, exploration, and disobedience.

The Acquisition

When MoMA began acquiring video games, in 2012, they were already being collected elsewhere—in museums dedicated to video games and in institutions such as the Museum of the Moving Image, in New York, and La Gaîté Lyrique, in Paris. An exhibition of games had been mounted at the Barbican Art Gallery, in London, in 2002, and one would take place at the Smithsonian American Art Museum in 2012.[15] But video games were relatively unexplored territory for museums of art. Their acquisition, especially in a museum of MoMA's authority and history,

14. Katie Salen Tekinbaş and Eric Zimmerman, *Rules of Play: Game Design Fundamentals* (Cambridge, MA: MIT Press, 2003), 61.

15. *Game On: The History and Culture of Video Games*, Barbican Art Gallery, London, May 16–September 15, 2002; *The Art of Video Games*, Smithsonian American Art Museum, Washington, DC, March 16–September 30, 2012. Both exhibitions traveled widely.

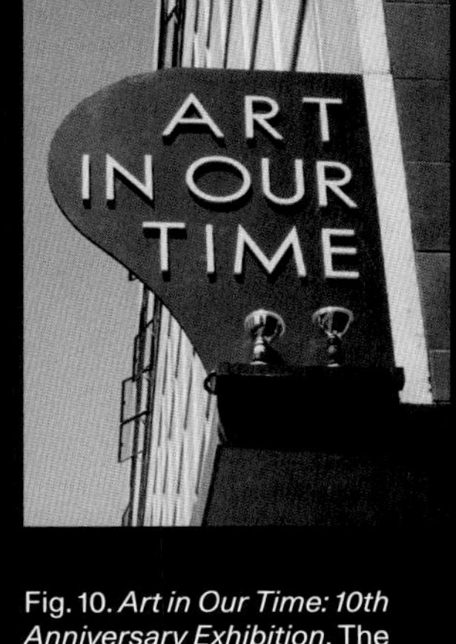

Fig. 10. *Art in Our Time: 10th Anniversary Exhibition*, The Museum of Modern Art, New York, 1939. Sign on the Museum's facade

16. One of Constantin Brâncuși's *Bird in Space* sculptures became the subject of a legal dispute when it was brought to New York in 1926 for an exhibition: was it an artwork, or was it a utilitarian object (and thus subject to import tax)? Brâncuși ultimately prevailed.

meant rethinking our practices of acquisition, conservation, and exhibition programming, as well as defying the dominant cultural attitude that games were mere entertainment or, at best, cultural artifacts.

To begin, in 2011 we—Senior Curator Paola Antonelli, Collection Specialist Paul Galloway, and former Curatorial Assistant Kate Carmody, all in MoMA's Department of Architecture and Design—drafted a checklist of forty games, with protocols for their acquisition. In this undertaking we were supported by a group of designers, gamers, critics, and historians, as well as dozens of our Museum colleagues. Our selection criteria included aesthetics, historical relevance, functionality, social significance, technological ingenuity, and economy—the same criteria we use to evaluate works of design—in addition to the games' success as interactive-design objects. These acquisitions posed questions about what constitutes an object worth collecting that struck at the heart of long-established museological practices, but it was not the first time that MoMA had been in this position in its ninety years of existence. The phrase "art in our time," from the title of the Museum's tenth-anniversary exhibition, in 1939 (fig. 10), has functioned as a kind of motto ever since, signaling MoMA's commitment to the idea that an art collection could be a mirror held up to a rapidly changing world and its rapidly changing culture. Such an embrace of evolution requires an embrace of uncertainty, even if such departures from tradition are met with disagreement and befuddlement—by other curators, viewers, trustees, and even customs officers.[16] And so our first step in working through the perplexities of acquiring video games was to define them as works of design, a category well established in the Museum's history. To articulate this definition, we focused on elements specific to the medium and critical for the design of a great game.

Behavior: A video game's scenarios, rules, and stimuli are given life through the behaviors they teach and elicit from players—with some results planned and others perhaps unexpected. Behavior in a game can be shaped through its logistics (by guiding players in basic navigational actions), through its emotional tone (by rewarding a particular attitude, such as altruism or aggression, with progress or satisfaction), and through choice (by giving players agency within the game's framework). The impact of behaviors learned while playing video games can extend beyond the screen. A game designed to encourage altruistic behavior might be used to train and educate, such as SimCity 2000

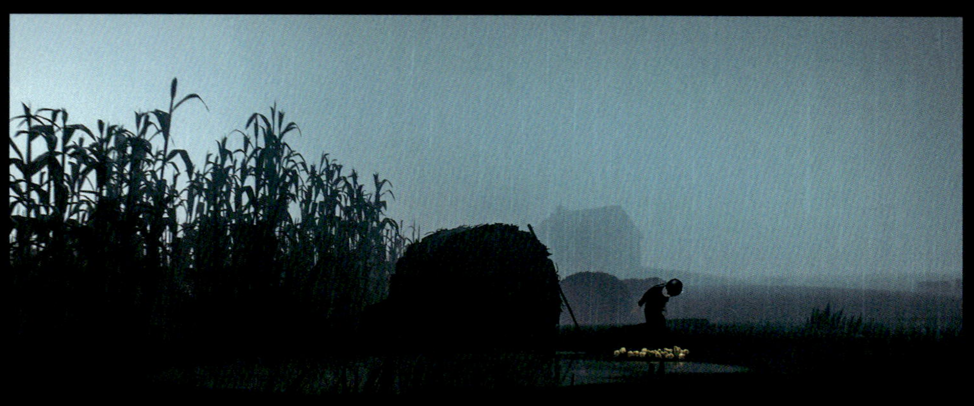

Fig. 11. Inside. 2016 (page 90)

(1993, page 110), which has been adopted for classes in STEM education: assuming responsibilities and making choices for digital avatars and communities might lead a player to question the way things are, and perhaps to envision how they could be otherwise.[17]

Aesthetics: Visual elegance is an important consideration: in design, it is not just a goal but also a tool. A video game's aesthetics can vary according to the available technology, the zeitgeist, and the designer's overall vision for the game, and elegance is manifested in the alignment of visual choices with intent. The graphic simplicity of Pong (1972, page 38) is as arresting as the far more complex visual style of Inside (fig. 11 and page 90); both clearly assert an aesthetic intention. Elegance has an additional meaning in electronic interactions: for programmers, "elegant code" is neat, well written, economical, and precise.

Space: The space in which a game exists is planned, designed, and constructed, much like architecture is in the physical world, although built with code rather than with bricks and mortar. Great video games manipulate and challenge our perceptions of space, in designs that push technology to its limits to create new frontiers of expressive and spatial freedom, such as games that take place in augmented and virtual reality. Video-game space can be experienced through a defined body—animal, human, or alien—or generated through godlike power, with players becoming architects, as they do in Minecraft (2011, page 120) or Dwarf Fortress (2006, page 74).

17. Matthew Cathell et al., "Using SimCity 4 Software as an Educational Tool to Complement Middle School Science and Mathematics," ASEE (American Society for Engineering Education) National Conference, Pittsburgh, June 22–25, 2008, peer.asee.org/using-simcity -4-software-as-an-educational -tool-to-complement-middle -school-science-and -mathematics.pdf.

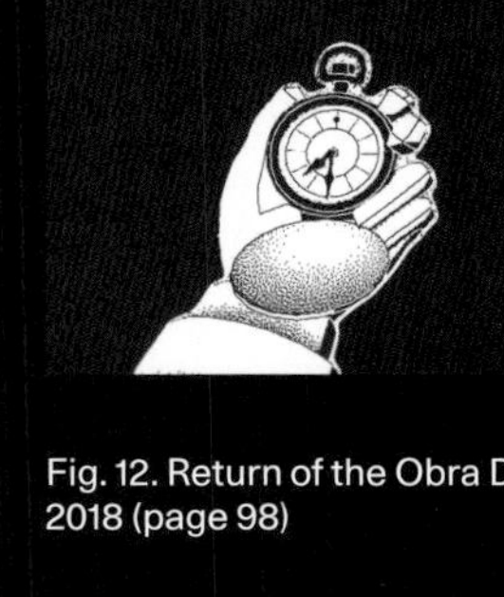

Fig. 12. Return of the Obra Dinn.
2018 (page 98)

Time: The passage of time in video games exists in tension between two Ancient Greek philosophical concepts: *chronos* (the shared convention of sequential time) and *kairos* (an individual's subjective experience of it). Playing a game in some cases means a commitment in conventional time that can extend over months and years. But within the game, time is subject to its designer's ability to manipulate reality. In Return of the Obra Dinn (fig. 12 and page 98), the tension between present and past drives both gameplay and narrative. The political machinations of Eve Online (2003, page 118) develop over years of real-time play, but in the quick five-minute game Passage (2007, page 76), a character's lifetime is condensed to a painful degree.

In addition to evaluating elements specific to video-game design, we applied the general criteria used to assess design objects in MoMA's collection, from posters and chairs to emergency rafts and typefaces. These include an object's historical, social, and cultural relevance, its functional and structural soundness, its technological innovation, and its synthesis of materials and techniques, as well as its potential to help people incorporate change and progress in their lives. In video games, programming language takes the place of wood, concrete, or plastic, and the quality of interaction is the virtual/digital translation of the modernist ideal of form married to function.

The next step was to address what it means to *acquire* a video game. Most of us understand ownership to be conferred by the act of purchase, whether of a physical disk, a downloaded digital file, a username and password, or a vintage machine. But a museum must also consider how it will ensure that a game will stay operable in the long run—for a decade or even for a century. The games of the last twenty years often have complex rights-management features built into them, such as constant requests for Internet verification, so that the player does not own the software so much as lease the experience. This lopsided arrangement represents a dramatic but common transfer of power from the player (who could previously sell, copy, and share games) to the publisher (who now keeps a tight grip on access and terms, and can even revoke permission to play).

The keys to the long-term health of a video game—its programming source code, the intellectual property rights, and the collective knowledge of its production—are held by its designers and publishers. Our approach was to involve these parties from the start, so that acquiring

End-User License Agreement (EULA) of Tetrageddon

This End-User License Agreement (henceforth referred to as "EULA" or "The Governing Law of the Land") is a legal, forever binding, agreement between you and the cursed website entity known as ARMAGAD.

Please read this EULA agreement out loud, maintaining a continuous low tonal pitch, while observing the incantations carefully. In the event that you do not correctly read this EULA there is a strong likelihood that a ghastly entity may be summoned. Once the incantation is complete, and this EULA has been read in its entirety, by clicking "accept" or visiting Tetrageddon, you are confirming your acceptance of said incantation and agreeing to become bound by the terms of this website. This binding is forever. It cannot be broken.

If you are entering into this EULA on behalf of a company or other legal entity, including illegal entities and void entities, you represent that you have the authority to bind such entities and their affiliate entities to this EULA. Once bound, the binding cannot be unbound. Adventurers much braver and much more heroic than yourself have tried. If you do not have such authority or if you do not agree with the terms set forth by this EULA, please seek the legal council of a higher website authority before entering this website. We do not accept responsibility for the unbound.

This EULA agreement shall apply only to Tetrageddon and any website visited hereonafter as a necessary precaution to those that have not yet read this EULA but may have come into contact with

Fig. 13. Nathalie Lawhead. Tetrageddon. 2015. The game's EULA is a satirical take on the typically dense legal language of user agreements.

Fig. 14. Pac-Man arcade cabinet. c. 1981. The Museum of Modern Art, New York. Gift of BANDAI NAMCO Entertainment Inc.

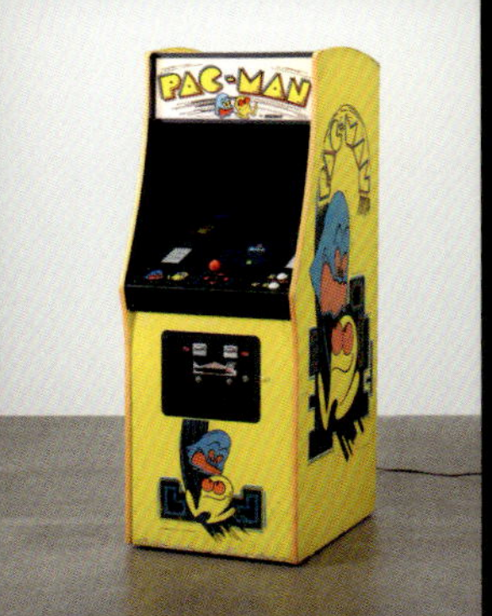

18. These steps were unnecessary in the case of NetHack (1987, page 46), which has been freely available since its beginnings. The game's public license is in keeping with the collaborative hacker ethos at its core.

a video game also meant acquiring a set of relationships. In terms of rights, it meant crafting a more solid and durable lease than those set out in a typical end-user license agreement (EULA)—that is, in the fine print that we as individual users tend to agree to without reading (fig. 13). Through each company's lawyers and MoMA's General Counsel, the games were acquired under exclusive, nonrevocable licenses that allow us to freely exhibit them, and that give us access to the software and hardware necessary for upkeep and display.[18] To their everlasting credit, every designer and publisher we worked with bent their rules to give us an unprecedented level of access.

Our acquisition protocols suggested that we obtain copies of the games in their original software format (such as cartridges or disks) and the original hardware on which they were played (such as consoles or computers) whenever possible. In addition to Pac-Man's secure software, BANDAI NAMCO, its producer, made a gift to the Museum of a fully operational vintage arcade cabinet (fig. 14 and page 44). Preserving these formats is useful for exhibitions and for helping future generations understand older games, especially given the rapid pace of techno-logical change and the rate at which hardware and software become

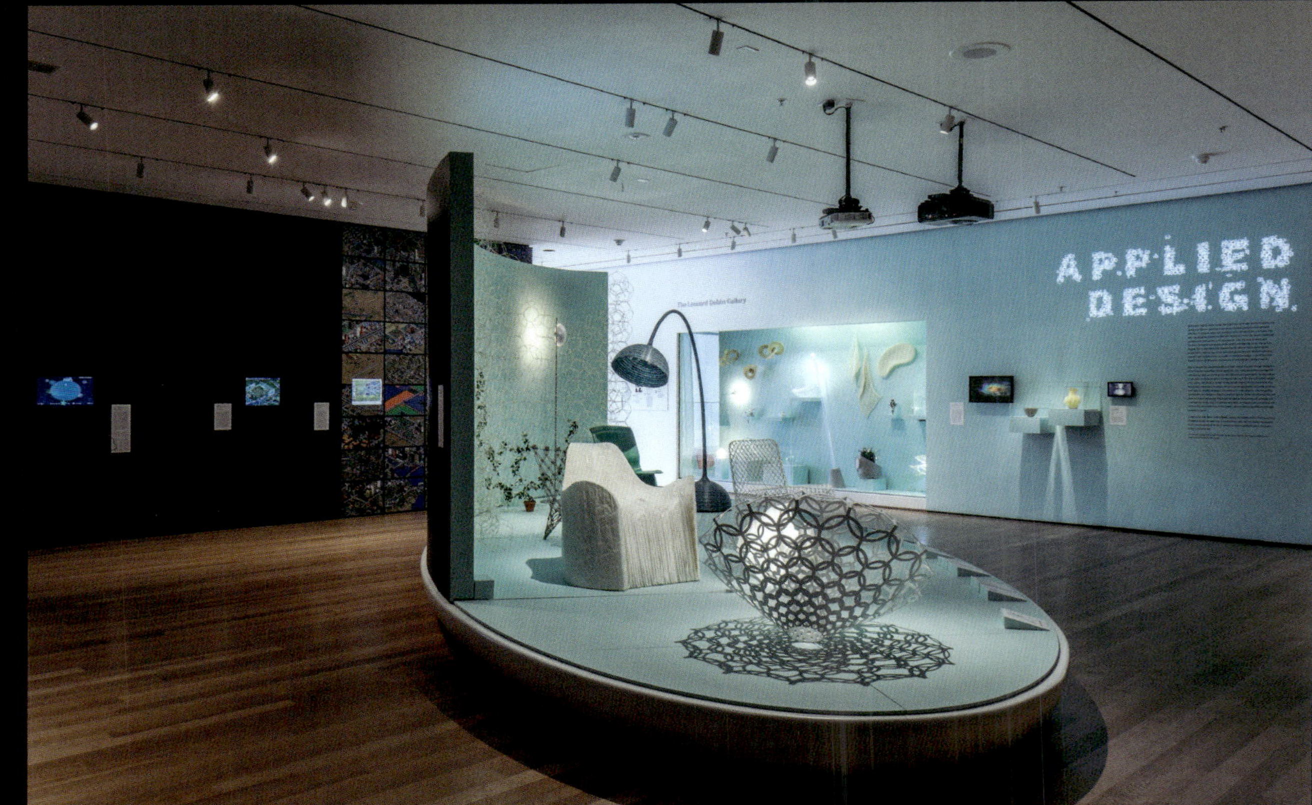

Fig. 15. *Applied Design*, The Museum of Modern Art, New York, March 2, 2013–January 20, 2014. Installation view

19. MoMA's video-game collection made its public debut in *Applied Design*, March 2, 2013–January 20, 2014. Interactive design such as Pac-Man, Eve Online, Portal, and The Sims were shown next to more traditional design objects such as chairs and lamps.

obsolete. To this end, we also requested each game's source code. This code, however, is guarded with extreme care in secure servers; to let it out into the world is considered a tremendous risk, making it vulnerable to hacking and pirating. We could sense the alarm, even over email, when we broached this topic. But in the end, many designers and publishers shared our conviction that video games are cultural products worth conserving, and they gave us the tools we needed to do just that. MoMA received full documentation and source code for about half the titles in its collection, including some blockbusters.

Installing the games in MoMA's galleries required fresh thinking about display. The elegance of interactive design is hard to convey without allowing the kind of interaction that is prohibited in traditional museum displays and enforced by stanchions, security tape, and "do not touch" signs. We wanted to let people play. The time-based, multidimensional, and collective aspects of many games, however, make them almost impossible to exhibit exactly as they are (or were) played. The solutions to this dilemma were imperfect. In the case of Eve Online, a massively multiplayer online role-playing game (MMORPG) in which campaigns take years to develop and play out, we collaborated with the developer and the game's community of players on *A Day in Eve Online*, a video that combines data visualization, recorded gameplay, and player commentary into a condensed window of twenty-four hours in this digital world of bewildering scope. We adapted Dwarf Fortress, an open-ended, constantly evolving game, into a more static form, turning some of its visual aspects into wallpaper. Our hope was that even if visitors came away with an incomplete understanding of a game, their curiosity would nonetheless be piqued, perhaps leading them to play the game after they leave the Museum.

We decided to install the games in screens of the same size as their original formats, and we set them cleanly in the gallery walls (fig. 15), connected to their controllers, either the originals or emulated versions. We opted not to show the original cabinets, home consoles, or computers at all: divorcing the game from the nostalgia around it would encourage viewers to focus on the controller and the screen—the game's primary input and output. This departure from exhibitions at other institutions, which tend to feature the hardware, posters, packaging, and other graphic ephemera, presents video games as exemplars of interactive design rather than as items of popular culture.[19]

Together, this book and the exhibition it accompanies consider video games as interactive design through three critical lenses. The first section looks at games as objects and as products, with a special focus on the input: the tactile element of the button, controller, or joystick that functions as the meeting point between the digital and the physical dimensions. The second section examines the creative strategies employed by designers to structure interactions and experiences that range from straightforward puzzles to sprawling online universes. In the last section, the camera spins around to look at the players—at their creative agency and at the role that choice and performance can play. As an alternative to the typical chronological, thematic, or genre-specific approaches to the history of video games, this taxonomy centers design as the most useful tool for understanding them.

Video Games IRL

The online world is seen as separate from and, by many, even secondary to what happens IRL, but is it actually unworthy of being called "real"? Considering how much of our lives takes place online—where we shop, make friends, find mates, navigate (fig. 16), learn, train, mediate, and design our identities—perhaps we should call it ORL, for "online real life," or perhaps, as some theorists suggest, the rest of life is really AFK, for "away from keyboard."[20]

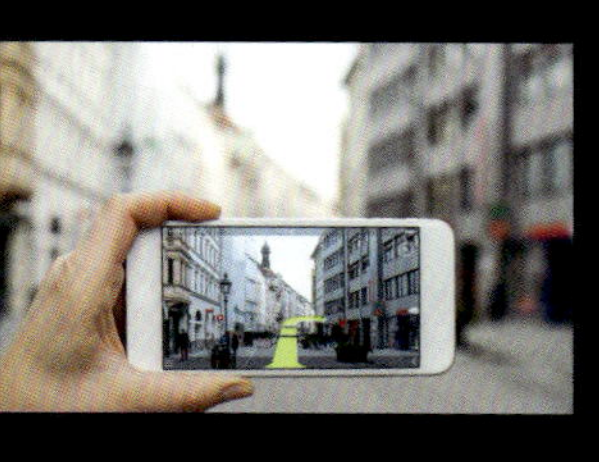

Fig. 17. Augmented-reality view of GPS location and directions on a smartphone, c. 2016

20. The social-media theorist Nathan Jurgenson coined the term "digital dualism" to describe the idea of online and offline lives as distinct realms. The binary idea that we can only inhabit one of them at a time, he says, "fails to capture the plain fact that our lived reality is the result of the constant interpenetration of the online and offline. That is, we live in an augmented reality that exists at the intersection of materiality and information, physicality and digitality, bodies and technology, atoms and bits, the off and the online. It is wrong to say 'IRL' to mean offline: *Facebook is real life*." Jurgenson, "The IRL Fetish," *New Inquiry*, June 28, 2012. For the writer and curator Legacy Russell, the term AFK "signifies a more continuous progression of the self, one that does not end when a user steps away from the computer but rather moves forward out into society away from the keyboard." Russell, *Glitch Feminism: A Manifesto* (London: Verso, 2020), 31.

21. "Video Games," Statista market- and consumer-data website, last update November 2021, statista.com/outlook /dmo/digital-media/video -games/worldwide.

22. "Roblox Reports August 2021 Key Metrics," Roblox news, September 15, 2021; Twitch advertising, twitchadvertising. tv/audience; "One Trillion Minecraft Views," YouTube Culture and Trends, December 2021, youtube.com/trends /articles/minecraft-trillion/.

23. "Kara Chung x Marc Goehring: Animal Crossing Runway Show for Reference Festival," Reference Festival, May 25, 2020, YouTube video, youtube.com/watch?v=P0xr 2zRpBZU; "French Connec- tion," official music video for Balenciaga x Fortnite, Placid, September 20, 2021, YouTube video, youtube.com/watch ?v=w5F77M_J1Cg.

24. Emma Westecott, "The Zero Game Manifesto," LiveJournal entry, August 27, 2005, monanobi.livejournal.com /20368.html. The manifesto sought to expand common definitions of gaming and its goals; according to Westecott it was "a collective effort of those of us at the studio, I was Studio Director so got to perform it. The zerogame studio was an applied research studio that was part of The Interactive Institute. We were based in Visby, Gotland [Sweden], and were in operation … 2000– 05ish." Westecott, email to the authors, April 25, 2022.

Whatever form their cultural innovations take, video games have a vast reach: it has been estimated that by 2023 there will be more than three billion active players around the world, and by 2026 a pro- jected economic impact of $239.7 billion.[21] In 2021, more than 40 million people used Roblox to make or play their own games, and an average of 31 million people per day came to Twitch for livestream action; since 2011, more than one trillion views of YouTube videos about Minecraft have accumulated.[22] Games such as Pokémon Go (2016) and Ingress (2013) are training for our hybrid lives to come, when the metaverse will be as fully inhabited (by corporations and institutions, as well as by individ- uals) as the physical world. When live fashion shows were canceled in 2020 and 2021 because of the Covid-19 pandemic, fashion brands found alternate ways of presenting new collections to the world, in some cases ingeniously relocating themselves on gaming platforms: Paco Rabanne and Chanel, for example, appeared in a runway segment in Animal Crossing (2001), and Balenciaga made high-fashion skins available to players in Fortnite (2017).[23]

In 2005, in "The Zero Game Manifesto," the designer and developer Emma Westecott declared that "games are *too powerful* to be regarded as merely entertainment"; they are, she insisted, a form of reality that inspires other realities.[24] Nearly twenty years later, this has proved to be the case: much of our world is shaped by infrastructures, languages, and cultures that were initially developed for video games. Social-media platforms use principles of gamification—and therefore interactive design—to encourage user engagement, with systems of rules, goals, and rewards (in the form of positive feedback such as likes and retweets) that hook users as neatly as an artfully constructed fantasy role-playing game. Shopping websites benefit from gaming technology in the form of augmented-reality changing rooms and live retail interactions; in matchmaking and hookup apps we can browse possible partners as carefully as we might choose the features of our avatars, or as breezily as we might leaf through an illustrated book, looking for a page for our eyes and mind to land on. The didactic tools that train players how to negotiate a game's space have been adapted for educational purposes, resulting, for example, in a version of Minecraft that teaches math, ecology, and other subjects to children, and the use of video games during basic training in the US military. The digital social interactions and mindfulness that can be achieved through playing games are being adapted for therapeutic uses, such as treating PTSD.[25]

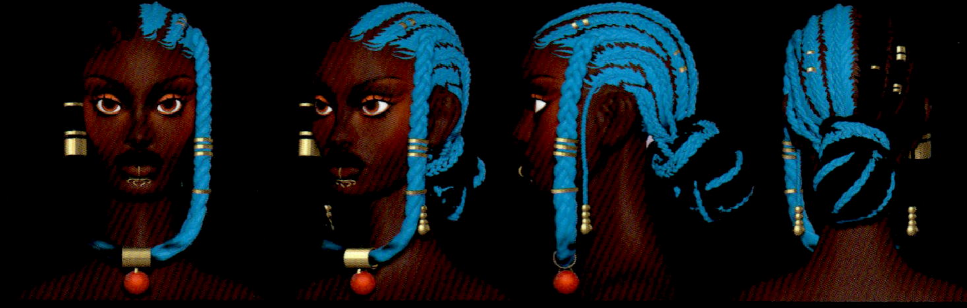

Fig. 17. Malika Mutombo. Design for the Open Source Afro Hair Library. 2022

Virtual realities, however, are not always innovative and, indeed, can be far from pleasant. During the Covid-19 pandemic, when humans of all ages and backgrounds—many of them children—were restricted to working and learning from home, online was, for millions, the *only* IRL. Gaming platforms, which are communal spaces not only for play but also for communication, promotion, shopping, learning, and socializing, also had to take the place of classrooms, playgrounds, sports fields, and street corners. Those who could not afford or access an online connection and, through it, community and resources, found them-selves isolated; those who were constantly online found themselves confronted by a dangerous escalation of propaganda, misinformation, conspiracies, trolling, bullying, and exploitation, both psychological and sexual—products of the anonymity and scarce regard for facts that define the online world. This behavior was hardly new in the world of gaming. In 2014, a campaign of online harassment against women in the video-game industry—now known as Gamergate—surprised many people with its vehemence; the harassers' culture-war stance of grievance and outrage—through ad hoc attacks, doxing, and threats— has been adopted by right-wing extremists on other platforms, often against individuals and groups that advocate progressive, inclusive ideals.[26] It is critical that we keep a spotlight on the ways in which online culture, whether gaming or otherwise, can dangerously amplify social pathologies.

The games in this volume reflect the flawed and fraught context in which they were created. Their creators are overwhelmingly male, and predominantly white. The characters in the games are frequently male and white. Even technology has skewed the gaming experience in favor of the already powerful: for decades, Black characters in video games were designed wearing helmets or with close-cropped hair because most programmers could not be bothered to write the complex coding

25. See, for example, Alex Miller, "How Video Games Are Saving Those Who Served," *Wired* online, October 20, 2020. A startup in the UK is developing AI-based games that are said to detect depres-sion, although they are as yet untested. Steven Zeitchik, "Can a Video Game Tell If You're Depressed?" *Washington Post*, April 28, 2022.

26. See Aja Romano, "What We Still Haven't Learned from Gamergate," Vox website, January 7, 2021.

27. To remedy this omission, a group of artists led by A. M. Darke is building the Open Source Afro Hair Library (afrohairlibrary.org), a data-base of 3D-modeled Black hair textures and styles, avail-able to digital artists for free. Darke, "Open Source Afro Hair Library," artist's website, prettydarke.cool/portfolio/open -source-afro-hair-library/. See also Trone Dowd, "Black Hair in Video Games Is Terrible. These 3D Artists Are Changing That," *Vice* online, January 7, 2022.

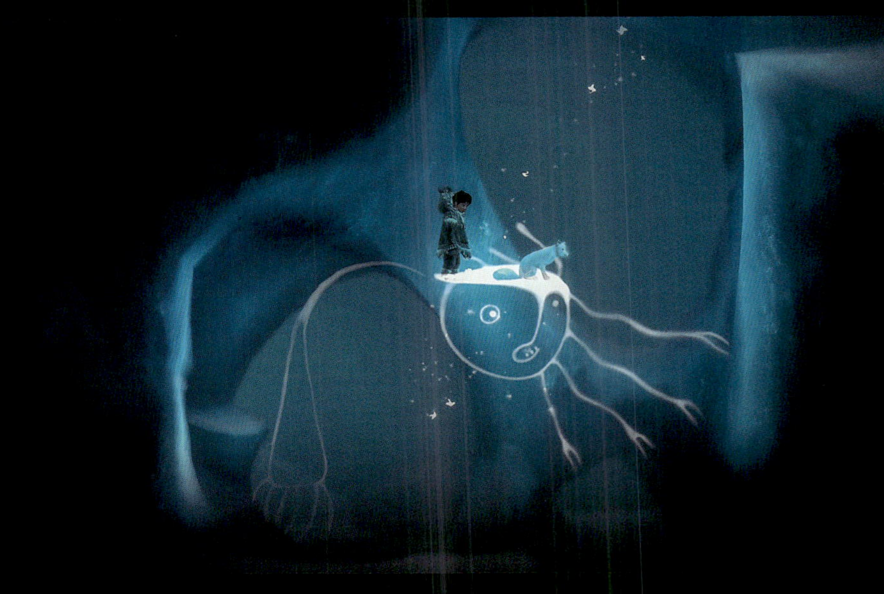

Fig. 18. Never Alone. 2014
(page 86)

necessary for the production of textured hair (fig. 17).[27] Female designers, queer designers, and designers of color working in the video-game industry face problems including discrimination, harassment, underrepresentation, and difficulty accessing financing.[28] Some games directly address these issues, such as Nathalie Lawhead's Everything Is Going to Be OK (2017, page 92), which was conceived as a cathartic project for its nonbinary artist, who had endured a great deal of abuse and harassment in the gaming world. In Journey, Jenova Chen pointedly removed markers of race and gender identity from the game's protagonist, a faceless robed figure.[29] These games are positive developments in the industry, and they present an imperative for our acquisition practices: MoMA's collection must fully represent the diversity of the designers working in the medium, and of the players who will translate and articulate their identities by interacting with the games.

28. Sexism and sexual harassment are also rife in the video-game industry. One of the most visible controversies involved Nolan Bushnell, the founder of Atari, who was accused of being responsible for the company's pronounced sexist culture. See Keith Stuart, "Atari Founder Nolan Bushnell Loses Award after Sexism Outcry." *Guardian* online,

February 1, 2018. The producers Riot Games (League of Legends) and Activision Blizzard (Call of Duty) were both sued by the California Department of Fair Employment and Housing on allegations of sexual harassment and employee discrimination, in 2018 and 2021, respectively. The 2018 suit was successful; the 2021 suit has not been resolved.

29. "We wanted the character to be an avatar which means it reflects the player's true nature. Therefore, it should not have any personality or any feature that misleads other [players'] perception on who might be controlling the avatar. No age, gender, racial definition. It can be anyone from anywhere on earth." Jenova Chen, "Journey's Enigmatic

Character: Its Six Iterations," interview, Control500: Game Development Stories, ctrl500 .com/art/the-main-character -of-journey/. See also Chen, "Designing Journey," Game Developers Conference 2013, San Francisco, March 25–29, 2013, gdcvault.com /play/1017700/Designing.

We believe that video games can be a vehicle for moving society forward; Steven Poole, at the turn of the twenty-first century, declared that they would "shape the worlds we will all inhabit tomorrow."[30] We would like to think that this is still true: That video games, through their nature as interactive design and their potential to shape behavior, can encourage tolerance, fluidity, and pluralism, and help societies withstand reactionary attacks against human and civil rights. That they can be testing grounds for the avant-garde, for notions still too radical for the wider public.[31] That they can model equitable and inclusive communities and challenge, in their imaginative spaces, previous modes of racial representation and gender construction. That they can give attention, acknowledgment, and respect to underrepresented cultures, as does Never Alone (fig. 18 and page 86), the game that gives this book its title. That they can bring us closer to nature and focus our awareness on climate change and the associated environmental crises.[32] That through them we can embody and empathize with other individuals and other species, and perhaps even will a more respectful and balanced reality into being. Through museums and other cultural institutions that look to the past to think about how the future might unroll, we may begin to comprehend the power of video games to surpass the hurdles we encounter IRL, and to harness that power for good.

32. See, for example, the exhibition *Eco Games*, at ZKM/Center for Art and Media, Karlsruhe, Germany, July 28, 2021–March 4,

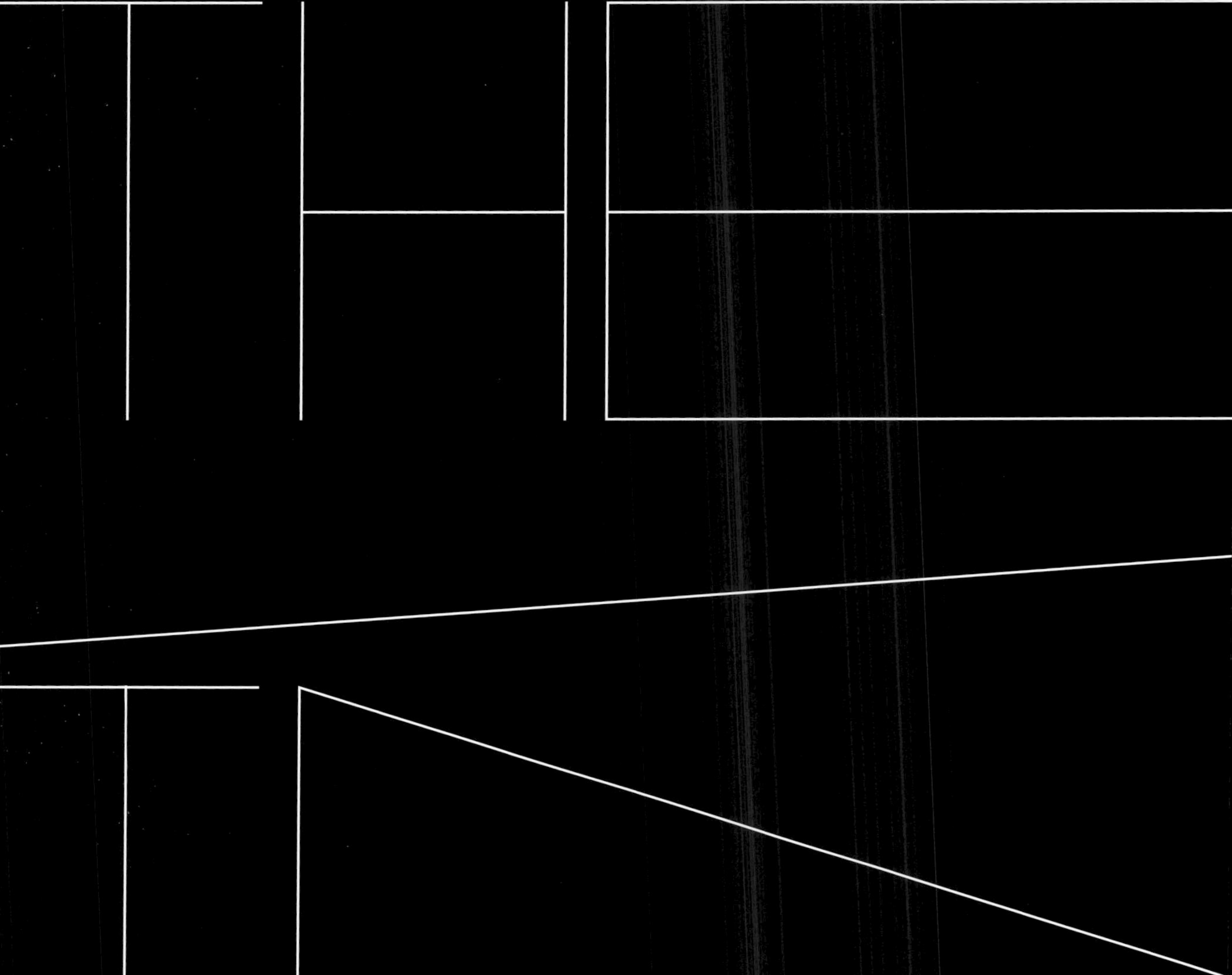

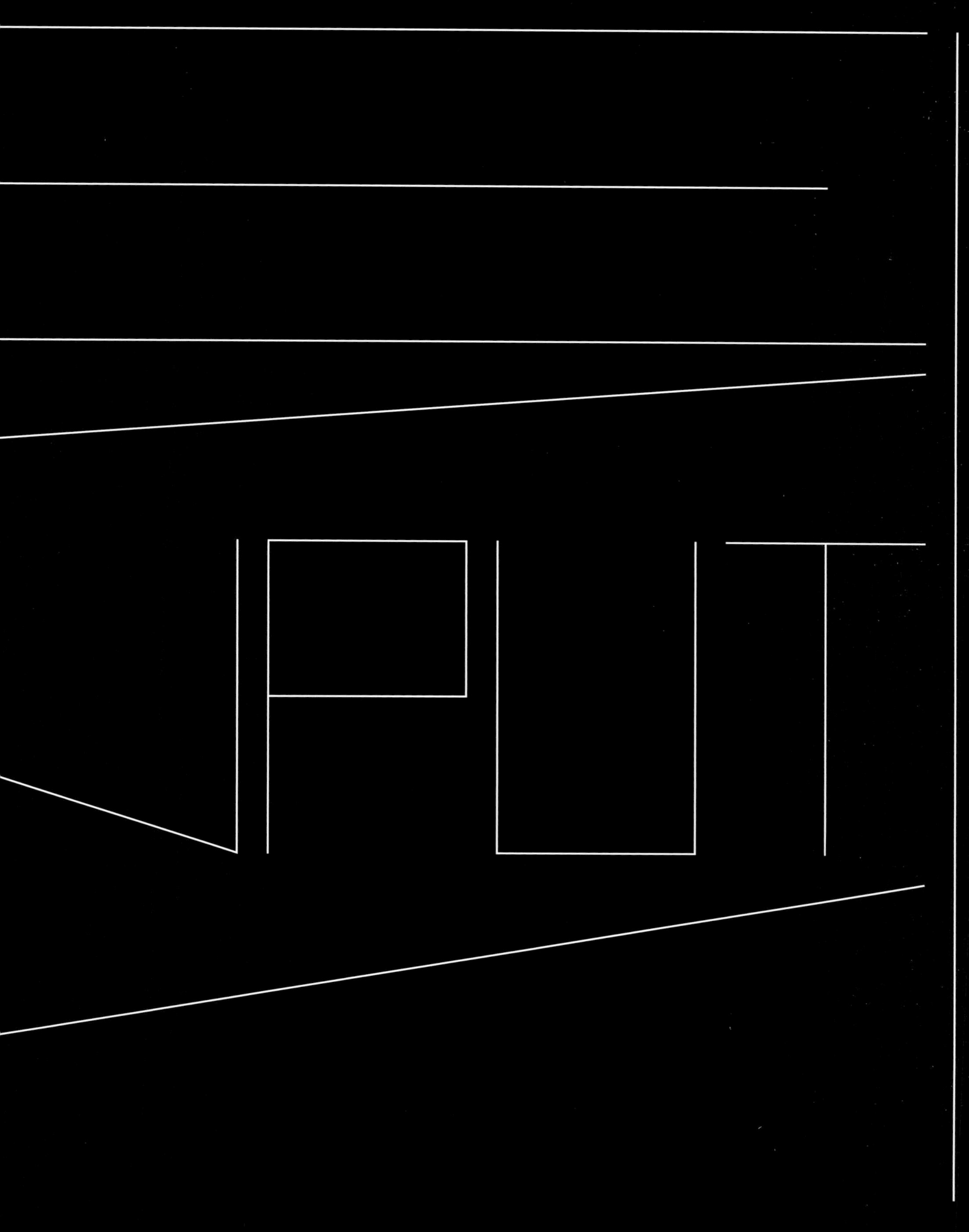

Paul Galloway

Fig. 1. Player 1 selection button
(1970s–present)

Consider the button.

This simple switch translates physical input—the pressing of a fingertip—into electronic signals (fig. 1). Through this small action, a button becomes a meeting place, a threshold between the realms of the corporeal and the digital. This is fitting: hands, for most of us, are our primary interface with the world; our eyes receive, our hands manipulate. Whether we are skillfully carving a block of marble or ineptly smashing a video-game controller button, it is through our hands that our will is physically exerted on the world, at least for now. The problem of how to most efficiently design tools and machines to do it for us has tasked designers for millennia, and the advent of computers has made this exchange both more convoluted and increasingly vital. Nevertheless, the unnatural-seeming input methods available for video games, from the keyboard to the joystick to the touchscreen, have not stopped designers from crafting interactions that engage the mind, the body, and the machine in progressively complex dialogues.

All input devices involve some level of practice to master. The standard layout of a computer keyboard, called QWERTY after the order of letters on the top row of keys, does not make sense at first glance, but with time and practice it becomes second nature to the user. So, too, does the layout of the modern video-game controller. The controls and functions for a contemporary military-combat video game, for example, achieve byzantine levels of complexity, on controllers with upwards of sixteen buttons crowded onto the surface of a small device, which are variously tapped, clicked, held, and double-tapped to navigate, display, move, and shoot (fig. 2). Players unaccustomed to crushing all ten digits in this mad embrace can find themselves utterly bewildered.

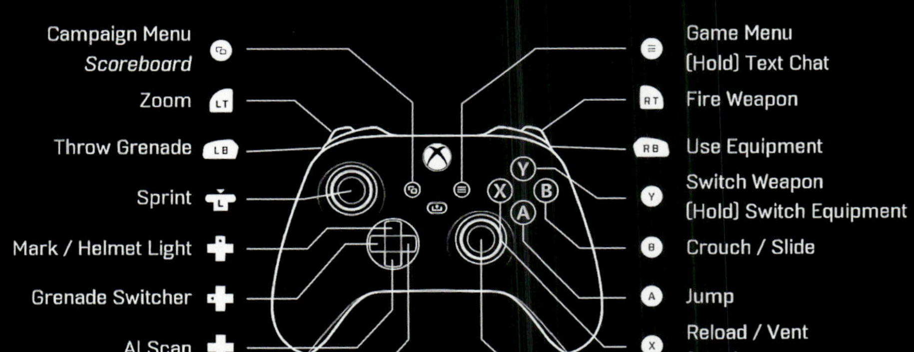

Fig. 2. Xbox controller layout for
Halo Infinite (2021)

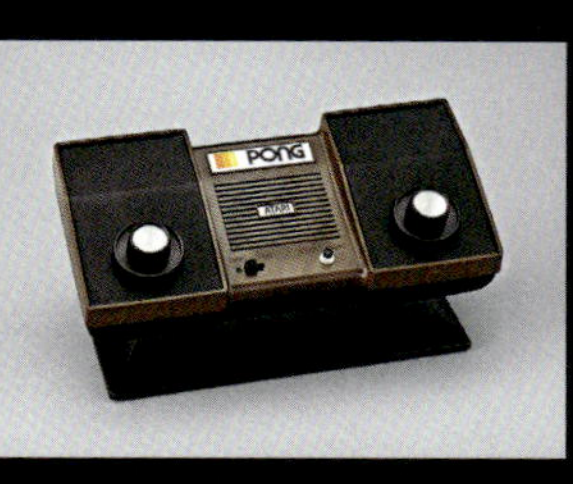

Fig. 3. Pong home console (1976)

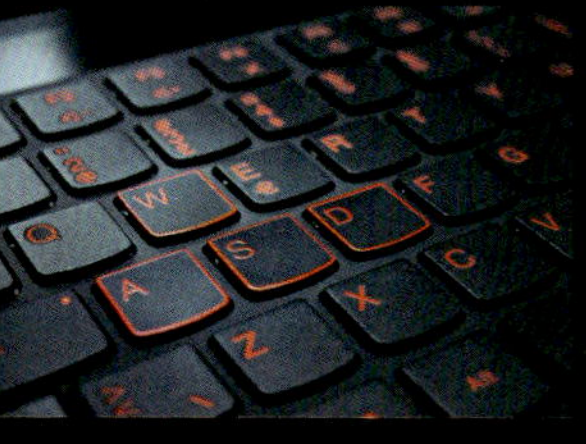

Fig. 4. WASD keyboard controls

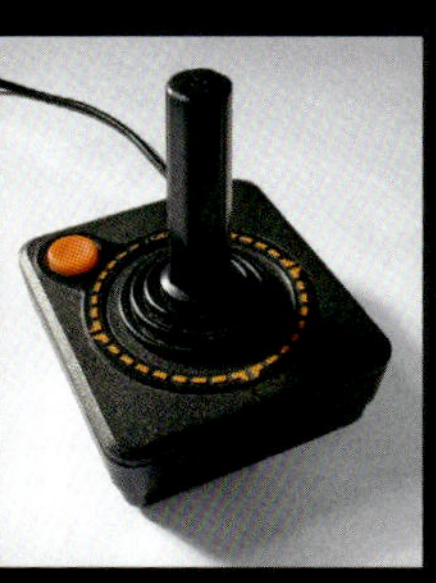

Fig. 5. Atari 2600 joystick (1980)

Early video games had the luxury (or extreme challenge) of controllers designed and built specifically for a single game. Atari's 1974 home version of its popular Pong has a two-person controller with a dial for each player (fig. 3 and page 38). Their function makes immediate sense: turn clockwise, and the on-screen paddle moves down; counterclockwise, and the paddle glides up. Motion in the physical world is neatly translated into motion in the digital in a masterpiece of interactive design. This perfect marrying of controller to game came, however, with a serious drawback: it is not easily adapted to other games. This is a Pong controller and a Pong controller only.

The keyboard, on the other hand, offers a multitude of possibilities for game input and has been adapted to thousands of games, even though it was not designed for this purpose. With its layout derived from the mechanical typewriter, the keyboard remains the primary computer-input device for both work and play. Video-game designers have taken advantage of this familiarity to enable a vast array of actions and interactions. In a commonly used scheme, for example, players move characters through a 3D environment with letter keys: W to move forward, S to go backward, A to go left, and D to go right (fig. 4). Avid gamers become accustomed to this arbitrary arrangement, but this and other layouts, like the keyboard itself, is not intuitive for a novice. This barrier limits the accessibility of many games, and it is an example of the drawbacks of designing a game around a universal input device.

The joystick, modeled on those used for piloting aircraft, may be the most intuitive of inputs. It emerged in the 1970s as a popular option for arcade machines and home-gaming systems such as the Atari 2600 (fig. 5). Like the dial for Pong, the joystick's use is readily apparent. The tactile feedback—you feel your arm and hand move in concert with the avatar on the screen—further immerses you in the game environment. When paired with one or more buttons, the joystick offers a range of options for game designers, but it is far from a subtle instrument. While it is ideal for steering Pac-Man around his simple 2D maze, the joystick, which you grasp in your fist, is not well suited to the kinds of subtle motion necessary for more complex games.

As gaming moved from public arcades into private homes, the design imperatives shifted as well. Controllers specific to each game were impractical, and game developers could not rely on a universal input if broad market appeal was the goal. As a result, the late 1980s and early 1990s saw a significant evolution in controller design. Developers moved

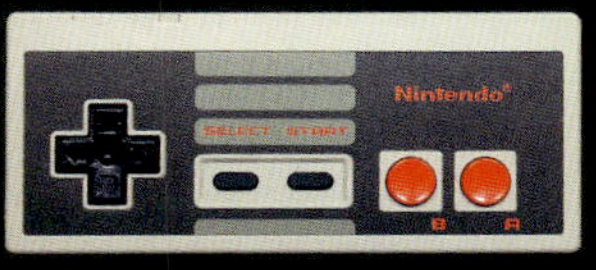

Fig. 6. Nintendo Entertainment System controller (c. 1986)

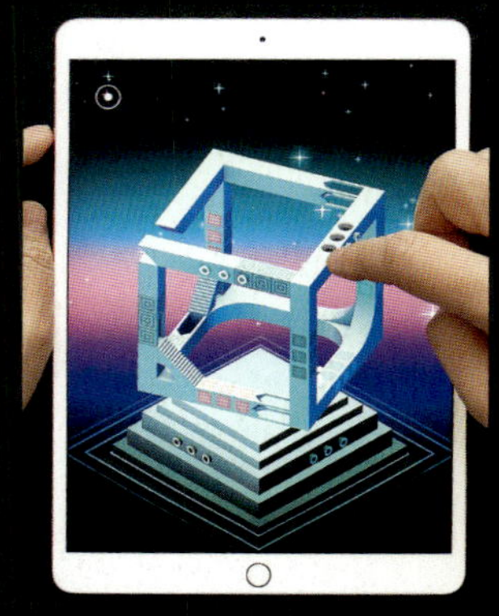

Fig. 7. Monument Valley (2014, page 56) on an Apple iPad

away from dials, knobs, and large joysticks toward smaller, more sensitive switches, such as those on the four-directional D-pad popularized by the Nintendo Entertainment System (fig. 6). This controller, whose descendants are still in use today, combines the best features of the joystick with an easy-to-understand directional system that reacts with greater sensitivity than a button (a finger is a much finer instrument than a fist). As games increased in complexity over the 1990s and 2000s, controllers followed suit, leading to the button-barnacled versions of today.

The rise of gaming on touchscreen devices, popularized first by the iPhone and now found everywhere, required designers to rethink how a player interacts with a game. Controlling a game by touching the screen on which it is being played inevitably resulted in the action being obscured by players' hands. Early attempts to resolve this issue led to unimaginative virtual re-creations of joysticks and buttons in the screen's corners, away from the main action. But some designers, such as those of Monument Valley (fig. 7 and page 56), took the design constraints imposed by the device as an opportunity to change the idea of game input entirely, by structuring gameplay around fingers directly on the screen. The game succeeds partly because solving the puzzles on the screen *feels* tactile: a player's fingers move elements around in a satisfying and instinctive manner. As with the dial for Pong, motion in the physical world is efficiently rendered in the digital. This return to the core principles of interactive design is a reminder that the richest experiences arise not from a better button layout but from a clear relationship between the actions of the body and the actions on the screen.

The past two decades have seen a profusion of new input devices that incorporate advanced hardware and software in new modes of interaction. Among the most influential are motion controllers, in which sensors and accelerometers translate body movements into game action, facilitating a more direct connection between physical and digital dimensions and—often, and thankfully—doing away with buttons. In addition, the growing sophistication of motion controls and new concepts for gaming inputs, including adaptive controls that can be customized by the player, has opened up gaming to players with a broader range of physical abilities, further expanding and enriching the community. Technological progress has also brought us closer to virtual reality—the dream of computer scientists, game designers, and science-fiction authors since the 1960s (fig. 8). The combination of motion controls, high computer-processing power, and advanced video screens has made this dream increasingly attainable. With a few more steps this "ultimate display" will look and feel exactly like reality, in the process obviating the need for controllers or physically manipulated inputs of any kind: within the world of a game, a player's hands, eyes, and gestures will precisely mimic their corresponding use in the physical world.[1] In this scenario, the aim of interactive design is for technology to disappear and the body to become almost irrelevant, while a different corporeal experience asserts itself in the digital realm.

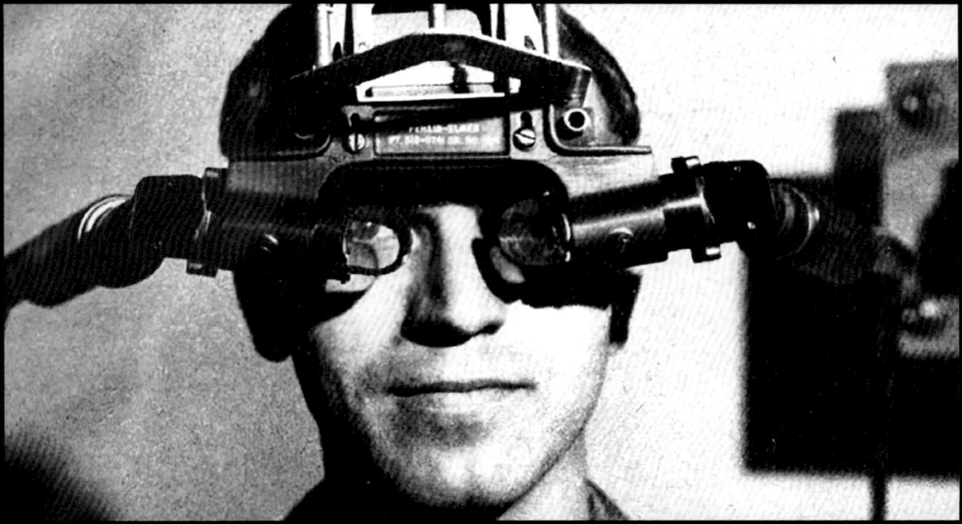

Fig. 8. Head-mounted display with tracking software designed by Ivan Sutherland and his students, 1968. With simple wireframe graphics responding in real time to the user's movements, this was the first successful demonstration of augmented reality.

1. "Ultimate display" is how the computer scientist Ivan Sutherland described the merging of real and simulated worlds. Sutherland was among the first to posit the idea of virtual reality, although the term itself wouldn't come into use until later. Sutherland, "The Ultimate Display," in *Information Processing 1965: Proceedings of the International Federation*

Magnavox Odyssey

Ralph Baer (American, born Germany. 1922–2014)
Magnavox (USA, est. 1917)

Magnavox Odyssey home video-game system 1972
The Museum of Modern Art, New York.
Gift of The Aaron and Betty Lee Stern Foundation

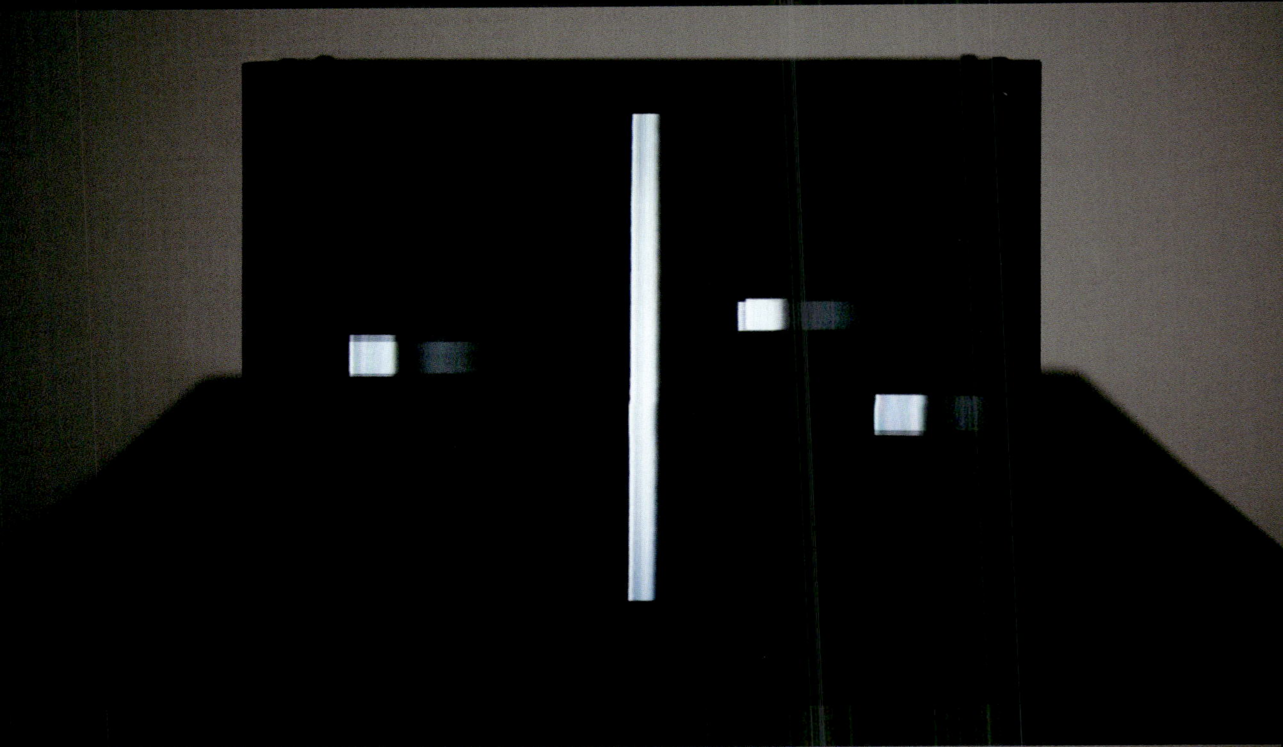

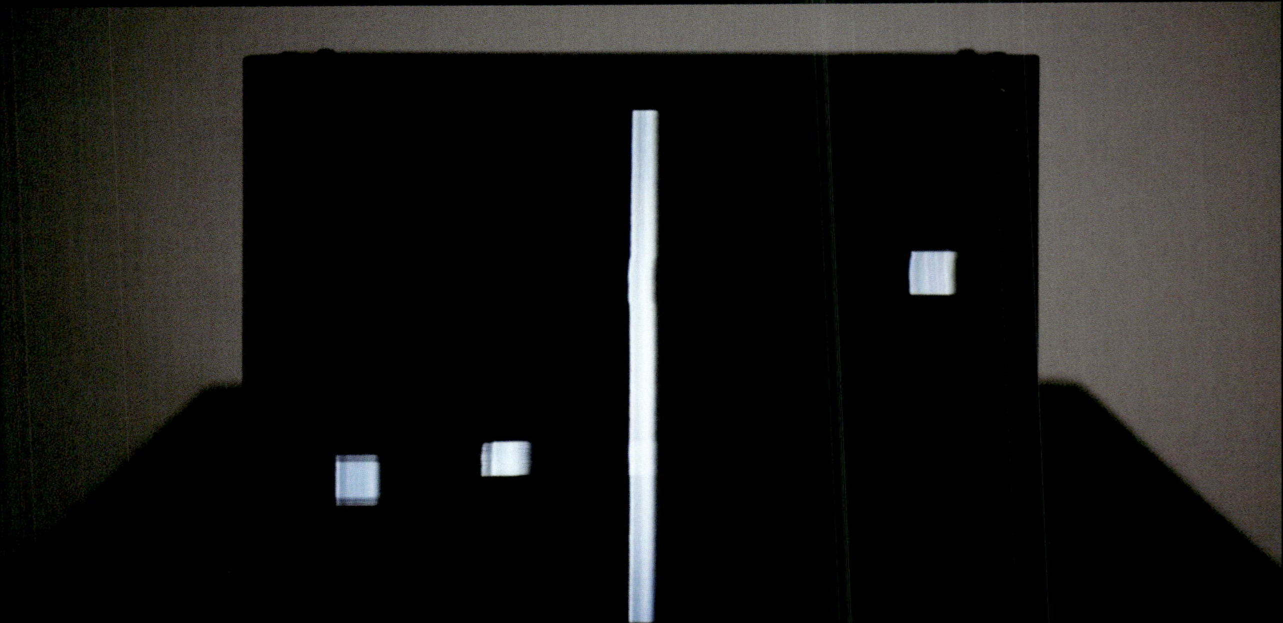

Prior to the arrival of the Magnavox Odyssey in 1972, few people had ever played a video game and almost none had done so at home on their own television set. While its commercial success was modest, the Odyssey gaming system nonetheless represents a crucial missing link in the history of video games, bridging the rarified academic and research worlds, where gaming had thus far lurked, and the domestic space. In doing so, it was instrumental in the formation of a new industry.

The Odyssey was the brainchild of Ralph Baer, an American inventor and engineer with long experience in the electronics industry. Creative and curious, Baer spent decades experimenting with ideas for interactive games for televisions. By the late 1960s his efforts had gained significant financial support, eventually leading to the television manufacturer Magnavox packaging and marketing the Odyssey as an "electronic game of the future" (the term video game was not yet in common use). The device arrived at a crowded, crucial moment in video gaming's origins. Ted Dabney and Nolan Bushnell's Computer Space had been released only a year earlier, and Atari's Pong (page 38) was released shortly after the Odyssey.[1] But both Pong and Computer Space were arcade machines, designed for public venues. The domestic aspirations of the Odyssey were, in many respects, ahead of their time. The subsequent arrival and wild success of the Atari 2600 console, in 1977, proved that Baer's instincts were correct: people wanted to play games at home.

The games available for the Odyssey are exceedingly simple, reflecting the limited technology of the time. Players use a controller featuring a set of dials to manipulate basic geometric shapes of light on the screen. There are no colors and no sound, and keeping score necessitates pen and paper. Indeed, the Odyssey needs a number of physical, analog tools to augment the system's limited capabilities, including colored plastic overlays that can be placed on the television's screen to enliven and change the look of the game, making the Odyssey a hybrid experience of futuristic technological format married to the more familiar practice of board games. As with the best of these, the Odyssey requires a leap of imagination: the white square on the screen can alternately represent a tennis racket, a hockey player, or a downhill skier. As game graphics improved over the ensuing decades, this leap became less and less necessary. But in 1972, for those lucky few who brought home a Magnavox Odyssey, the future was revealed to be a fertile ground for play, imagination, and exploration.

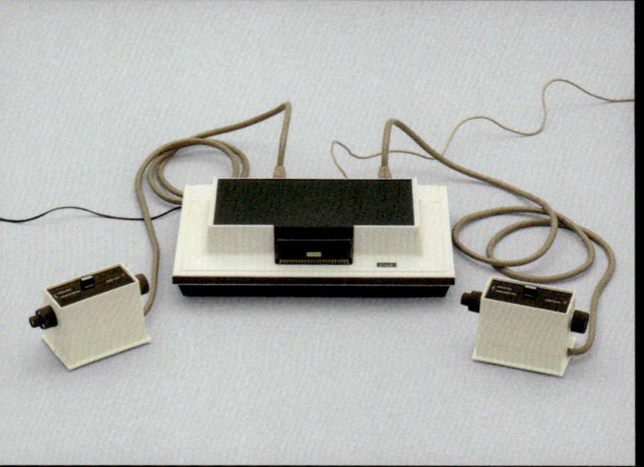

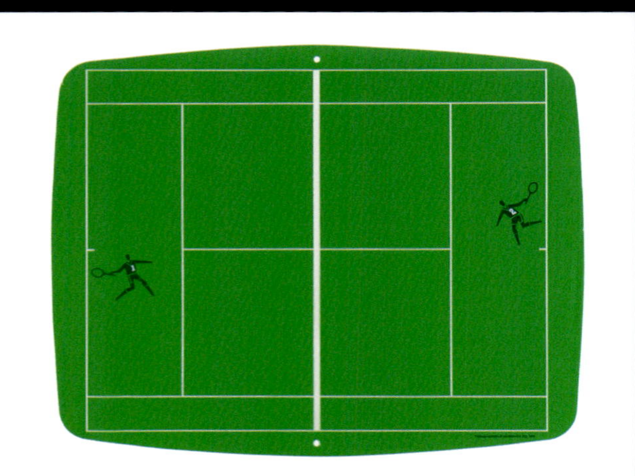

Screen overlay for Magnavox Odyssey Tennis

Pong

Allan Alcorn (American, born 1948)
Atari, Inc. (USA, est. 1972)

Pong 1972
The Museum of Modern Art, New York.
Gift of Atari Interactive, Inc.

Pong was a game for drunks—like all coin-operated amusements (pinball, billiards, claw machines), a way to extract as much money as possible from bored, tipsy patrons. The connections between alcohol, gaming, and gambling—and with shakedown rackets by the Mafia—had been long established by the early 1970s, and so seedy was the association that many cities outlawed pinball machines. This did not stop entrepreneurial creators from envisioning new diversions, however, and in August 1972 the first Pong machine was installed at Andy Capp's Tavern in Sunnyvale, California.

The game was conceived by Nolan Bushnell, the founder of Atari and a pioneer of video-game development. Inspired by the Magnavox Odyssey (page 36), which had been released earlier the same year, Bushnell hired Allan Alcorn to create the first game for the company. Initially, to evaluate the young engineer's computer skills Bushnell tasked Alcorn with creating an arcade version of the Odyssey's table tennis game (originality and copyright were not concepts the nascent industry was yet concerned with). In just three months, Alcorn produced a game that was a marked improvement on the Odyssey's version: Atari's Pong featured sound, finer control, and on-screen scorekeeping. Alcorn's game so impressed Bushnell that he organized a public test at Andy Capp's, installing it in a decidedly DIY arcade cabinet. After two weeks, the game broke down, and Alcorn was dispatched to repair it. He was surprised to discover an electrical short caused by an overflow of coins in the collection tray—a repurposed bread pan. The game was clearly a hit, and for the next two years Atari could not manufacture Pong cabinets fast enough to keep pace with demand. For the first time, a video-game arcade machine generated massive profits. With it, the video-game industry exploded into the world.

Pong's success owed no small amount to its brilliantly simple design. The players control on-screen paddles with dials that move them up and down, gestures that would have been instantly familiar to anyone who had changed channels on a television set. Alcorn added finesse to the act of bouncing the ball back to an opponent by programming a range of zones into the controls that affect the angle and speed of the ball's return. This combination of simple

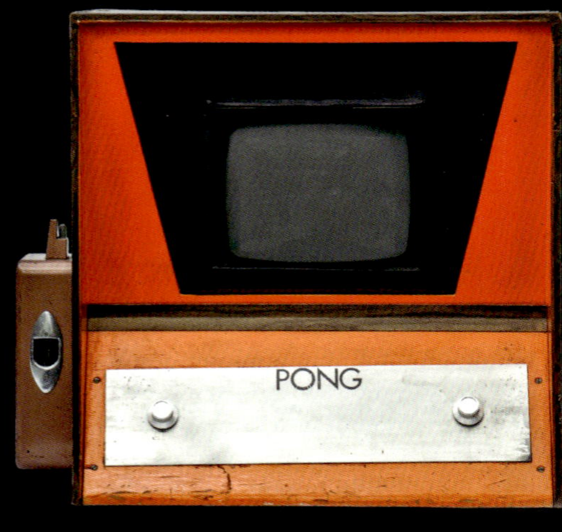

Pong arcade cabinet prototype (1972)

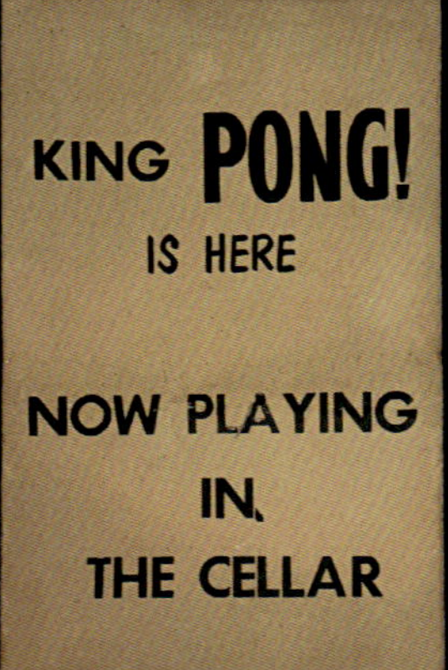

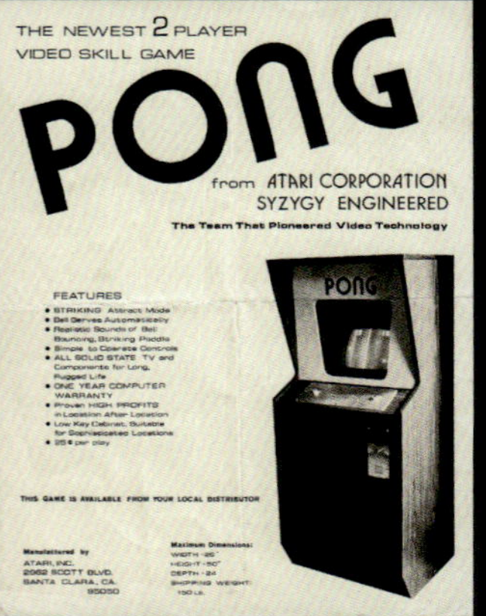

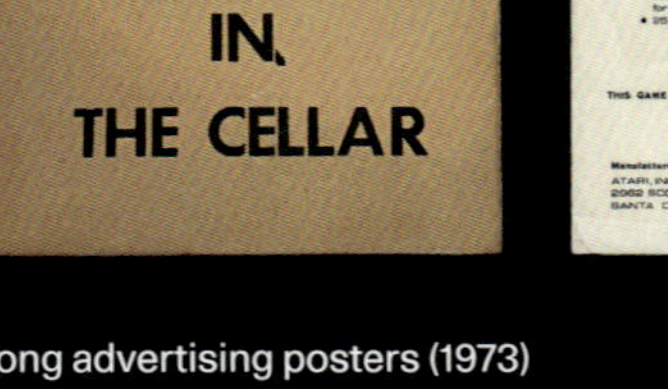

Pong advertising posters (1973)

Space Invaders

Tomohiro Nishikado (Japanese, born 1944)
Taito Corporation (Japan, est. 1953)

Space Invaders 1978
The Museum of Modern Art, New York.
Gift of the Taito Corporation

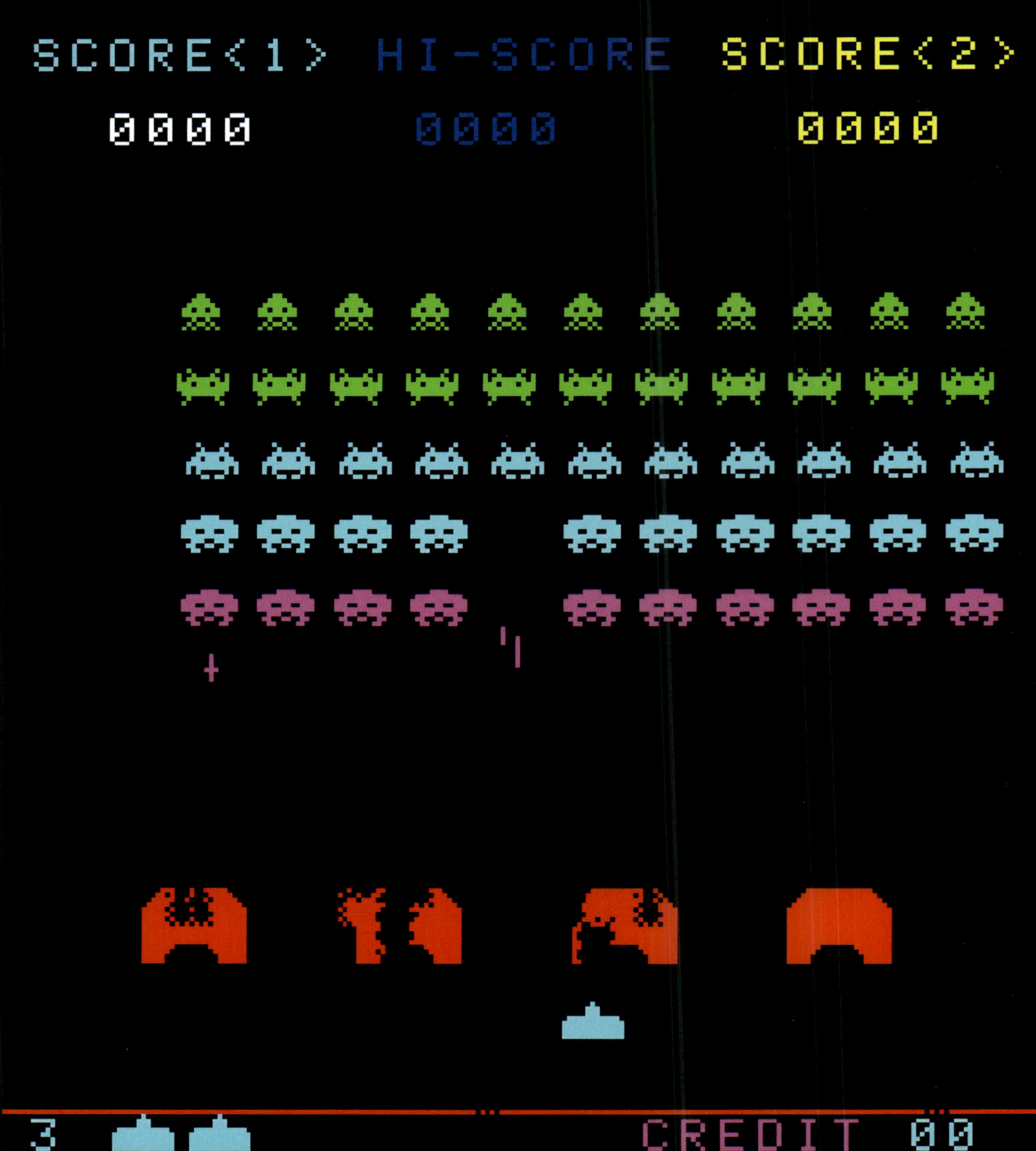

A relentless enemy army descends from the heavens. A lone gun turret frantically pivots from left to right, firing on as many attackers as possible while avoiding being shot in return. Four ominous bass notes, thumping like a heartbeat, increase in tempo as the horde comes closer and closer. A sense of doom, a fear of not being fast enough or accurate enough, grows with every beat. Tomohiro Nishikado's Space Invaders ratchets up the tension of combat to a fever pitch and achieves an emotional intensity that was, in the late 1970s, without precedent in video games.

Early in the game's development the approaching throng was made up of tanks, airplanes, and soldiers. For the people of Japan, however, the threat of unstoppable death from above was a traumatic and recent memory. Popular movies such as *Godzilla* and manga titles like *Akira* focused on the collective horror of destruction and offered—through Godzilla stomping Tokyo—a kind of catharsis. But passively watching such an onslaught is one thing; being put in the position of a lone warrior staving off catastrophe, even in a game, is far more emotionally fraught. Perhaps sensing this unsettling potential, Taito, the game's developer, insisted that Nishikado remove direct references to actual war. Inspired by *The War of the Worlds*, H. G. Wells's 1898 novel of a martian invasion of Britain, Nishikado substituted gyrating aliens that look like weird sea creatures for the familiar terrestrial threats, simultaneously distancing the violence from the real world and making the enemy all the more threatening in its inhumanity.

Gameplay is straightforward: a joystick moves the turret from left to right, and a button fires the gun. Players can quickly master the basic controls, and this ease of entry made the game accessible to the masses, most of whom had limited experience with video games. Space Invaders changed that, particularly in Japan, where it was an unparalleled hit. This extraordinary success led to the creation of Invader Houses in many urban centers—essentially cafes packed with Space Invaders cabinets. When Taito exported the game, the phenomenon was duplicated internationally. Video games were no longer found only in bars; they could also be played in quotidian places such as restaurants, movie theaters, stores, and arcades.

Space Invaders offered a host of innovations: it was the first game with a continuous soundtrack; the first to feature a high-score posting, creating intense competition among players; and one of the first to reach more than a billion dollars in sales. But for many players, it was the game's powerful emotional pull that proved the most enduring. Many legendary designers cite Nishikado's captivating, claustrophobic pressure cooker as their introduction to video games.

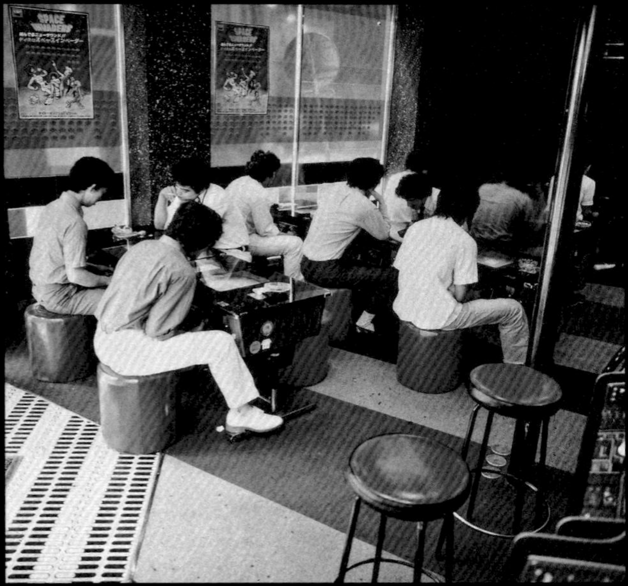

Invader House, Tokyo, 1978

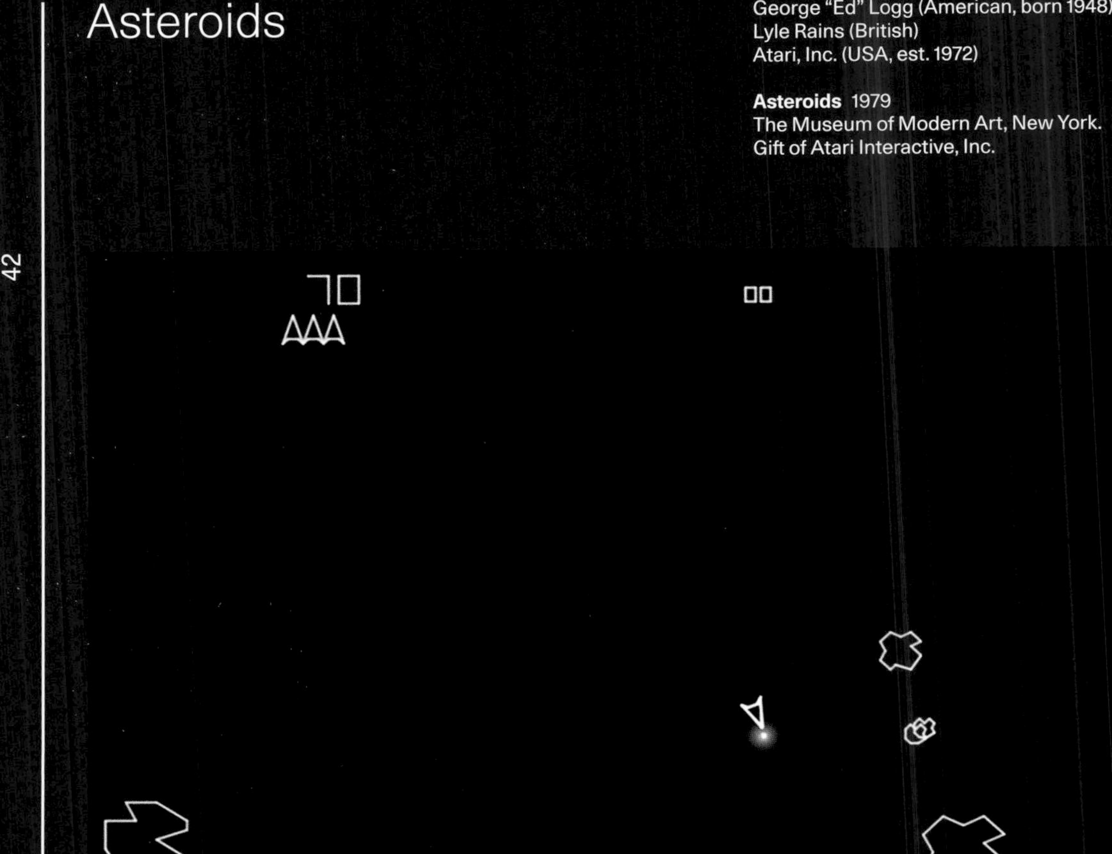
Asteroids

George "Ed" Logg (American, born 1948)
Lyle Rains (British)
Atari, Inc. (USA, est. 1972)

Asteroids 1979
The Museum of Modern Art, New York.
Gift of Atari Interactive, Inc.

42

Although it shares DNA with many games that came before it, Asteroids introduced a novel approach to the tried-and-true formula of piloting a spaceship around a black-and-white screen and firing at oncoming threats. Rather than focusing on combat with another player, as its antecedents did, Asteroids focuses on single-player action, with floating celestial bodies adding chaotic unpredictability. The multiple demands on a player's attention—chasing down the enemy's flying saucers, destroying asteroids, and dodging shrapnel from their destruction—result in a game of tremendous tension. Like Space Invaders (1978, page 40), the game features a relentless, menacing soundtrack that amplifies the suspense.

Asteroids is a prime example of iterative game design, in which a core concept is altered and refined through its development in subsequent games. A descendant of Spacewar! (1962), one of the first computer games, Asteroids might also be viewed as an update of Computer Space (1971), an arcade version of Spacewar! But don't confuse it with other Spacewar! variants such as Galaxy Game (1971), Orbit War (1974), Star Cruiser (1977), or Space Wars (1977). And certainly don't confuse Asteroids with that other popular space conflict from 1977, the film *Star Wars* (the sequel to which features spaceships crashing into, yes, asteroids). Space was a busy place in the 1970s.

To a player encountering Asteroids in an arcade in 1979, the game would have stood out dramatically from the other screens around it. It deployed an advanced vector monitor, which, unlike the industry-standard raster monitors used by most games at the time, has far higher resolution and the ability to include more complex shapes and motions. The result is gameplay that feels more fluid and lifelike. Its controls are direct descendants of the Spacewar! setup: five buttons control thrust, left and right rotation, firing, and a new hyperspace button, which grants an escape, albeit an unpredictable one, for players in desperate straits. These complex controls demanded greater dexterity and attention from the player, and they foreshadowed the intricate controller layouts that would become common in the decades to come.

Asteroids was designed by Lyle Rains and Ed Logg, the latter a formidable figure in Atari history who had a hand in major commercial hits such as Centipede (1981) and Gauntlet (1985). Their creative reinterpretation of the Spacewar! model arrived at a moment when arcade games were approaching the zenith of their popularity. Asteroids was Atari's second vector-graphics game, but it would become the company's greatest success, further establishing it as the leading force in the rapidly expanding business of video games. But Asteroids was also a coda to the era of simply drawn geometric space combat played on black-and-white monitors. There would be more to video games than wars in space.

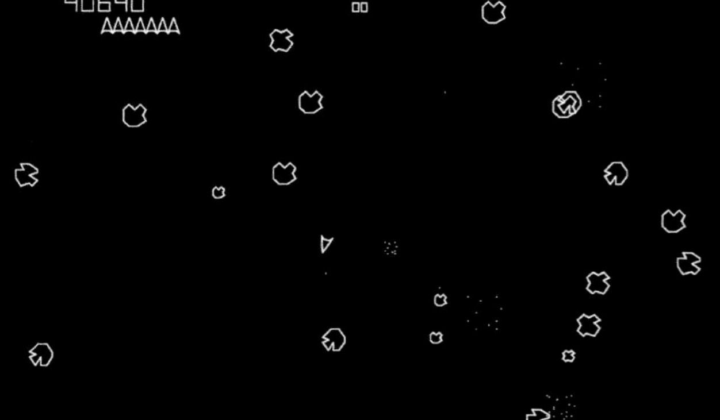

Pac-Man

Toru Iwatani (Japanese, born 1955)
NAMCO LTD. (Japan, est. 1955)

Pac-Man 1980
The Museum of Modern Art, New York.
Gift of BANDAI NAMCO Entertainment Inc.

Toru Iwatani knew there could be more to video games than violence. Aware that most games at the time skewed toward themes assumed to be attractive to men (shoot-'em-ups, car racing, sports), he sought an approach that would appeal to broader audiences, and to women in particular. With the idea that women might prefer fruit to laser guns, Iwatani crafted a game about eating. Although his severely gendered assumptions are dismaying, he was onto something. Within a year of its release, Pac-Man had earned more than a billion dollars, driving the arcade business into the stratosphere.

Iwatani's colorful, cheery game took visual inspiration from the Japanese cultural obsession with cuteness, or *kawaii* culture. Pac-Man, its voracious hero, is a vivid yellow circle with a mouth. His antagonists are four adorable, brightly colored ghosts called Inky, Pinky, Blinky, and Clyde. The setting for the action is a circuitous maze filled with dots, all of which Pac-Man must devour, while also avoiding the ghosts, in order to advance to the next level. By consuming one of the four "power pills" located in the maze's corners, Pac-Man briefly becomes capable of eating the ghosts, turning the tables for a few seconds. The characters overflow with personality; even the ghosts follow distinctly programmed behaviors. Blinky, for example, doggedly pursues Pac-Man all over the maze, whereas Clyde wanders in a haze of confusion. This lends a sense of chaotic unpredictability, especially in the higher levels, when the action dramatically speeds up. The nuances of the ghosts' behavioral patterns imbue the game with a partylike atmosphere, as though Pac-Man is part of a group of friends playing tag. The player controls Pac-Man with nothing more than a joystick, piloting him around the maze to the accompaniment of upbeat, bouncing sound effects.

The confluence of playfulness, personality, and whimsy make the game's characters tremendously appealing. To veteran arcadegoers, Pac-Man was a welcome burst of joy after years of white-knuckled space combat and alien invasion. To new players, the cute, cartoonish game was fun, easy to master, and a rewarding diversion. The game was an enormous hit, and, in a first, its characters became global icons, appearing on printed clothing, as plastic toys in McDonald's Happy Meals, and in pop music. Pac-Man

arcade cabinets showed up in laundromats, hotel lobbies, and stores, inserting video gaming further into everyday life. The video-game industry had never experienced anything like it. The cult of Pac-Man foreshadowed the global reach of later characters such as Mario, Sonic the Hedgehog, and Lara Croft, but the result was not entirely positive: the saturation of the market with Pac-Man cabinets helped push the arcade business past the point of economic sustainability, contributing to its spectacular collapse only a few years later as home-console gaming surged in popularity. Nevertheless, Iwatani's humble eating game profoundly influenced the direction of video games in the following decade, inspiring designers to consider new ways of shaping character behavior.

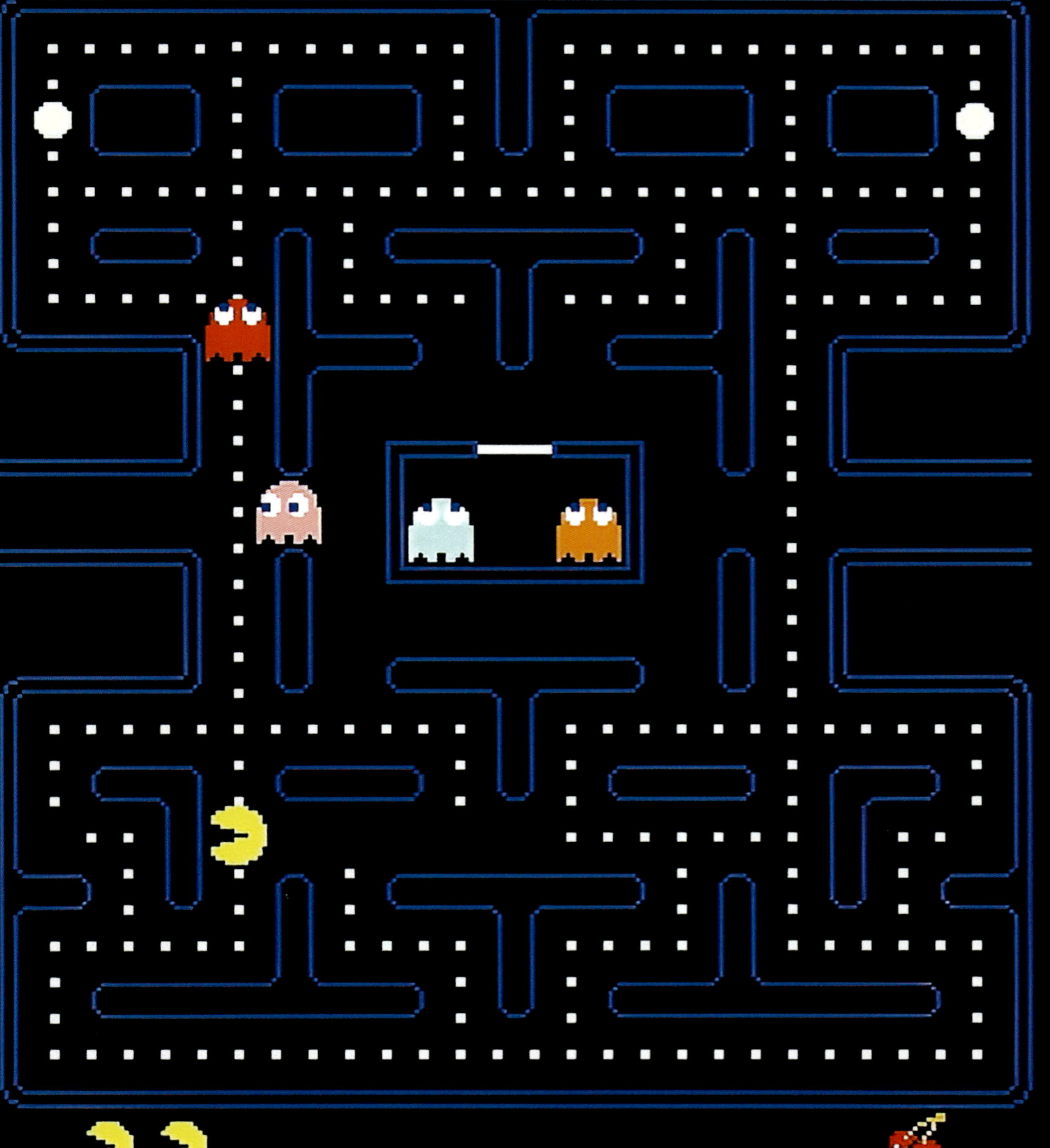

1UP
220
HIGH SCORE
1000
2UP
290

NetHack

NetHack DevTeam (USA, est. 1987)

NetHack 1987
The Museum of Modern Art, New York

Calling a video-game player a nerd reduces a vast and varied community into a broad stereotype. Calling a NetHack player a nerd, on the other hand, is a plausible and accurate use of the word. There are few video games that so successfully combine the rarest elements in the periodic table of dorkiness: the role-playing game Dungeons & Dragons (D&D), Usenet newsgroups, communal computer programming, and obscure references to the fantasy novels of Terry Pratchett. NetHack is inscrutable, enormously difficult to master, and impenetrable for the novice player. Abandon all hope, ye noobs who enter here.

Much like Asteroids (1979, page 42) evolved from Spacewar! (1962), NetHack is descended from Rogue (1980), a game so widely imitated that it led to an entire genre dubbed "roguelikes." The essential feature of all roguelikes is the D&D–style exploration of dungeons in which players gather items, battle monsters, and, often, fulfill quests. NetHack's procedurally generated dungeon levels are ambitiously enriched, with greater complexity, unpredictability, and healthy servings of humor. Created and still maintained in the present day by a collaborative group of programmers known as DevTeam, the game is a software fork (or altered copy) of the 1982 game Hack, one of the first successful online games. Led by Mike Stephenson, DevTeam worked together, altering and improving the code over Usenet. In keeping with its hacker ethos, the game was released freely and with full permission for other programmers to participate. The "net" in NetHack is a testament to the role that the burgeoning capabilities of online communication played in fostering collaboration.

Playing NetHack demands a great deal of facility with its only input: the computer keyboard. As we might expect of a game created by computer programmers, it assumes an expert level of familiarity with arcane key combinations and the cause-and-effect nature of coding; it is not designed with the general public in mind. Instead, the game drops a player into a dark dungeon that is slowly and unforgivingly revealed through exploration. To avoid dangers and locate treasures, players need to memorize more than seventy commands and actions—a skill requirement that scoffs at the more friendly visuals and sound effects of Atari and Nintendo games. Items and monsters are represented by dizzying constructions of ASCII text, in a visual system that players must learn in order to be able to navigate. Through trial and error, they come to recognize, for example, that a white *f* represents a friendly house cat while the yellow *f* is a dangerous tiger. Only with patience and determination do players master the game and its vocabularies.

NetHack was a turning point in video-game history, segmenting the community into hardcore gamers, who were willing to invest time and effort into complex and obscure systems, and those drawn to the mass-market delights of Pac-Man (1980, page 44) and other colorful games. For the former, it was and remains one of the most rich and challenging role-playing games.

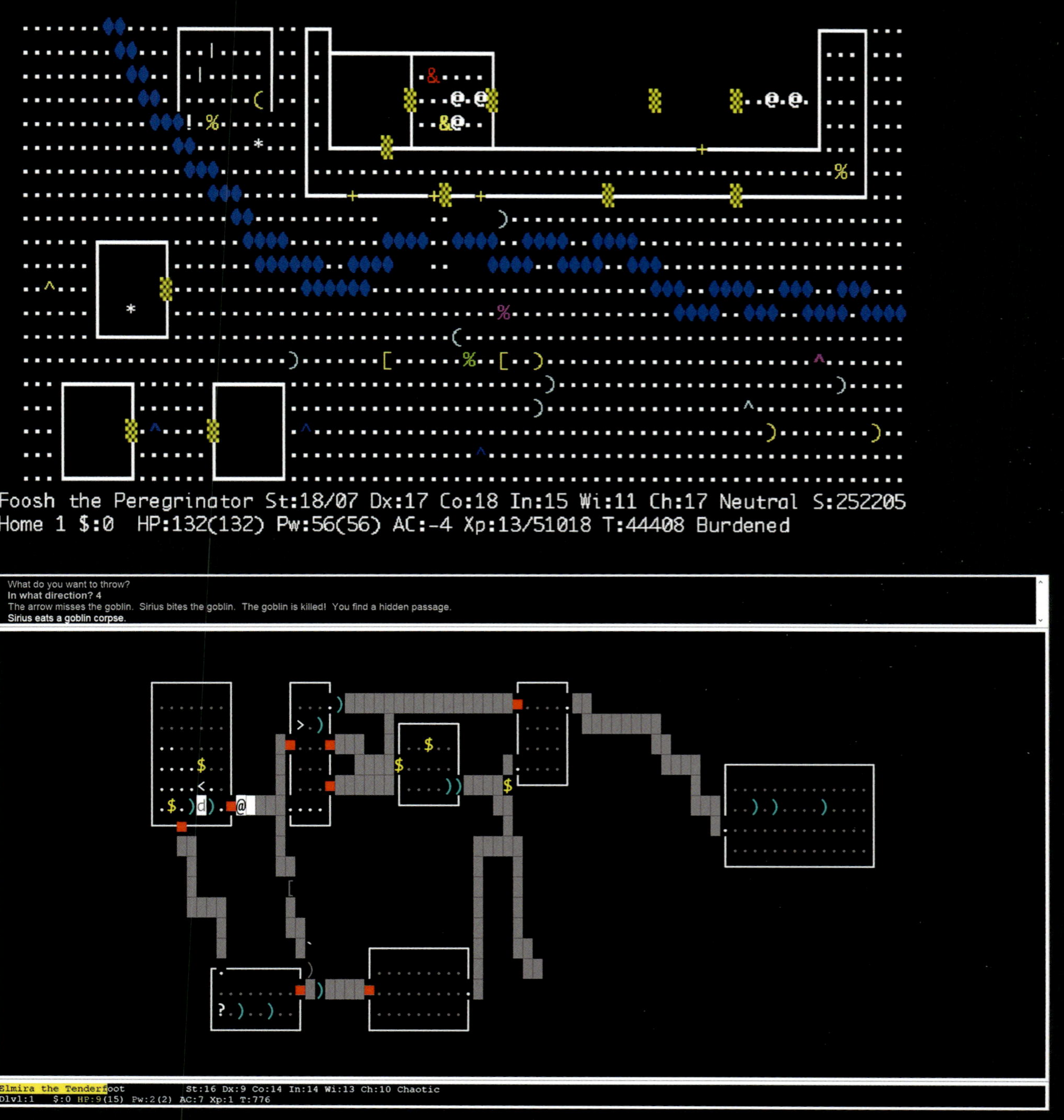

The djinni speaks. "I am in your debt. I will grant one wish!"--More--
Foosh the Peregrinator St:18/07 Dx:17 Co:18 In:15 Wi:11 Ch:17 Neutral S:252205
Home 1 $:0   HP:132(132) Pw:56(56) AC:-4 Xp:13/51018 T:44408 Burdened
What do you want to throw?
In what direction? 4
The arrow misses the goblin. Sirius bites the goblin. The goblin is killed! You find a hidden passage.
Sirius eats a goblin corpse.
THE INPUT
Elmira the Tenderfoot   St:16 Dx:9 Co:14 In:14 Wi:13 Ch:10 Chaotic
Dlvl:1 $:0 HP:9(15) Pw:2(2) AC:7 Xp:1 T:776

Tetris

Alexey Pajitnov (Russian, born 1955)

Tetris 1984
The Museum of Modern Art, New York.
Gift of The Tetris Company, LLC

For one of the most successful games of all time, Tetris had surprisingly humble beginnings. Like the games developed decades before in North America and Europe, it emerged from an academic computer lab and, for quite some time, was freely shared and played by the select few who had access to a computer. That it was developed in the Soviet Union, on computers far weaker than those available everywhere else, is a twist on this familiar story. After lurking for years behind the Iron Curtain, in the late 1980s Alexey Pajitnov's addictive, maddening game found its way to the rest of the world, where it would influence game design for generations.

Pajitnov was a typical computer programmer, plugging away late into the night at the Moscow Academy of Science. Inspired by board games, he came up with the idea for a computer game in which a player must stack varying shapes composed of four square blocks, or Tetriminos. The player rotates the shapes as they drop into a grid, attempting to fit them in among those already in place. Filling a row of blocks from side to side clears the whole line, making more room to accommodate the never-ending cascade. The game rapidly becomes a race against time: as the blocks pile up in impossible configurations the player has to clear as many lines as possible before the screen fills. The relentlessness of the falling shapes demands quick thinking, lending a pronounced tension to an otherwise straightforward puzzle.

Pajitnov worked on an Elektronika 60 computer, which was state of the art in the Soviet Union but incapable of graphics or sound. To get around this, he employed keyboard characters (brackets, slashes, and exclamation points) to create the game's grid and delineate shapes and borders. This was a familiar workaround for the programmers of video games (see NetHack [1987, page 46] and Dwarf Fortress [2006, page 74]), who used ASCII character encoding to approximate pictures and graphical shapes. When Tetris finally emerged from Russia, Pajitnov's simple

Tetris has been presented in countless formats, but whether on a Russian computer's fuzzy screen in the 1980s, a Nintendo Game Boy in the 1990s, or a modern smartphone, the game hooks its players through challenging yet easy-to-understand gameplay. Fitting shapes together and stacking blocks are among the first games children learn. Pajitnov's creative reinterpretation of this dynamic offered a return to one of childhood's simple joys and gave rise to legions of puzzle games desperate to imitate Tetris's success.

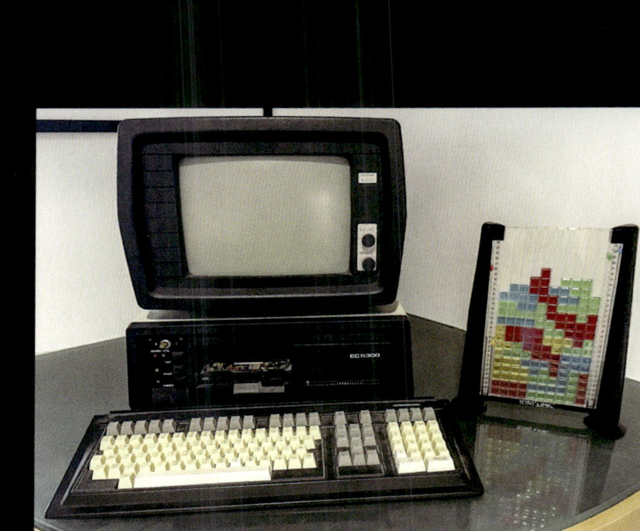

Elektronika 60 computer (early 1980s)

```
FULL LINES: 0      <!. . . . . . . . . . .!>     BEST LINES:
LEVEL: 1           <!. . . . . . . . . . .!>     1:  76
SCORE: 156         <!. . . . . . . . . . .!>     2:  44
TIME: 2:52         <!. . . . . . . . . . .!>     3:  34
                   <!. . . . . . . . . . .!>     4:  31
                   <!. . . . . . . . . . .!>     5:  22
                   <!. . . . . . . . . . .!>     6:  6
                   <!. . . . . . . . . . .!>     7:  6
                   <!. . . . . . . . . . .!>     8:  5
          [][][]   <!. . . . . . . . . . .!>     9:  2
          []       <!. . . . . . . . . . .!>     10: 1
                   <!. . . . . . . . . . .!>
                   <!. . . . . . . . . . .!>
                   <!. . . . .[] .[] .[] .!>
                   <!. . . .[] .[][][] .!>
                   <!. . .[][][][][][] .!>
                   <!. . .[][][][][][] .!>
                   <!.[][][][][][][][][] .!>
                   <![][][][][][][][][][] .!>
                   <![*********************]>
                    \/\/\/\/\/\/\/\/\/\/\/
```

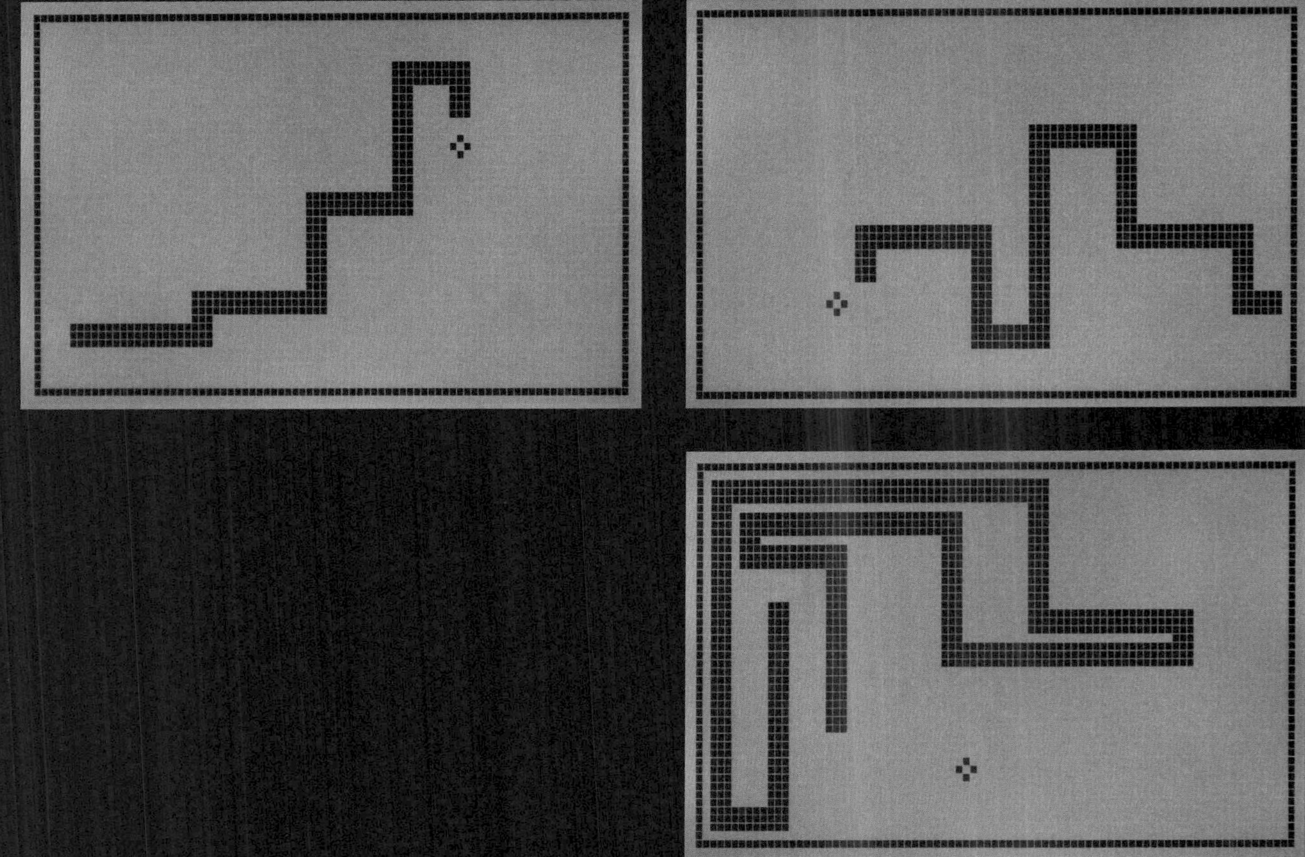

Staring down at a cell-phone screen is now so commonplace that it is taken for granted. Earlier in the age of mobile communication, however, cell phones were used primarily for calls—held up to the ear rather than in front of the face. The evolution from cell-phone-as-telephone-device to cell-phone-as-*everything*-device (with the arrival of the smartphone in 2007) contains multiple landmarks. One such moment was the 1997 release of Nokia's model 6110, which came with an added bonus: Snake.

A throwback to the simple designs of the early era of gaming, Snake was instantly iconic, and it forever altered the mobile-phone industry. Cellular phones had been on the market since the early 1980s, but their high cost kept them out of reach for most people. For those who could afford them, however, the ability to make a call from anywhere was a stunning feat of technical wizardry. Nokia, the Finnish multinational communications corporation that came to dominate the market, was a key player in the mass manufacture of affordable cell phones in the 1990s. To gain a competitive advantage, Nokia tasked the programmer Taneli Armanto with creating a game for their upcoming flagship phone. Working within the 6110's stifling constraints (of memory, processing, and display) forced Armanto to economize his design. The phone's maximum resolution of 48 by 84 pixels was less than half of what the Atari 2600—a system from twenty years before—could produce on a television screen. In a best-case scenario, he might manage to squeeze a 1970s game onto a 1990s phone.

Taking inspiration from the 1976 arcade game Blockade, Armanto created a game in which the player, using only the number keypad, directs an always-in-motion snake around the screen, turning at right angles to eat items for points. Hitting a wall or its own tail results in the snake's instant death. As the game progresses, the tail grows longer, becoming an increasingly challenging obstacle to navigate around. The snake's death is a foregone conclusion; eventually the screen is filled by its massive tail, and there is nowhere left to turn. The goal, then, is to achieve the highest score possible before expiring. There is no color, and the only sound is a harsh beep whenever the snake eats an item. Snake was a basic game designed for brief play sessions—a rewarding diversion between calls.

Snake is a monument in the history of game (and mobile-phone) design not only because it was among the first video games on a cell phone but also because, like any design masterpiece, it transformed its constraints into strengths. In an era when games on consoles and PCs were becoming more operatic and complex, Nokia's humble digital reptile charted the way for a new kind of play.

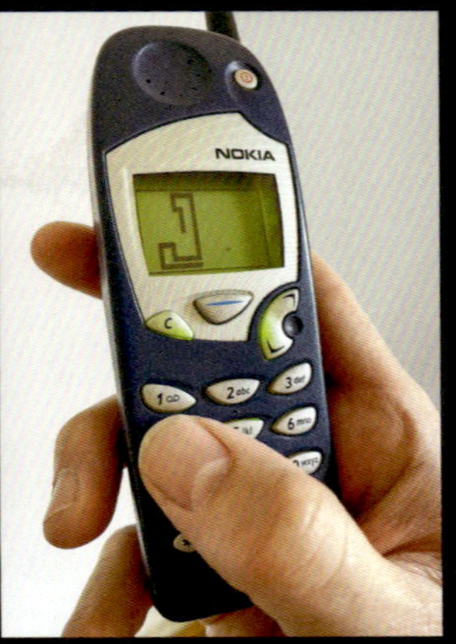

Nokia model 5165 (c. 1999)

Katamari Damacy

Keita Takahashi (Japanese, born 1975)
NAMCO LTD. (Japan, est. 1955)

Katamari Damacy 2004
The Museum of Modern Art, New York.
Gift of BANDAI NAMCO Entertainment Inc.

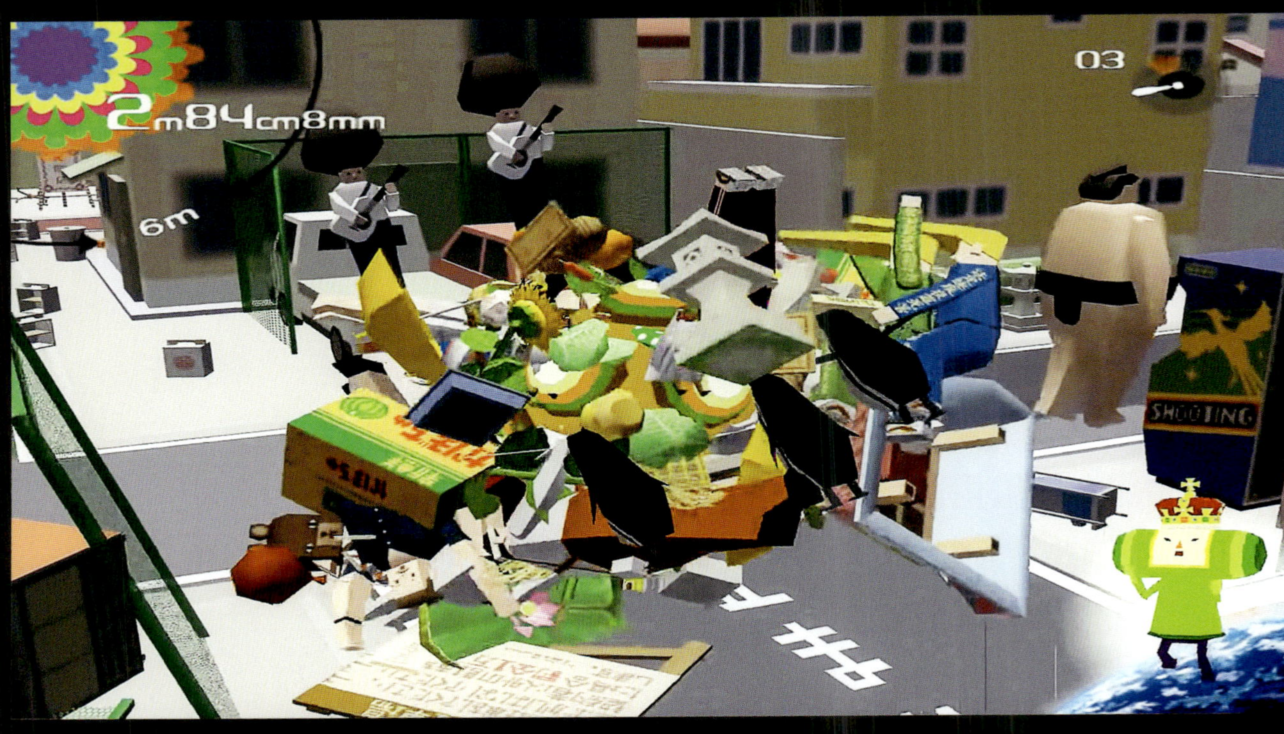

Your august father, the King of the Cosmos, needs you to help repair the universe, which he wrecked while on a drunken spree. As the young prince, you are tasked with mending the damage, which you do by rolling the mess into giant balls that are later transmuted into new stars and constellations, thereby restoring the heavens. These sticky balls start out small, beginning with plants and bits of sushi, and are progressively built up into giant orbs composed of people, buildings, and mountains. This is the twisted logic of Katamari Damacy, one of the most bizarre, humorous, and influential games of the early 2000s.

Designed by Keita Takahashi for the Sony PlayStation 2, Katamari Damacy (Japanese for "clump spirit") revels in the absurd and the surreal. In addition to jettisoning typical story arcs, in which a hero rescues a princess or defeats an evil enemy, the game also dispenses with the system of rewards (points, lives, or achievements) ordinarily used to encourage play. Instead play becomes just that—play. The basic act of pushing a ball, albeit a magic, supersticky one, becomes a pleasure in and of itself, inviting the player to experience the the simple joy of moving around

and delighting in the weird. With two joysticks, the player manipulates the direction and speed of the ball as it rolls about picking up stuff. As the ball grows, its mass exerts a corresponding gravity, increasing its ability to attract larger and larger objects. This fidelity to physics makes the preposterousness of the game's overall premise stand out all the more. Why did I just capture an old lady with a walker? Why does the king want me to collect pairs of twins? Why am I being serenaded by a Japanese version of a Las Vegas lounge act as I gather the detritus of modern civilization?

In Katamari Damacy, the game is an excuse for *playing*. The enormous success of Takahashi's creation opened the door to designers willing to reconsider the received wisdom about which kinds of stories sold best, which game structures were most rewarding, and what players wanted out of a video game. By foregrounding humor and joy, Takahashi reminds us what we most desire from a game: fun.

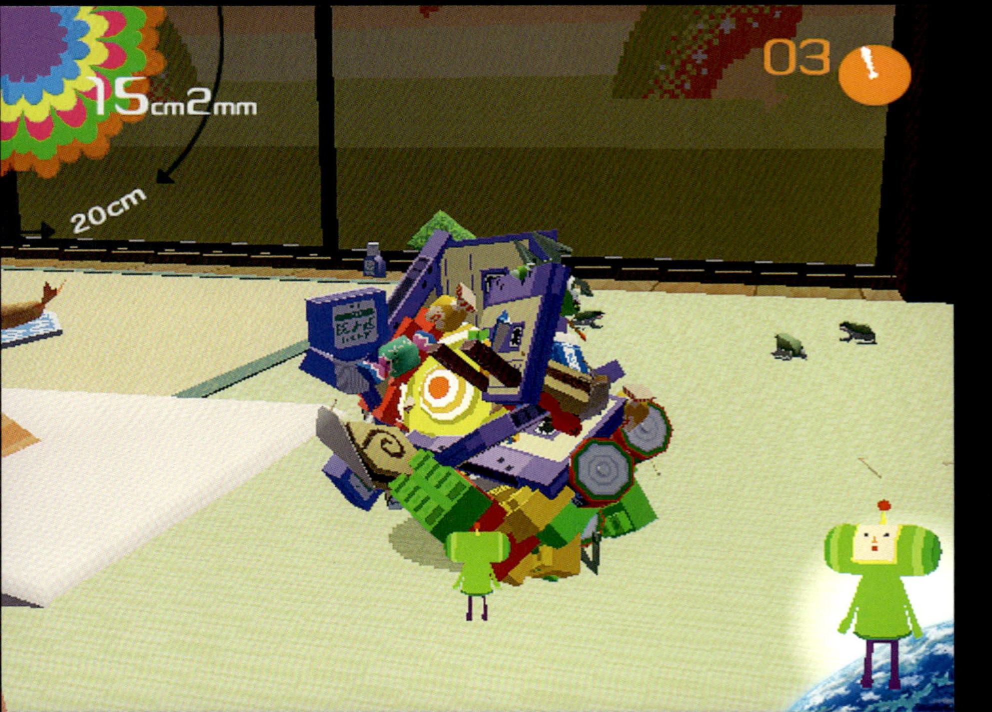

Canabalt

Adam Saltsman (American, born 1982)

Canabalt 2009
Music by Daniel Baranowsky (American, born 1984)
The Museum of Modern Art, New York.
Gift of the designer

Canabalt is an exemplar of the fertile field of web-based video games that flourished in the first decade of the twenty-first century. Programmed in JavaScript and playable on web browsers through an Adobe Flash plug-in, these free games blazed a trail for independent developers working outside of the large, highly capitalized business ecosystems of consoles and corporate developers. Canabalt also arrived at a fortuitous moment: its app version was a natural match for the recently released iPhone. Its simplicity of action and frenetic, relentless gameplay proved enormously successful and spawned a multitude of imitators eager to join the gold rush of gaming on touchscreen devices.

Designed by Adam Saltsman with a distinct spatial and architectural flair, Canabalt employs stylized graphics in a grayscale palette to create a film-noir atmosphere. This visual setup is an appropriate accompaniment for an action-packed, suspenseful race, in which players direct a suited businessman who has plunged from a skyscraper window and is desperately sprinting across rooftops to escape some unseen menace. The game scrolls to the right, and players must jump the businessman over buildings and obstacles while dodging collapsing structures, traps, and debris crashing down from the sky—running as far as possible before falling from a rooftop. The player's distance and score are revealed after each round, providing a mark to surpass in the next one. The game's controls are reduced to one action: making the man jump. Whether done with the click of a mouse (on a web

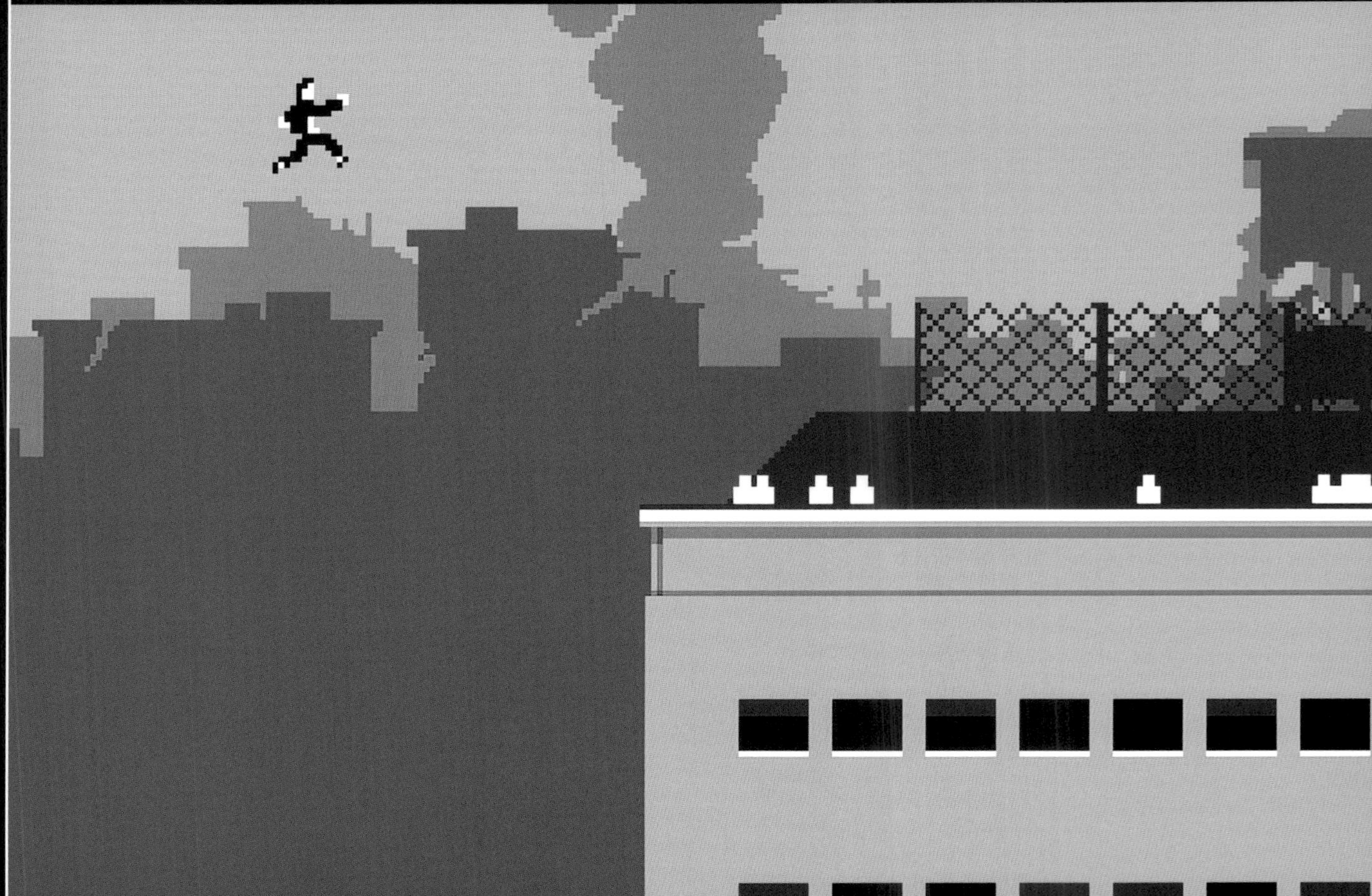

browser) or the tap of a finger (on a touchscreen), this minimalist control system allows players to focus on the increasing difficulty of correctly timing the jumps. With an ominous soundtrack augmenting the feverish pace of the game, players find themselves fully immersed in an unremitting race against death.

The success of Canabalt popularized a form of gaming known as "endless runner," in which the player controls a figure that runs and avoids obstacles. These games and their straightforward control schemes were perfect fits for the exploding market for touchscreen smartphones and tablets, which in the first years of their availability favored atmospheric music, strong visuals, and brief play sessions over complex control strategies and long, drawn-out stories. Their simplicity also drew in people who had not avidly played video games before, further broadening the market and community of gamers. As with Nokia's Snake (1997, page 50), Saltsman's deft combination of economic design and compelling gameplay made the case for a kind of "light" gaming, in which Canabalt and titles like it laid the groundwork for an entirely new, independent ecosystem of video-game production.

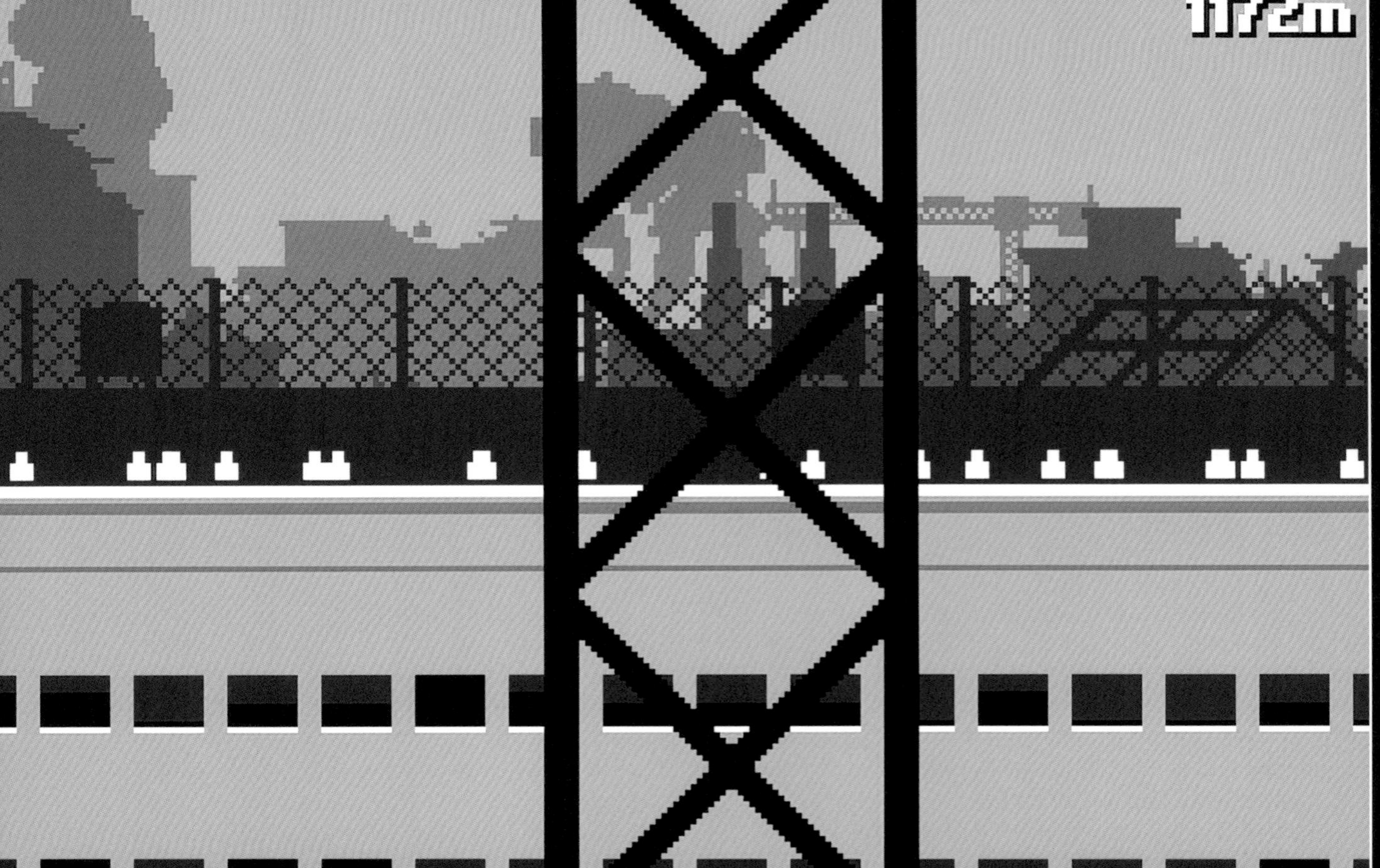

Monument Valley

ustwo games (UK, est. 2004)

Monument Valley 2014
The Museum of Modern Art, New York.
Gift of Ustwo Games

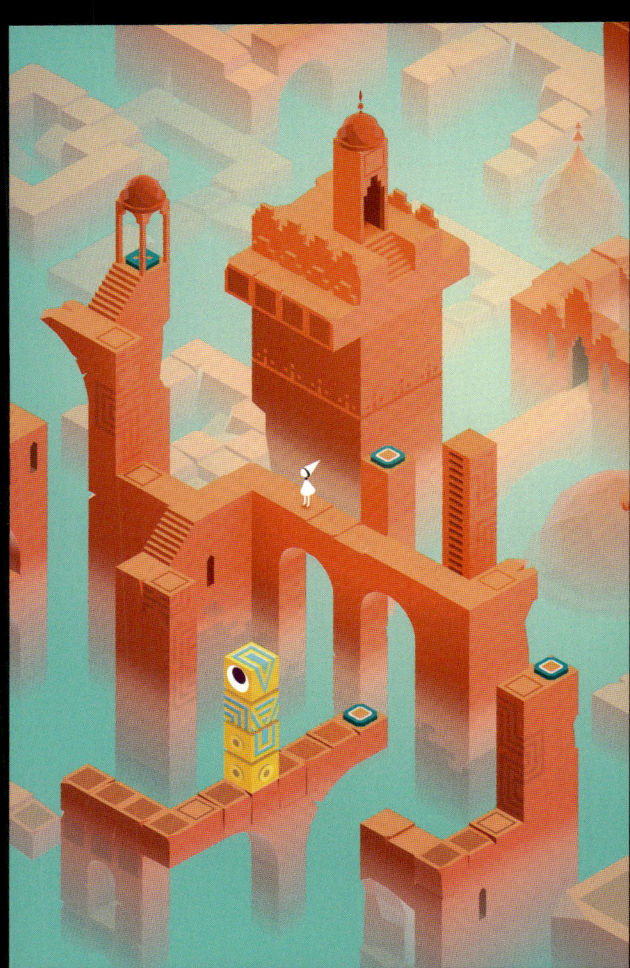

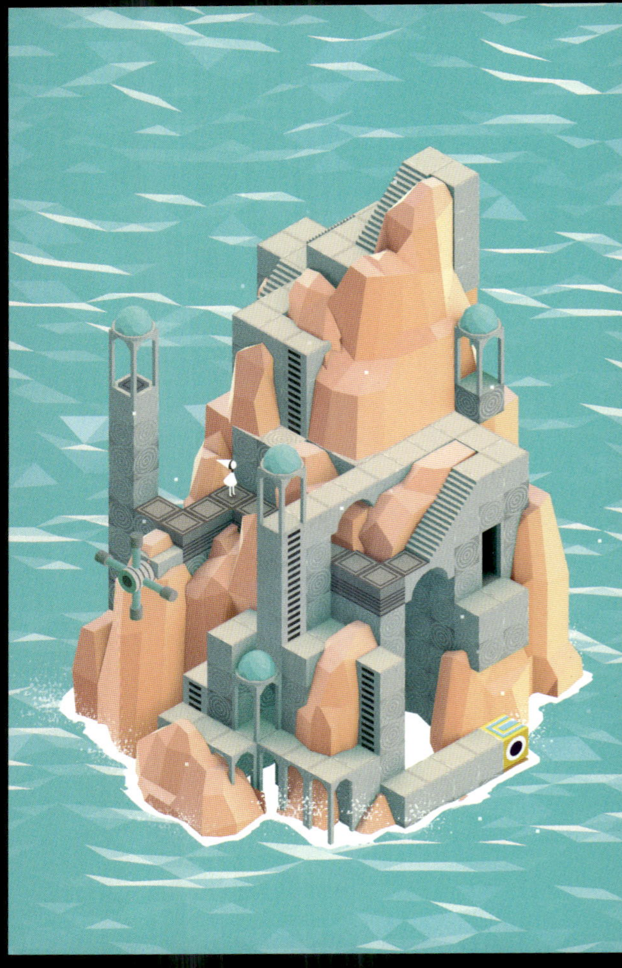

The arrival of Monument Valley signaled that smartphones and touchscreen tablets could provide rich experiences on par with those offered by consoles and PC gaming. Its combination of stunning visuals, challenging puzzles, and intuitive gameplay produced one of the first games to fully and successfully embrace the new touchscreen format.

Developed by the British indie developer ustwo with Ken Wong as its lead designer, the game follows Princess Ida as she navigates dreamy isometric landscapes filled with complex structures. Inspired by the works of the Dutch artist M. C. Escher, who was himself influenced by Moorish architecture and the eighteenth-century Italian architect Giovanni Battista Piranesi, the buildings in Monument Valley are made

up of impossible geometries and structural forms. Waterfalls cascade in endless Möbius loops; twisting balconies are linked in improbable ways; and rotating staircases connect walls and ceilings. Through a series of touches and swipes, players lead Princess Ida around this bewildering landscape, solving puzzles that require moving various building elements around in order to open new paths, and in the process reconsidering the rules of gravity, physics, and perception. With its soft, soothing soundtrack, the game feels like a beguiling and relaxing dream.

Gaming on a touchscreen device presented novel problems to designers accustomed to the conventions of gameplay on PCs (mouse and keyboard) or consoles (joystick and button controller). How would

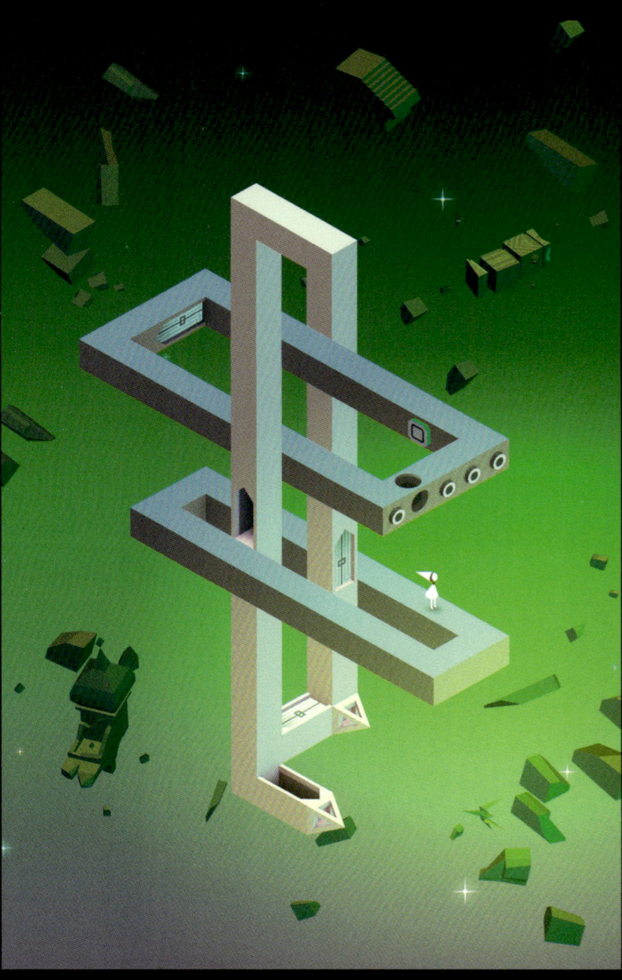

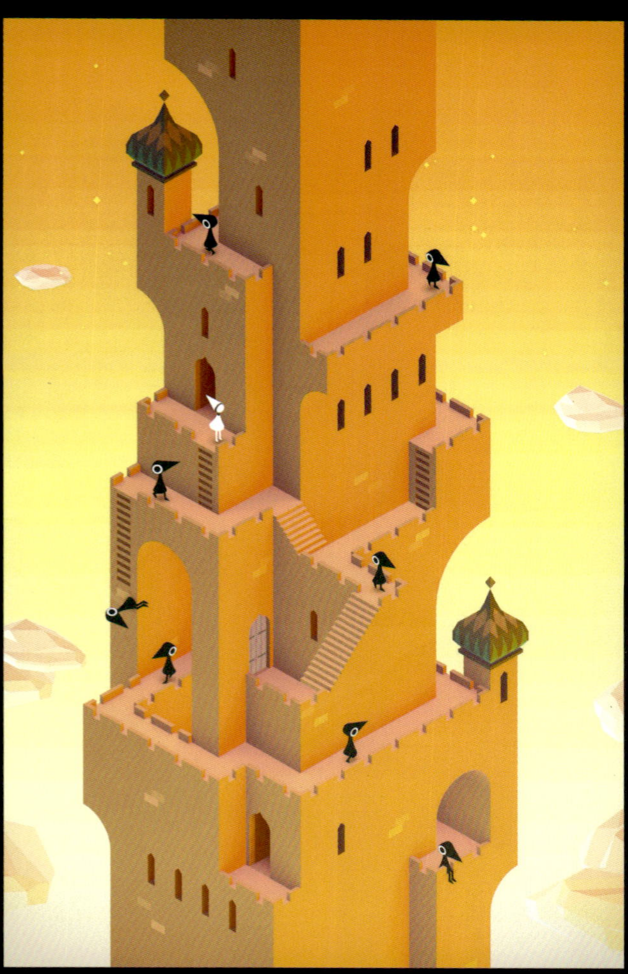

the player direct the avatar around the screen? Would a virtual re-creation of a joystick suffice, or would it consume valuable on-screen real estate? How does a designer keep the player's fingers from obscuring the screen and interfering with the game? Monument Valley demonstrates a way of rethinking game design for a device in which the input and output have been merged. In having the player swipe and drag the puzzle structures around the screen, the game mimics the forms of navigation used for other pro-grams on the device, such as browsing the Internet and text messaging. Rather than trying to shoehorn a control strategy from one context into another, on an altogether different device, the game's design seam-lessly adapts to the environment in which it is played.

Monument Valley's marrying of form to function, of game design to game input, marked a return to the core principles of interactive design: controls that are simple, direct, and, above all, intuitive. When added to sophisticated and beautiful visuals, a compelling narrative, and moving music, this approach yields powerfully affecting experiences. Getting lost in a maze has never been so much fun.

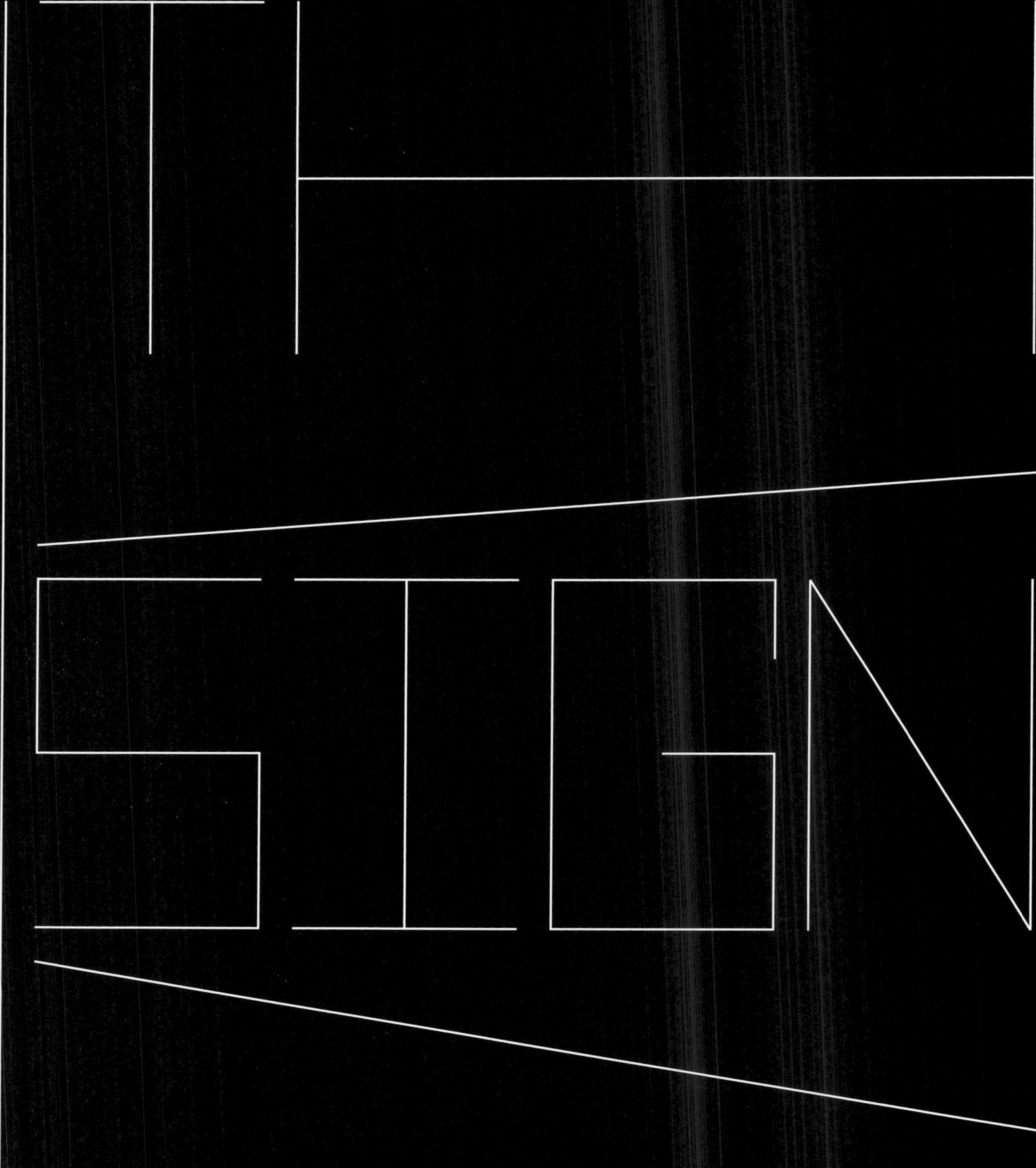
THE
SIGN

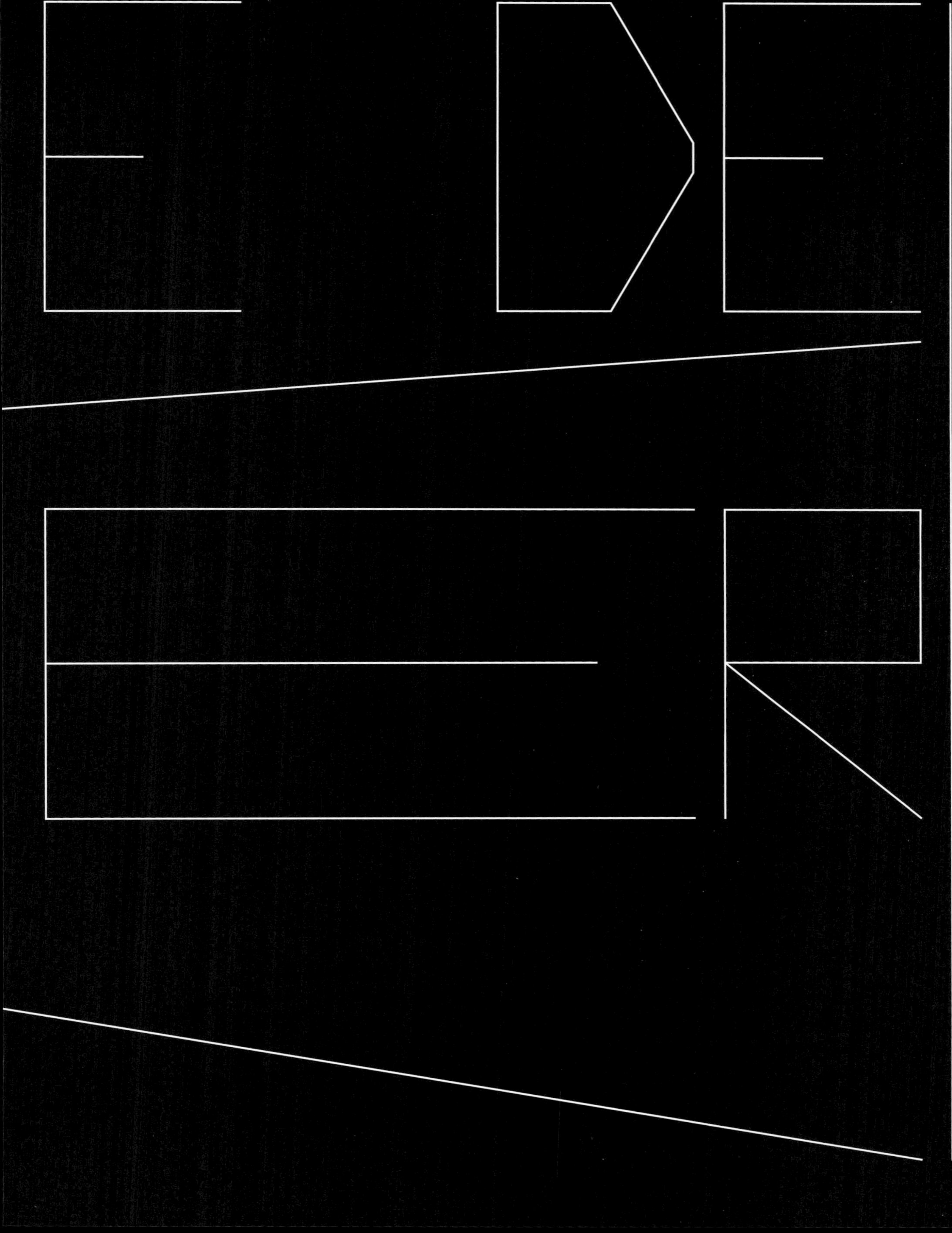

Anna Burckhardt

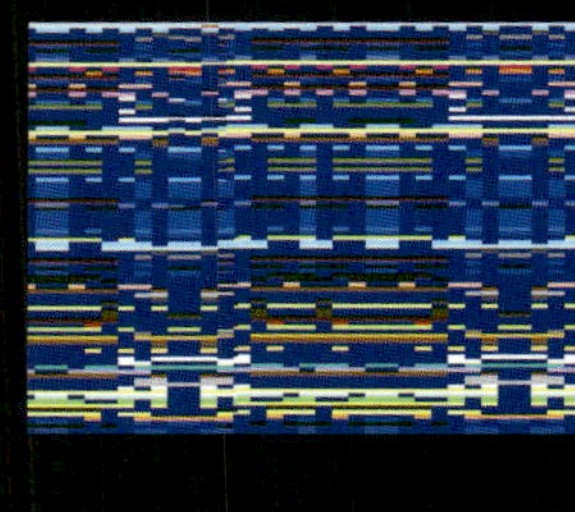

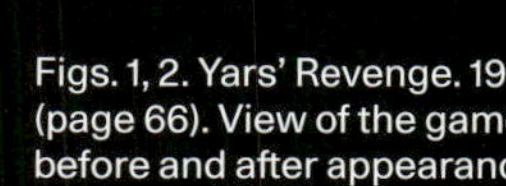

Figs. 1, 2. Yars' Revenge. 1982
(page 66). View of the game
before and after appearance of
the Easter egg

1. In 1980 the designer Warren
Robinett inserted his name in
the Atari 2600 game Adventure,
in the form of giant flashing
letters in a secret room, to
protest the removal of developer credits from Atari games
by its parent company Warner
Communications. When a
teenaged fan discovered the
hidden room and broke the
news to the company, Warner,
in an unsurprising (and grabby)
move, developed a marketing
strategy around it, and programmers were instructed to
add Easter eggs to every game.
Adventure's hidden element
was not the first, but it was the
first be called an Easter egg.
See Seth Porges, "The True
Story behind the Original Video
Game That Inspired 'Ready
Player One,'" *Forbes* online,
December 20, 2017.

For many designers, a great video game is one that thoroughly immerses the player in another world—pushing aside everyday life, even if briefly. Others delight in the opposite: sudden disruptions, hidden rabbit holes, and abrupt breaches of the fourth wall, which test our need to control the game, reminding us that we are at the mercy of someone else. One such surprise emerged in 1982, in the game Yars' Revenge (page 66); after players completed a particularly complex maneuver, the screen went dark and the letters HSWWSH appeared, interrupting gameplay and restarting the game (figs. 1, 2). Those curious and dedicated enough to investigate learned that these were not random letters caused by a glitch; they were the initials of Howard Scott Warshaw—the game's designer.

Designers, developers, and programmers have used messages, features, or images hidden in a game's software (known as Easter eggs) since the early days of video games, to connect directly with players and in particular with ardent fans. The first ones were a way for designers to assert their authorship in defiance of the corporations that took credit for their work. In the 1980s, when Atari reigned over the industry, every aspect of a game's design—from coding to scoring and graphics—was typically handled by a single person who seldom received any recognition (or royalties) for it. By tucking his name deep in the game, only discoverable by accident or insider knowledge, Warshaw thumbed his nose at the empty suits at Warner Communications—Atari's owner, a company with a reputation for treating developers poorly.[1] Since then, Easter eggs have become more and more common in video games, as inside jokes, keys to hidden levels, and attention-grabbing tricks. Even though they halt a game's progression, they have proved so enormously popular that they have become an industry standard, expected by new and seasoned players alike.

Interruptions and irritations, however, run counter to almost everything interaction designers are taught, which is that engagement with phone apps, vending machines, and any object or software requiring human interaction should be free of frustration-causing friction or disturbance.[2] Moreover, negative features or effects make easy tasks harder to accomplish, while positive ones make difficult tasks easier. This ethos, of course, applies to video games as well—until it doesn't. In general, designers aim to write elegant code—neat, precise code—that economically elicits specific behaviors from players. But as designers expand the idea of what a video-game experience is, efficiency and immersion are not always the end goal.

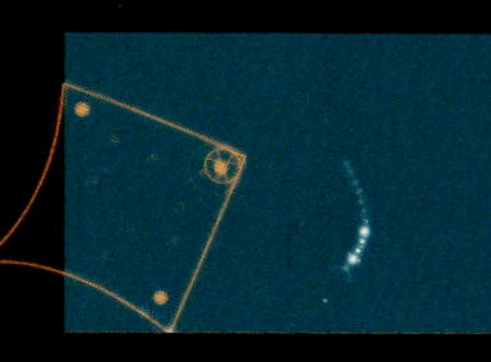

Fig. 3. flOw. 2007 (page 78)

2. See, for example, the usability texts often assigned to design students, including Donald Norman, *The Design of Everyday Things*, rev. ed. (1982; Cambridge, MA: MIT Press, 2013); and Alan Cooper, Robert Reimann, David Cronin, and Cristopher Noessel, *About Face: The Essentials of Interaction Design*, rev. ed. (1995; Indianapolis: Wiley, 2014). Gillian Crampton Smith, a pioneer in the field, wrote, "In the past, those who built interactive systems tended to focus on the technology that makes them possible rather than on the interfaces that allow people to use them. But a system isn't complete without the people who use it. Like it or not, people—irritable, demanding, and often distracted people like ourselves—and their goals are the point of our systems, and we must design for them." Smith, "What Is Interactive Design?," foreword to Bill Moggridge, *Designing Interactions* (Cambridge, MA: MIT Press, 2007), xii.

3. Jenova Chen, "Flow in Games," master's thesis (University of Southern California, 2006).

Immersion is traditionally produced by minimizing distractions. With thatgamecompany, his independent studio, the designer Jenova Chen pursues engrossing, emotional experiences brought about by serene and continuous design. Players guiding microorganisms through a liquid plane or directing the wind through fields of flowers encounter no jarring elements. flOw (fig. 3 and page 78), as its name suggests, exemplifies this design philosophy, in a game inspired by the Hungarian psychologist Mihaly Csikszentmihalyi's concept of mental flow. Chen, with the programmer Nicholas Clark, created a game that automatically adjusts the level of gameplay in order to keep players absorbed; for this to be possible, Chen has written, "The activity needs to reach a balance between the challenges of the activity and the abilities of the participant."[3] Players who are adept at flOw's tasks find that with each successful maneuver the game becomes increasingly difficult. The interface continues to challenge them, encouraging their attention to the game and preventing boredom from setting in. For less-practiced players, who might find the game difficult from the start, flOw sets up obstacles at a slower speed. For Chen and designers like him, immersion is a positive state, in which players can temporarily forget their burdens and responsibilities (and, for better or worse, time) without finding themselves frustrated, bored, or defeated.

Not every designer believes in full immersion and optimization (the continual updating of a game in order to improve its performance and visual quality). Like those who embraced Easter eggs, some designers, many working independently, believe that interruptions can keep players fully engaged. Their games deliberately elicit feelings we might otherwise try to avoid, such as boredom, annoyance, and even failure, as well as situations we would prefer not to have to confront. In Papers, Please (fig. 4 and page 84), Lucas Pope turned the ostensibly straightforward

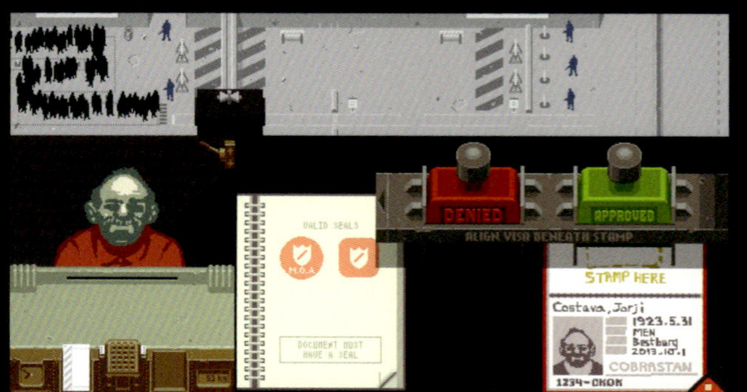

Fig. 4. Papers, Please. 2013 (page 84)

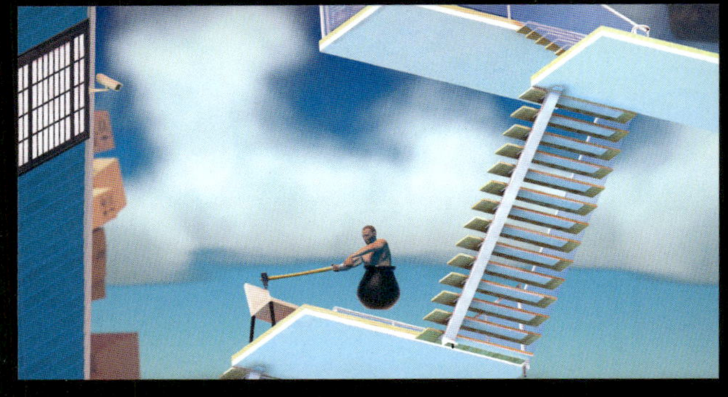

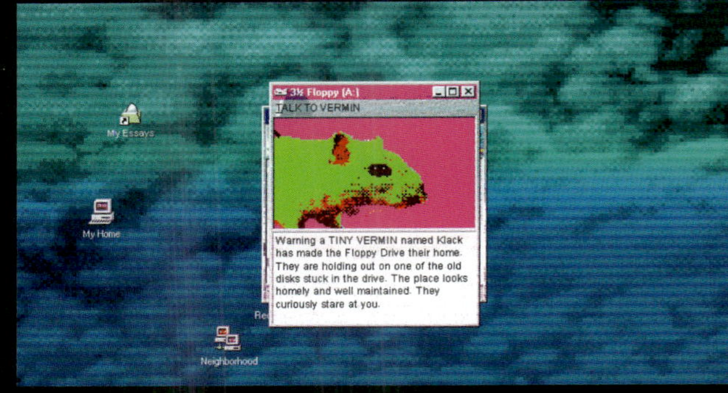

Fig. 5. Getting Over It with Bennett Foddy. 2017 (page 96). "When games were new they wanted a lot from you. Daunting you, taunting you, resetting and delaying you."

Fig. 6. Everything Is Going to Be OK. 2017 (page 92)

4. Patrick Begley, "'Empathy Gaming' Focuses on Emotions and Moral Decisions," *Sydney Morning Herald*, October 20, 2014.

5. See Bennett Foddy, interview by Jesper Juul, in *Handmade Pixels: Independent Video Games and the Quest for Authenticity* (Cambridge, MA: MIT Press, 2019); full interview at jesperjuul.net/handmade pixels/interviews/foddy.html.

act of exchanging documents—in this case, immigration papers—into a role-playing scenario that forces players into uncomfortable ethical territory. In the form of an immigration official in a fictional totalitarian country, players make choices that have inevitably negative implications, either for the official or for the individuals he interacts with. The game offers no possibility of a rewarding victory; instead, players make morally ambiguous decisions over and over and over again before arriving at one of several equally bleak endings. Games such as Papers, Please are known, for better or worse, as "empathy games," the goal of which, as the journalist Patrick Begley wrote in 2014, defining it in print for the first time, is to have a player "inhabit their character's emotional worlds, confronting themes such as poverty, sexuality and mental illness"; whether or not they regard the experience as a positive one is irrelevant.[4]

Bennett Foddy's design philosophy edges closer to something like cruelty. He believes that video games should disobey and even antagonize the player, and he takes every opportunity to provide friction, to taunt, and to play tricks.[5] The design of Getting Over It with Bennett Foddy (fig. 5 and page 98) produces the opposite of flow: it is a hilariously frustrating game accompanied by the designer's frustrating commentary. For Foddy, only the very real possibility of failure can produce a realistic sense of developing stakes. In QWOP (2008), his previous (equally absurd and enraging) game, players control a runner with Q, W, O, and P keys on a computer keyboard; the keys correspond to the runner's right and left thighs and calves, and keeping them coordinated is ridiculously hard. Like QWOP, Getting Over It uses rudimentary programming to simulate an activity that seems easy, but which turns every interaction into a painfully difficult experience. Instead of sophisticated graphics, a powerful soundtrack, or intricate puzzles, players get a clumsy avatar that seldom reacts to input commands in expected ways, and no guarantee that any progress will be saved. The only thing that matters is how much effort they put into it—the kind of effort that results from knowing at any minute they could lose it all.

Some designers remove themselves from the debate about immersion versus frustration by discarding the label of "game" altogether. Nathalie Lawhead's Everything Is Going to Be OK (fig. 6 and page 92), for example, is a disorienting and deeply personal interactive work that explores trauma and abuse. Through misbehaving commands and funny, painful vignettes, it rejects baseline tenets of software usability such as the existence of comprehensible rules and easily understood instructions. "Art on computers, games especially, lend themselves well to reversing the power dynamic a computer user expects," Lawhead has said, "control becomes loss of control."[6] The role of the player is merely to click along and set the work in motion, but without any say in how it unfolds; here, as in life, the player grows through surviving experiences rather than controlling them.

Some games require a mutual and cooperative relationship between their algorithms and their players. No game depends on this dynamic more than the long-lived and obscure yet widely influential Dwarf Fortress (2006, page 74).[7] Its software generates a world of forests, mountains, and rivers; as players build thriving dwarf colonies in this landscape, they develop their own narratives out of whatever information has been made available. At the heart of Dwarf Fortress is the concept of emergent narrative, a design approach in which players influence and change a game's story and outcome.[8]

This interdependence speaks to a larger principle of interactive design: video games—no matter how elegant the code, how realistic the animations, how witty the dialogue—cannot play themselves. All designers make a tacit agreement to collaborate to varying degrees with players, because a video game, like a theatrical production that only comes to life with an audience, depends on its players to give it meaning. An Easter egg needs to be activated in order to reveal its message; the sense of failure at being sent back to the beginning of a game can only be grasped by a real human being, who has the power to press Pause in order to recover from it. As Foddy kindly reminds us in that moment, "Feel free to go away and come back. I'll be here."

6. Nathalie Lawhead, "Artist Profile: Nathalie Lawhead," interview by Ryan Kuo, Rhizome website, February 1, 2022.

7. Dwarf Fortress paved the way for games such as Minecraft (2011, page 120) and Fortnite (2017). See Evan Urquhart, "The Dwarves Who Built the Road to Fortnite," Slate online, June 6, 2019.

8. See Tarn Adams, "Characterization and Emergent Narrative in Dwarf Fortress," in Beat Suter, René Bauer, and Mela Kocher, eds., Narrative Mechanics: Strategies and Meanings in Games and Real Life (Bielefeld, Germany: transcript, 2021), 151–60.

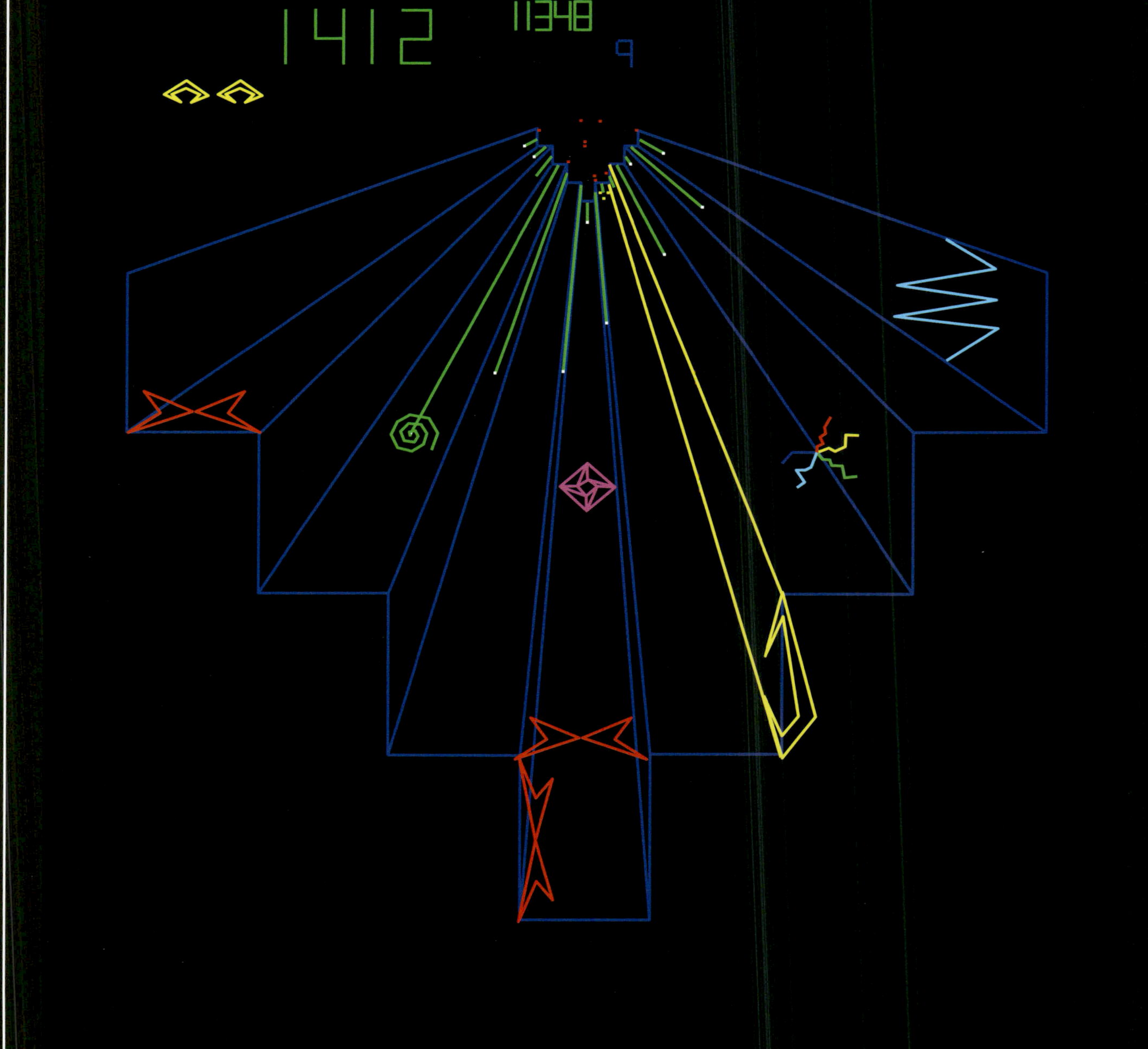

1412
11348
9
NEVER ALONE

Dave Theurer, a designer at Atari in the early 1980s, conceived Tempest as a first-person version of the popular Japanese game Space Invaders (1978, page 40). He had come to the company after graduating from Wheaton College and quickly made a name for himself with arcade games such as the classic Missile Command (1980), in which players defend six West Coast cities from ballistic missiles. He has attributed his quick success to his undergraduate degree in psychology and his research into motivation and addiction.[1]

Thanks in part to Missile Command's popularity, Atari gave Theurer free rein to develop his next project. Space Invaders was one of his favorite video games, and he thought he could reproduce it with an entirely new graphical perspective—with the player viewing the game through the shooter's eyes. In market testing, however, the game proved unpopular; players did not find it *fun*. Rather than giving up, Theurer changed course. For an altogether new arcade game he drew inspiration from a recurring childhood nightmare about having to smash monsters crawling out of a dark hole in the ground—the entrance to a tunnel leading down to the center of the earth. To turn the nightmare into a game, Theurer bent the customary flat vertical plane of the playing space into a tube, so that players appeared to be firing (by hitting a button) into a tunnel out of which various enemies were emerging; spinning a knob, the game's other control, caused both the tunnel and the targets to rotate. This idea was well received, although the revolving elements left the testers nauseated. Theurer modified the game to limit the rotation to the player's line of fire and to keep the tunnel stationary. The changes were a success.

Tempest became one of the first video games to make the leap into graphics drawn in one-point perspective. It was also one of the first to feature a 3D color-vector display and the first of its kind to allow players to select the difficulty of their starting level, using a system known as SkillStep that is now an industry standard. Theurer's goal was to elevate players to a trancelike state that could temporarily block out the struggles of daily life. Rather than simply increasing the number of opponents as players advance, Tempest has levels that are visually and navigationally distinct, with the sides of the tunnel variously curved, flat, or set at different heights. These progressively difficult forms prompt players to alter their behavior and strategy as they move through the game. The success of Tempest, like that of Space Invaders before it, speaks to how gripping a game can be when it combines smooth input, artful graphics, and engaging gameplay.

1. Dave Theurer, "Blowing Things Up," interview by Ken Loge, *Dreamsteep* blog; originally printed in *Morph's Outpost on the Digital Frontier*, May 1994; blog and magazine discontinued, see diginoodles .com/writing/interesting /blowing-things-up.

Yars' Revenge

Howard Scott Warshaw (American, born 1957)
Atari, Inc. (USA, est. 1972)

Yars' Revenge 1982
The Museum of Modern Art, New York.
Gift of Atari Interactive, Inc.

1. See Howard Scott Warshaw, "Yars' Revenge: Classic Game Postmortem," GDC, Game Developer's Conference, August 10, 2015, YouTube video, youtube.com/watch?v=aqH4k_OEqhY.
2. Warshaw, "Classic Game Postmortem."

Howard Scott Warshaw might be best remembered as the designer of E.T. the Extra-Terrestrial—a much-maligned video game, based on the hit movie of 1982, that has often (perhaps unjustly) been credited with destroying the economic growth of the video-game industry in the early 1980s. Before this unfortunate claim to fame, however, Warshaw was a respected programmer at Atari. In 1981 he was tasked with adapting the arcade game Star Castle for the Atari 2600 home console. After many failed experiments, he realized that the higher processing power and multibutton controller of the arcade game were ill-suited to such a conversion; moreover, Star Castle's vector-based graphics were nearly impossible to replicate on a television set. Warshaw did not give up. Instead, he reimagined the game completely, changing its concept as well as the playing scenario.

In Star Castle the player pilots a spaceship charged with destroying an enemy cannon, but in Yars' Revenge the player controls a Yar—an insectlike creature that must break through the defenses of the Qotile, an alien attacker, by shooting or nibbling at its shield. For Atari's at-home controls—a joystick with a single button—Warshaw incorporated into the game the Zorlorn Cannon, which the player fires by pulling back on the joystick when the Qotile's field has been breached. The Qotile, positioned on the screen's right-hand side, can shoot beyond its own shield and kill the Yar, but the player can move the Yar into a multicolored band at the screen's middle left, where it is protected from the Qotile but unable to fire. This neutral field, an essential aspect of the game, was also an inventive way to adapt to the limitations of the 4K bytes of ROM and 128 bytes of RAM in which Yars' Revenge was coded. In a method Warshaw sometimes called "cheap graphics," the pixelated animations are produced by the game's code, randomly generated by its cartridge and appearing on-screen in lieu of memory-wasting graphics.[1]

Warshaw has often said that his bachelor's degree in economics has been far more helpful to his career as a video-game developer than any programming knowledge.[2] It taught him that in situations of scarcity every element counts: the constraints he encountered while trying to translate a game from one form to another led him to an entirely original result. Yars' Revenge was the first game to display programming code on the screen, the first to feature a pause mode, and the first to offer an enhanced gameplay experience by adding layers of sounds to cue events in the game. Through its graphics, audio, and gameplay, it is an example of the way technology's limitations can

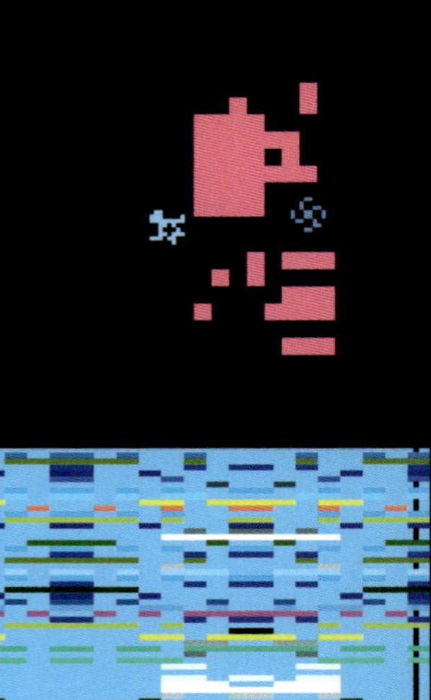

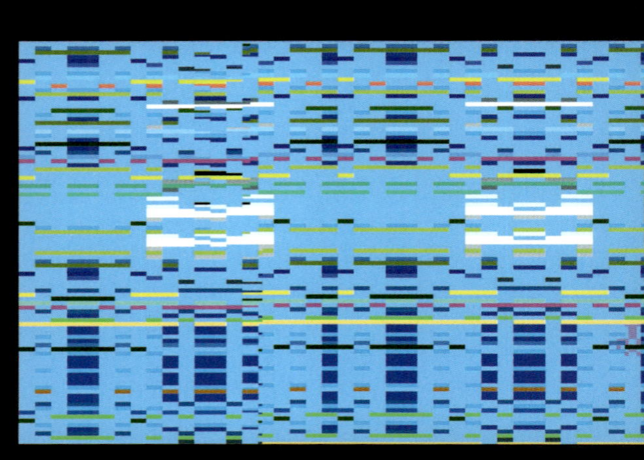

Another World

Éric Chahi (French, born 1967)

Another World 1991
The Museum of Modern Art, New York.
Gift of the designer

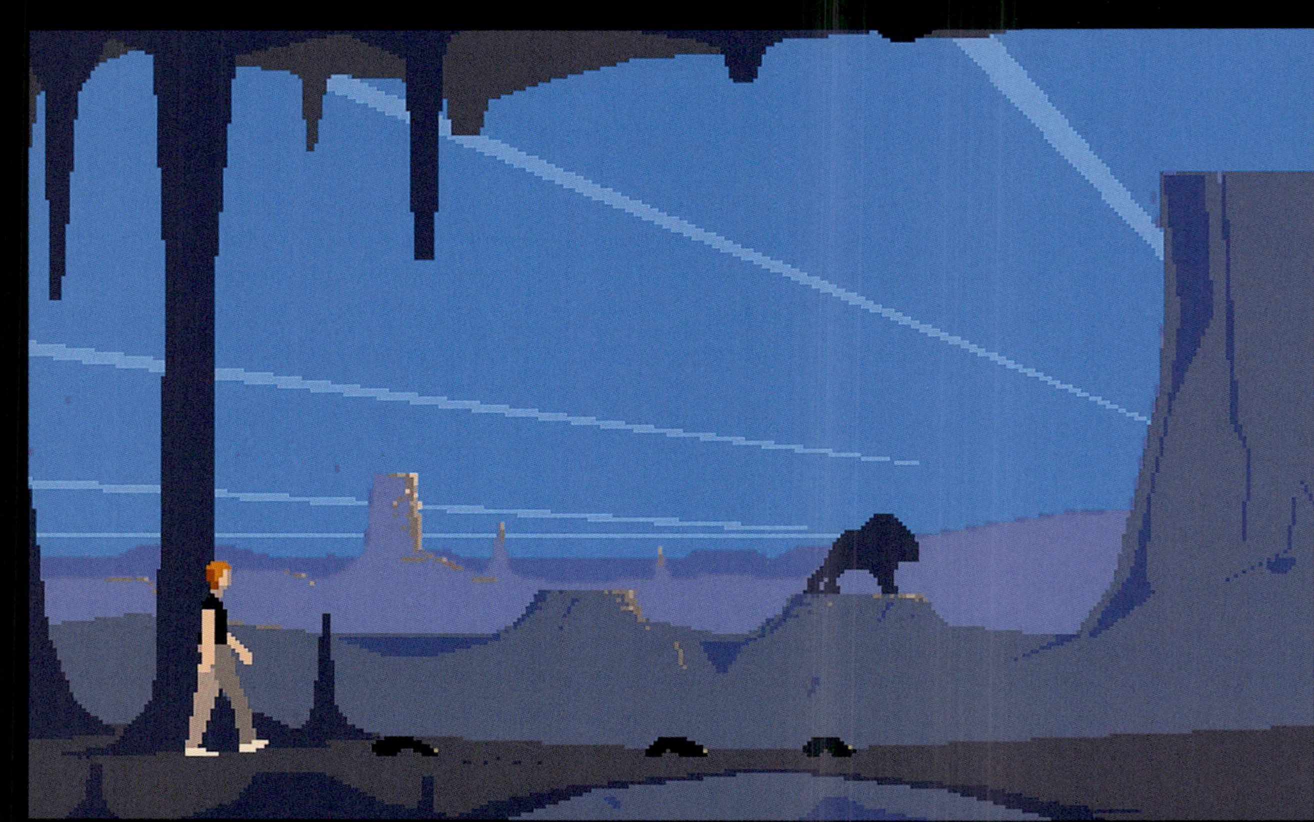

In the cinematic opening to Another World, Lester Chaykin, after a failed particle-accelerator experiment, finds himself on an unknown and eerily quiet planet—a barren, rocky landscape populated by a race of humanoid aliens. The player is tasked with guiding Lester through this world, from challenge to challenge, using a joystick or keyboard to jump, shoot, and steer clear of obstacles. Lester's survival also depends on an unexpected friend: Buddy, an alien prisoner who helps him evade capture and avoid death. Buddy and Lester communicate nonverbally, via gestures and actions rather than relying on text—a rare feature in a platform game at the time. The game ends when either Lester or his friend is wounded or killed.

With Another World (originally released in North America as Out of This World, and in Japan as Outer World), Éric Chahi distilled the essence of what makes movies compelling—the rhythm, the drama—into game form. Instead of advancing Lester through

levels, the player moves him through beautifully rendered landscapes that are both expansive in scale and spare in style. To produce realistic graphics during key segments of the game, such as the opener, Chahi used rotoscoping, a technique that involves extracting an object's silhouette from a moving image and creating a new animation in a new setting with it. But he also wanted to engage the player's imagination with evocative (rather than highly detailed) content.

The game's unique tension between the sparse and the complex is the result of Chahi's inventive and economical use of technology. As a young developer, he had played a version of the 1983 arcade game Dragon's Lair on an Amiga personal computer, and he had been inspired by its vivid full-screen action scenes, which were composed of bitmaps (compressed grids of squares in various colors) read directly from a floppy disk. To create a similar effect for Another World, he used polygon graphics— straight-sided 2D shapes (usually triangles) that

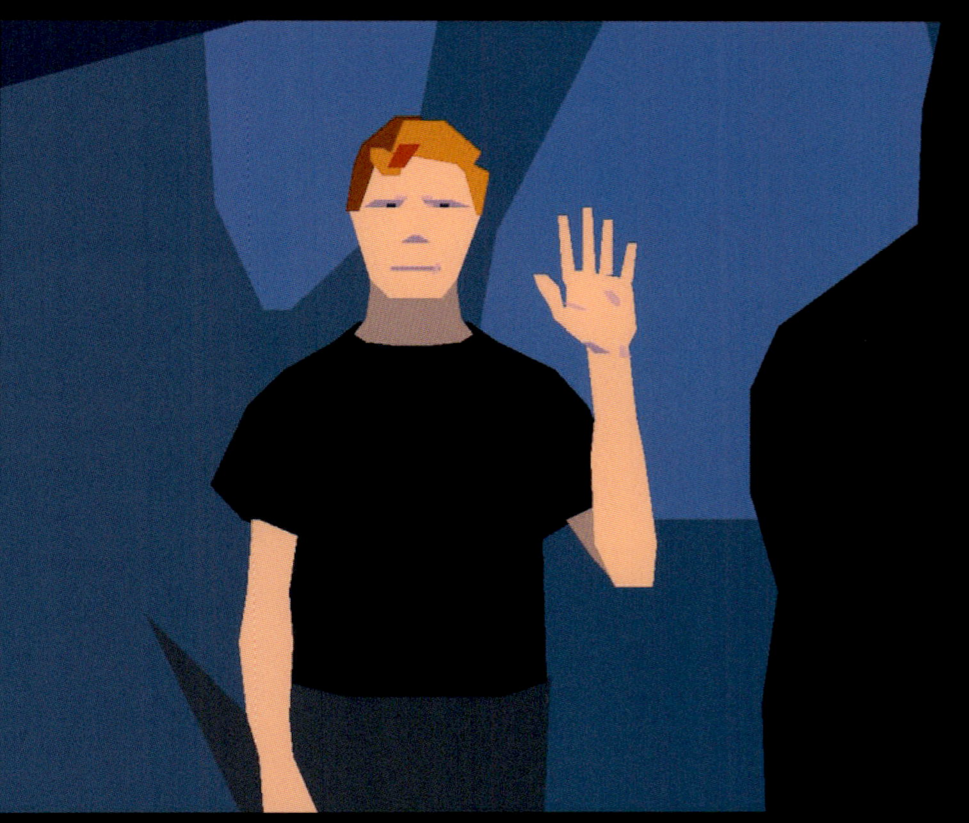

approximate 3D graphics when locked together—
in vector-based code that produced lifelike animations and took up very little disk space but did not
allow for great complexity in details and textures.
This technical limitation, however, became part of
the game's core concept: players provide their own
interpretations and meanings for the various figures
they encounter—a large beast, for example, is nothing
more than a menacing wolf-shaped outline. To rein-
force the flow of the experience, Chahi supplied
none of the customary information—energy-level
indicators, score, or other icons—that typically
disrupts gameplay.

   Chahi developed Another World independently,
and to this day he retains creative control of it. He has
said that through his long solitary hours of working
on the game, he came to relate to Lester's lonely
journey.[1] With an unlikely interspecies friendship at its
center, Another World is a quiet exploration of friendship and connection in the midst of isolation.

1. Éric Chahi, "Another World:
The Creative Process," Dotemu,
March 8, 2018, YouTube video,
youtube.com/watch?v=MraFN
8sNghs.

Myst

Rand Miller (American, born 1959)
Robyn Miller (American, born 1966)
Cyan (USA, est. 1987)

Myst 1993
The Museum of Modern Art, New York.
Gift of Cyan Worlds, Inc.

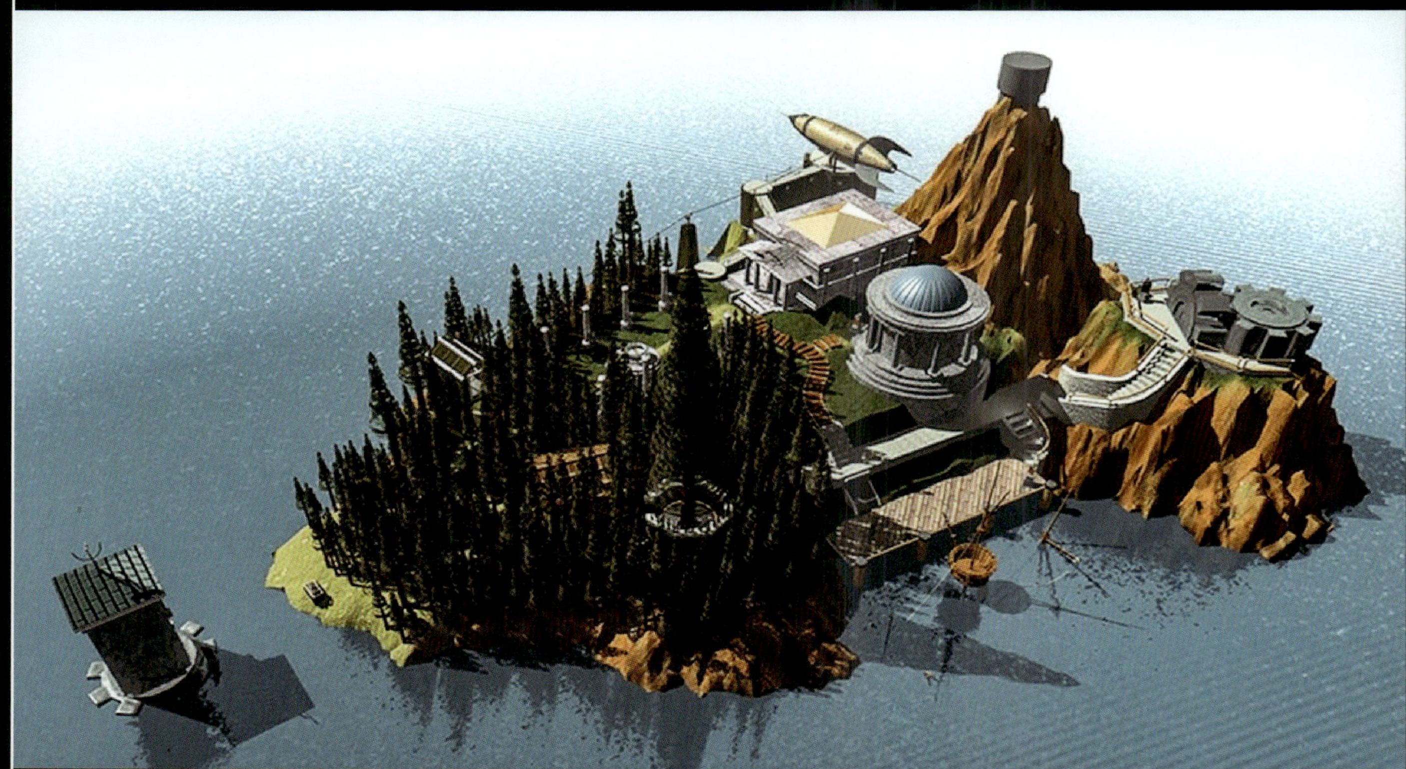

In the late 1980s and early '90s, the experience of playing video games at home was changed by a single technology: the CD-ROM. The compact disk read-only memory, introduced in the early 1980s, held significantly more data than a floppy disk or cartridge, in high-memory files that computers read by shining laser light on them. By the end of the decade, when personal computers with CD drives, made by Apple, IBM, and other companies, became more widely available, the CD-ROM found all sorts of practical applications. Its storage capacity proved revolutionary for the video-game industry, thanks in large part to Myst, a point-and-click fantasy adventure puzzle that was the highest-selling PC game of the 1990s.

The brothers Robyn and Rand Miller were already familiar with the advantages of CD-ROM technology when they set out to design Myst. In 1988, with the Macintosh-based application HyperCard, they had developed The Manhole, an interactive children's book in which players access different scenarios by clicking on various animated objects on the screen.

Clicking on a manhole, for example, makes it slide open to reveal a growing beanstalk. Instead of a straightforward digital children's book, The Manhole is an exploratory adventure—a world-within-a-world experience that laid the groundwork for what Myst would eventually become. After an initial version on five floppy disks, which required players to continually pause to eject and reload disks, The Manhole was made available on CD-ROM in 1989.

With Myst, the Millers created an adventure on a grander scale; its advanced graphics and 3D animations were so hefty and complex that only a CD-ROM could hold them. They spent months designing the game's landscape. Working exclusively with Macintosh computers, HyperCard, and Photoshop, they used heightmaps—grayscale textures that store surface elevations and other landscape data—for Myst's basic terrain. With the graphics software StrataVision 3D they filled in textures and details to create the game's complex puzzles and engrossing animations.

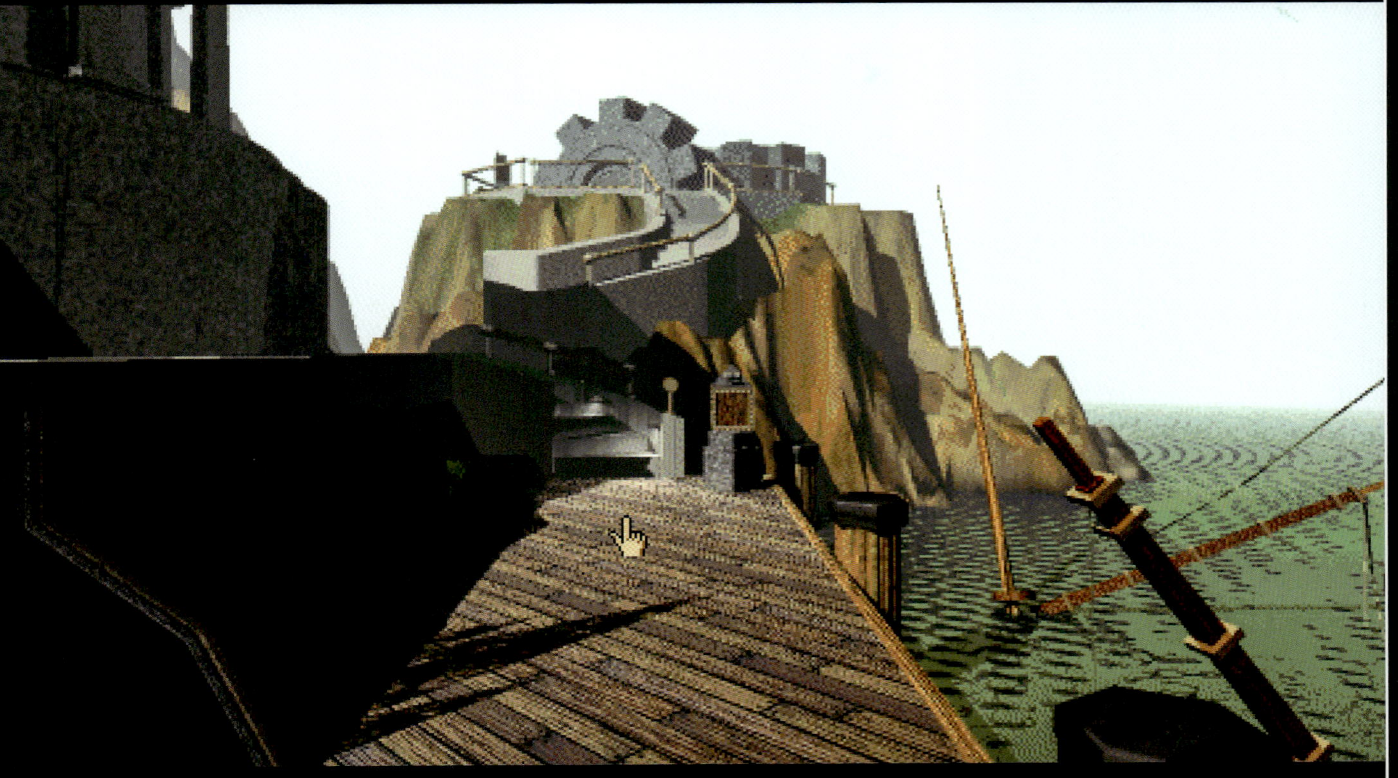

The player controls the Stranger, who is taken by an enchanted book to Myst, a mysterious unpopulated island filled with more charmed books by an explorer named Atrus. By piecing together puzzles hidden around the island, the Stranger can travel to other worlds, known as Ages, where more clues are revealed by clicking on or dragging objects. The goal is to discover what has happened to the characters that once inhabited the Ages, and there are a number of possible outcomes, depending on which clues are decoded and which actions are taken. For millions of players in the 1990s, however, the true thrill of the game was exploring the strange and lonely island, with some fans referring to it as mystical, or even religious. Through their commitment to weaving narrative into an intricate interactive game, the Millers produced what has been called the "first convincing virtual reality experience … of feeling physically present in a fictional world."[1]

1. Benj Edwards, "Myst at 25: How It Changed Gaming, Created Addicts, and Made Enemies," *Fast Company* online, September 24, 2018.

Portal

Valve (USA, est. 1996)

Portal 2005–07
The Museum of Modern Art, New York.
Gift of Valve

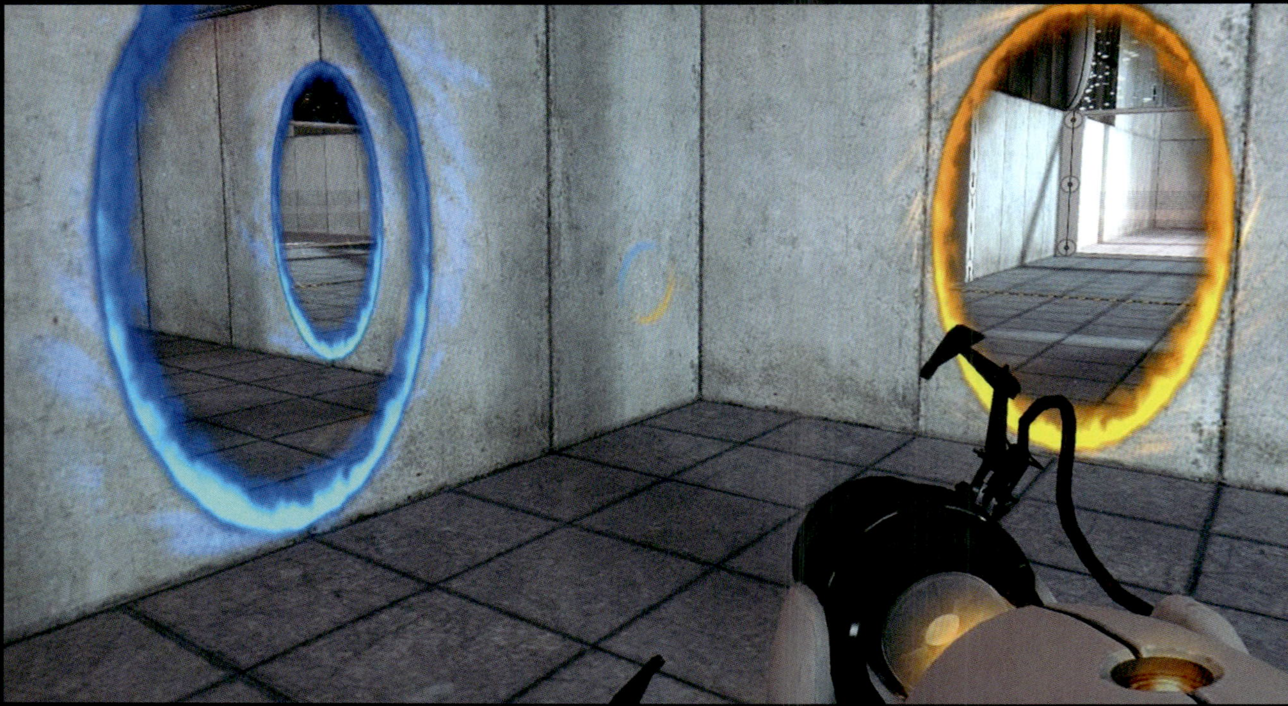

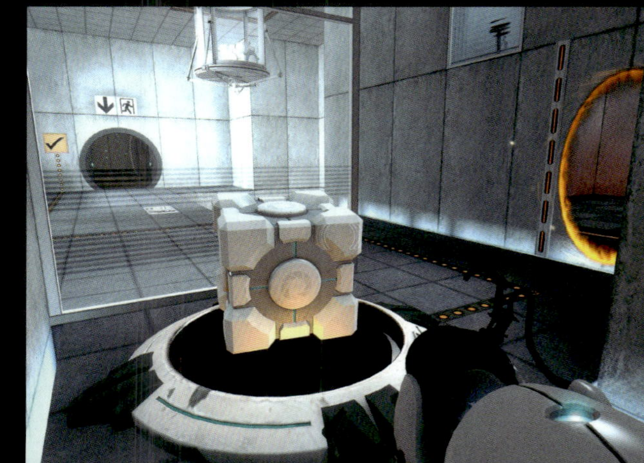

You wake up in a bare glass cage. You look around
for any clues to your location or any possible ways
to escape but can see only a radio and a toilet bowl.
Suddenly a menacing yet strangely soothing voice
announces, "The portal will open in 3, 2, 1." Two oval
holes, one blue, one orange, appear—one inside the
cage and the other outside of it. Through the portals
you see a woman in a cage identical to yours: you
are looking back at yourself. This woman is Chell, the
central character of Portal, a groundbreaking first-
person puzzle-platform game. You, the player, control
Chell as she works her way through an endless-
seeming string of enclosed spaces, instructed by a
disembodied (and surprisingly witty) artificial intelligence called GLaDOS (Genetic Lifeform and Disk
Operating System). The key to completing GLaDOS's
tests and continuing to move through the space is
the Aperture Science Handheld Portal Device, or
ASHPD, which creates interspatial portals through
which Chell can pass by shooting at the walls,
ceiling, and floors. Throughout, GLaDOS taunts Chell
with the promise of chocolate cake. (Spoiler alert:
The cake is a lie.)[1]

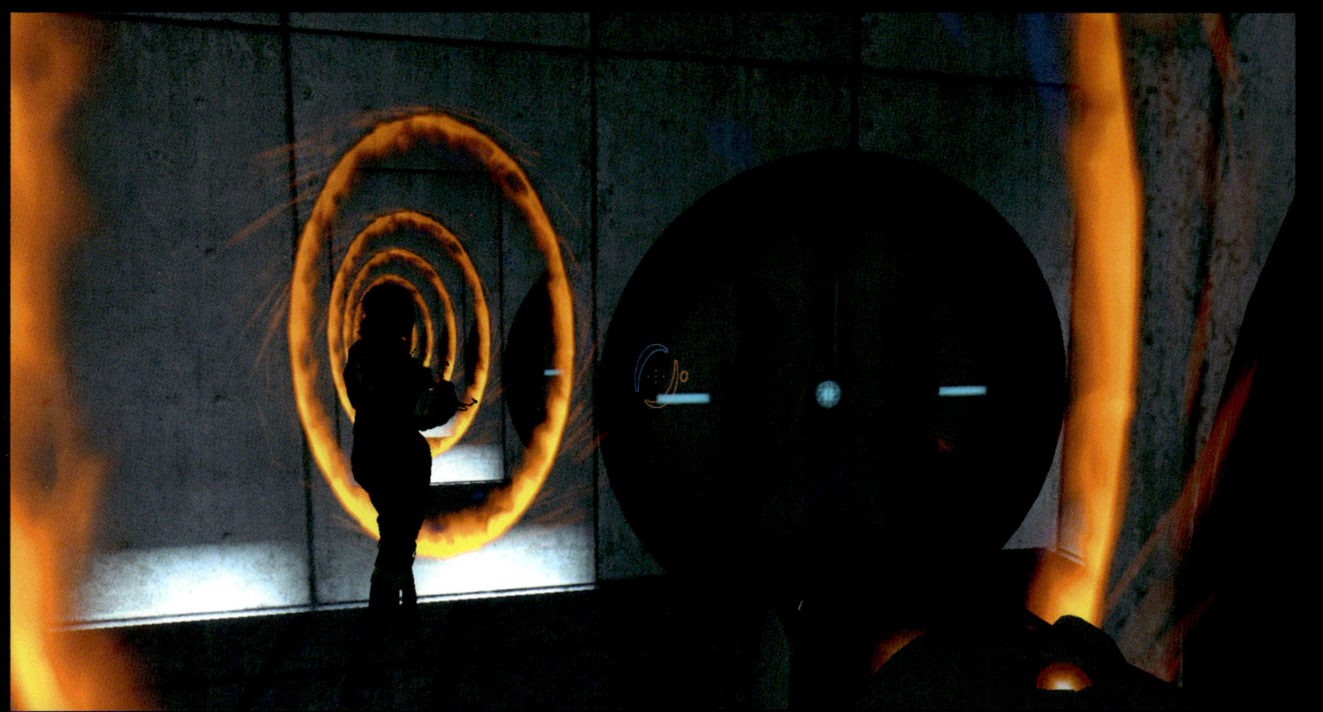

One of the most sophisticated and original video games of the early 2000s, Portal is, at its core, about physics and spatial awareness. Shooting open a blue portal produces only a swirling hole that goes nowhere, but when Chell opens an orange portal on another surface, a connection between them is established—a wormhole through which she can jump from one to the other. The player controls Chell's entry angle and speed, and the velocity and direction of her entry determine the velocity and direction of her exit (or, as GLaDOS mockingly puts it, "Speedy thing goes in, speedy thing comes out"). With these complex maneuvers and precisely positioned portal entries, the player can manipulate Chell's momentum, allowing her to travel longer distances or even to defy gravity by jumping from a portal on the floor through one on the ceiling.

The idea for Portal originated with Narbacular Drop, an independent freeware game in which a character called Princess No-Knees (due to her inability to jump) uses magically interconnected portals to escape a trap-filled dungeon. Narbacular Drop was released in 2005 by a group of eight students at the DigiPen Institute of Technology in Redmond, Washington; they were later invited to present it to executives at Valve—including its CEO, Gabe Newell. Newell was so impressed that he asked the group to develop the game at his company, with Kim Swift as its lead designer. With the writers Erik Wolpaw and Chet Faliszek, the group transformed their clever bare-bones puzzle into an intricate game whose mechanics, engrossing narrative, and compelling antagonist have inspired professional gamers and physics teachers alike.[2]

1. "The cake is a lie" became a catchphrase among Portal fans, as well as a popular meme.

2. Katie Salen, "How Portal 2 Developers Became the Best Sixth Grade Physics Teachers Ever," *Fast Company* online, November 13, 2012.

Dwarf Fortress

Tarn Adams (American, born 1978)
Zach Adams (American, born 1975)
Bay 12 Games (USA, est. 2000)

Dwarf Fortress 2006
The Museum of Modern Art, New York.
Gift of the designers

The creative and technical force behind the single-player fantasy game Slaves to Armok: God of Blood, Chapter II: Dwarf Fortress—known to most players simply as Dwarf Fortress—are the brothers Tarn and Zach Adams, who have been working on it steadily for almost twenty years. As longtime fans of classic fantasy novels such as J. R. R. Tolkien's *Lord of the Rings* and role-playing games such as Dungeons & Dragons, they were inspired by dungeon-crawling "roguelike" games such as Rogue (1980) and NetHack (1987, page 46). For their own game, the Adamses developed an open-ended story generator: a simulation game in which players build and oversee a dwarf settlement in a vast software-generated world that conjures up a slightly different scenario each time.[1] Every patch of land provides what is necessary for the dwarves to thrive—rocks, minerals, healthy soil for growing mushrooms (a key food in the dwarven diet)—but as the ecosystem grows, so do the challenges: floods, competing settlements, and vampire dwarves.

The interface uses tiled 2D building blocks instead of the 3D animations favored by contemporary designers; its text-based graphics, elegantly rendered in ASCII characters, recall the computer games of the 1980s; and dwarves are represented by smiley faces, and trees by brown or green zeroes. The dynamic between the algorithms and the player is collaborative. After the software configures the landscape, generating mountains, woodlands, and dwarf profiles, the player fills it out, putting up fortresses and towers, brewing alcohol, and designing dwarf clothing. This dynamic is indicative of what Tarn Adams has referred to as the "emergent narrative" that drives the game; instead of following a predetermined storyline or controlling a scripted character, the player creates a unique story—choosing sites for construction, assigning tasks to the dwarves, deciding which foods to grow—by following the different pieces of information provided in each new scenario.[2] There are no prizes to win or levels to progress through. The only goal, emphasized by the game's unofficial slogan ("Losing is fun!"), is to build as inventively as possible until the settlement is inevitably destroyed by some external factor, forcing the player to start over.

Dwarf Fortress has amassed a cultish following of gamers who possess the keyboard skills and patience necessary to master the game. These dedicated souls are active on message boards, write comic books and fan fiction about their dwarf civilizations, and, perhaps most important, support the Adamses through individual donations, which allow them to maintain the game and continue developing increasingly complex worlds and features.[3] Since its release in 2006, Dwarf Fortress has been available at no cost, accessible to anyone curious about exploring one of the most intricate fantasy-world simulators ever created.

1. Jonah Weiner, "Where Do Dwarf-Eating Carp Come From?," *New York Times Magazine*, June 21, 2011.

2. Tarn Adams, "Characterization and Emergent Narrative in Dwarf Fortress," in Beat Suter, René Bauer, and Mela Kocher, eds., *Narrative Mechanics: Strategies and Meanings in Games and Real Life* (Bielefeld, Germany: transcript, 2021), 151–60.

3. The Adamses are funded almost exclusively by donations through the electronic payment platforms PayPal and Patreon, in exchange for stories and art drawn by the brothers.

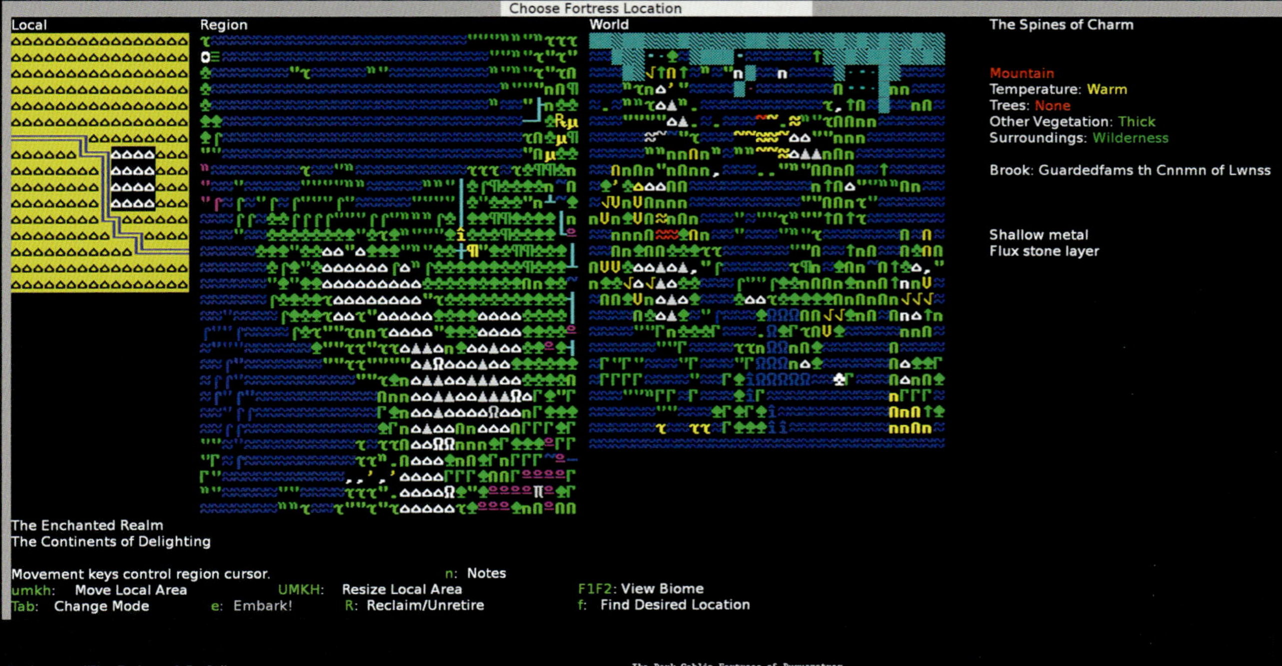
Choose Fortress Location
Local
Region
World
The Spines of Charm
Mountain
Temperature: Warm
Trees: None
Other Vegetation: Thick
Surroundings: Wilderness
Brook: Guardedfams th Cnnmn of Lwnss
Shallow metal
Flux stone layer
The Enchanted Realm
The Continents of Delighting
Movement keys control region cursor.
n: Notes
umkh: Move Local Area
UMKH: Resize Local Area
F1F2: View Biome
Tab: Change Mode
e: Embark!
R: Reclaim/Unretire
f: Find Desired Location

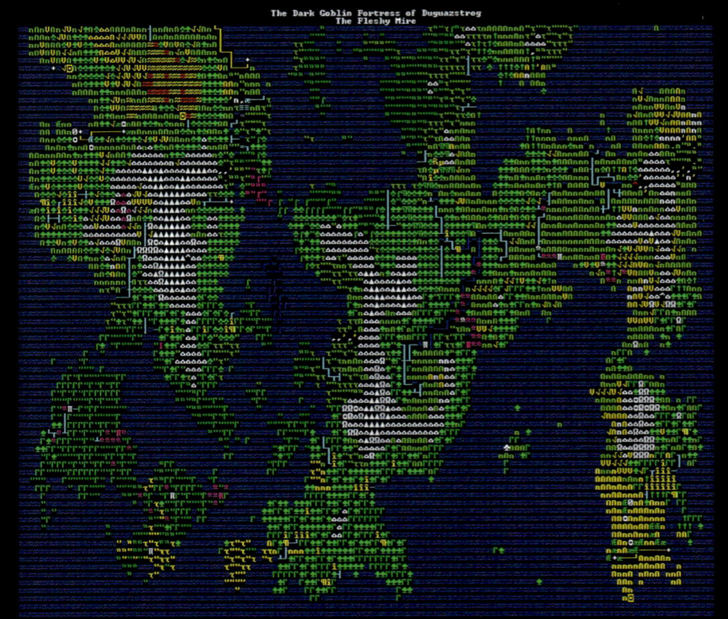
The Dark Goblin Fortress of Duguazstrog
The Fleshy Mire
Iadinomon, "The Enchanted Realm"
Creating New Region (2 Rejected)
Preparing elevation...
Setting temperature...
Running rivers...
Forming lakes and minerals...
Growing vegetation...
Verifying terrain...
Importing wildlife...
Recounting legends...
The Age of Myth
Year 72
Hist Figs: 8834
Dead: 1856
Events: 35511
Enter or ESC to pause/finish.

Passage

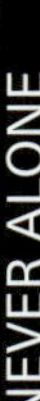

Jason Rohrer (American, born 1977)

Passage 2007
The Museum of Modern Art, New York.
Gift of the designer

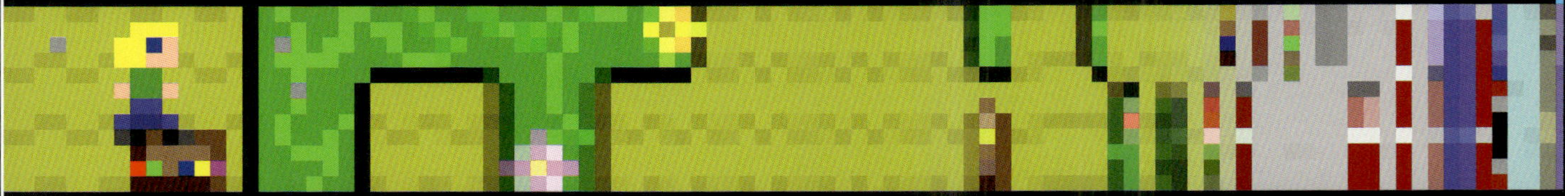

Passage is a very short game about life. The player controls a character that begins as a young adult, grows older while being relentlessly pushed through a narrow pixelated corridor, and then eventually dies, all in the span of five minutes. Throughout the experience, the character faces obstacles and makes choices that shape the brief remainder of the game. Rewards can be found in treasure chests along the way, but the value of the points fluctuates depending on the life decisions the player has made. Undertaking the journey with a partner may earn more points, but moving through the game and gathering points is smoother when traveling solo, and a character's speed is also slowed by the grief that follows a partner's inevitable death. And as in life, there is only one possible outcome, inexorable and absolute.

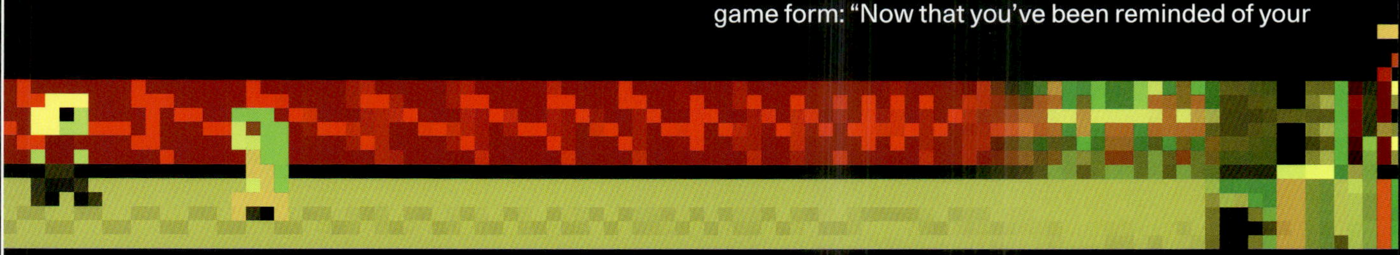

Taking up no more than 500kb of memory space and displaying the action inside a field of a mere 100 by 16 pixels, Passage is a memento mori in video-game form: "Now that you've been reminded of your

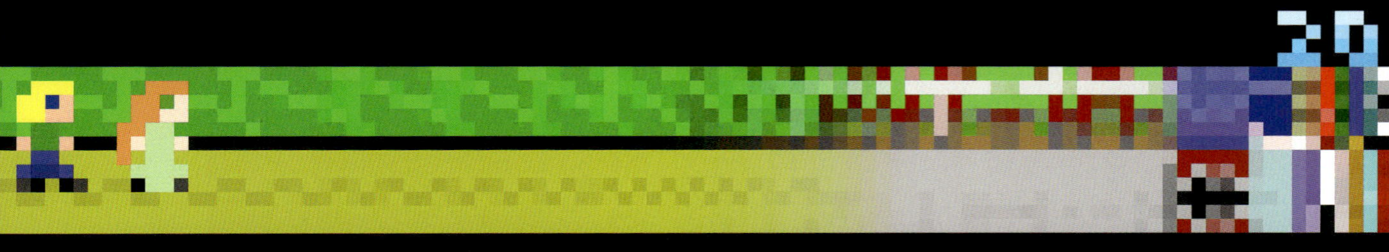

own mortality," Jason Rohrer, the game's designer, has asked, "what are you going to do with the rest of your life?"[1] The game distills some of life's biggest choices into what Rohrer calls "mechanical meta-phors," allowing players to consider different answers to this existential question.[2] The character's position at the game's beginning, on the left side of the screen, leaves room for a wide, blurry future, visible on the horizon toward the right. As time passes, this posi-tion gradually moves toward the horizon, bringing the character closer to it, with less future ahead and more space — representing memories of a life lived — accumulating behind. The risk of venturing into the the unknown is depicted as a maze with limited visi-bility, while the short, strict time limit is, of course, a reminder that every life is finite.

Rorher creates games that speak to a shared human experience, and he sees them as powerful tools for exploring — and questioning — the interac-tions necessary for living in society and in the world, from our daily conversations with strangers to our silent relationships with nature. Passage has been breezily labeled an "art game" for its use of video-game tools and technology to consider larger ideas rather than functional and entertaining pastimes, but it is among the games that have truly broadened the possibilities for the medium. It opened the door to the independent designers and experimental games that shaped the industry in the decade following its release.

1. Jason Rohrer, "Between: An Interview with Jason Rohrer," by Patrick Jagoda, *Critical Inquiry* online, University of Chicago, May 2011.

2. Rohrer, "Between."

flOw

Jenova (Xinghan) Chen (Chinese, born 1981)
Nicholas Clark (American, born 1984)
thatgamecompany (USA, est. 2006)

flOw 2007
The Museum of Modern Art, New York.
Gift of Sony Computer Entertainment LLC

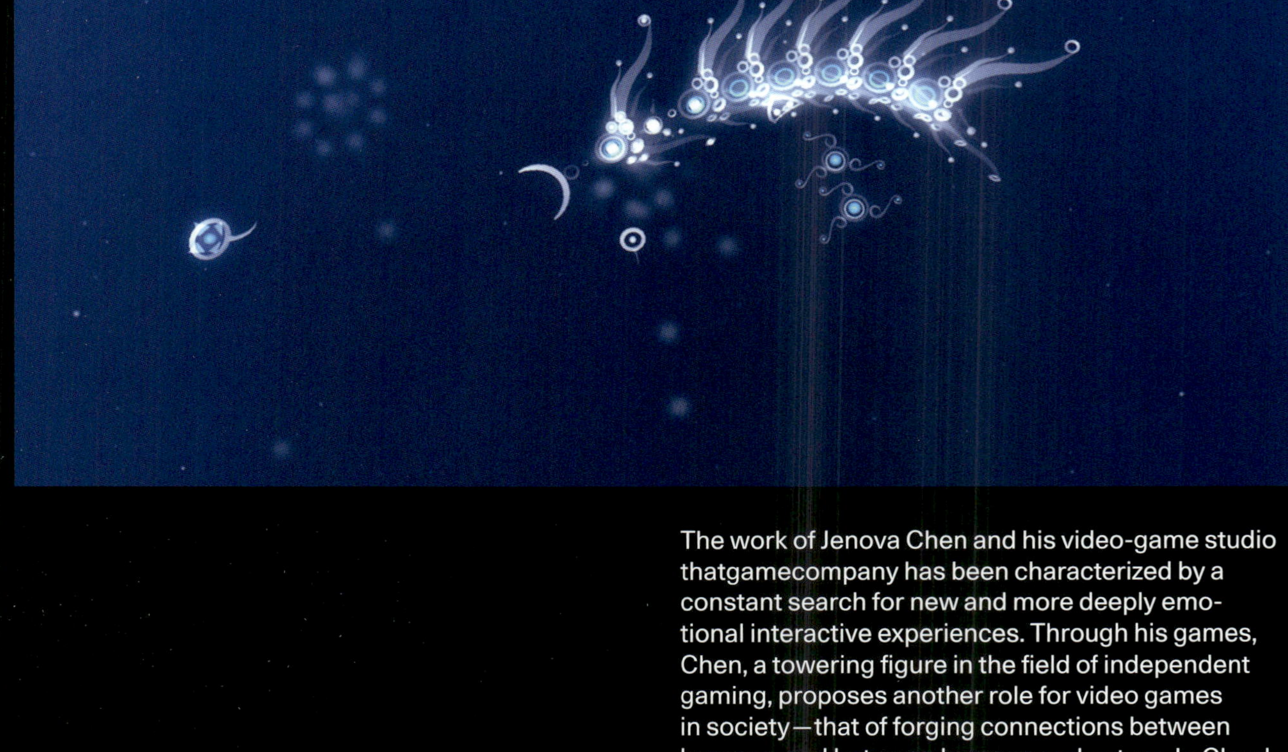

The work of Jenova Chen and his video-game studio thatgamecompany has been characterized by a constant search for new and more deeply emotional interactive experiences. Through his games, Chen, a towering figure in the field of independent gaming, proposes another role for video games in society—that of forging connections between humans, and between humans and nature. In Cloud, his first project, designed while he was still a student, players fly over oceans, islands, cities, and valleys, manipulating clouds in order to clean the world with rain. This basic but powerful idea of connection set Chen on a quest to expand the spectrum of emotions that video games can evoke, informing much of his subsequent work.

With the designer and programmer Nicholas Clark, Chen created flOw for his master's thesis; it was available to the public as free Flash-based software in 2006 and was reworked for the Sony PlayStation 3 in 2008. The idea was to design a game that would adapt to players with different levels of skill. In Chen's view, traditional video games are produced with experienced players in mind and are therefore inaccessible

iliar with the basics of the medium.[1]
ored the concept of dynamic difficulty
DA), in which a game's programming
adjusts itself to a player's abilities and
g its reactions to the player's choices.
yer controls an evolving serpentine
g through water, helping it consume
s in order to grow larger and advance
nt levels, each one introducing dif-
es that present new challenges. If a
s the tasks quickly, the game becomes
fficult in order to prevent boredom
, while for a less-adept player it adopts
n order to prevent the frustration that
ed by a task that is too hard. Navigation
endeavor—directing the creature
nore than a click and swift move of the
of the joystick—and is accompanied by
re composed by Austin Wintory.
spired by the Hungarian psychologist
entmihalyi's theory of mental flow: the
g immersed in an activity for its own
egard for time, ego, or reward.[2] By
layer's abilities, flOw encourages this
offering a spectrum of challenges and
nts players a sense of control over the
ence.[3]

1. Howard Wen, "Go with the flOw: Jenova Chen on Console Independence," Game Developer, January 2, 2007, gamedeveloper.com/design/go-with-the-i-flOw-i-jenova-chen-on-console-independence.

2. Mihaly Csikszentmihalyi, "Go with the Flow," interview, *Wired* online, September 1, 1996.

3. Jenova Chen, "Flow in Games," master's thesis (University of Southern California, 2006).

Flower

Jenova (Xinghan) Chen (Chinese, born 1981)
thatgamecompany (USA, est. 2006)

Flower 2009
The Museum of Modern Art, New York.
Gift of Sony Interactive Entertainment LLC

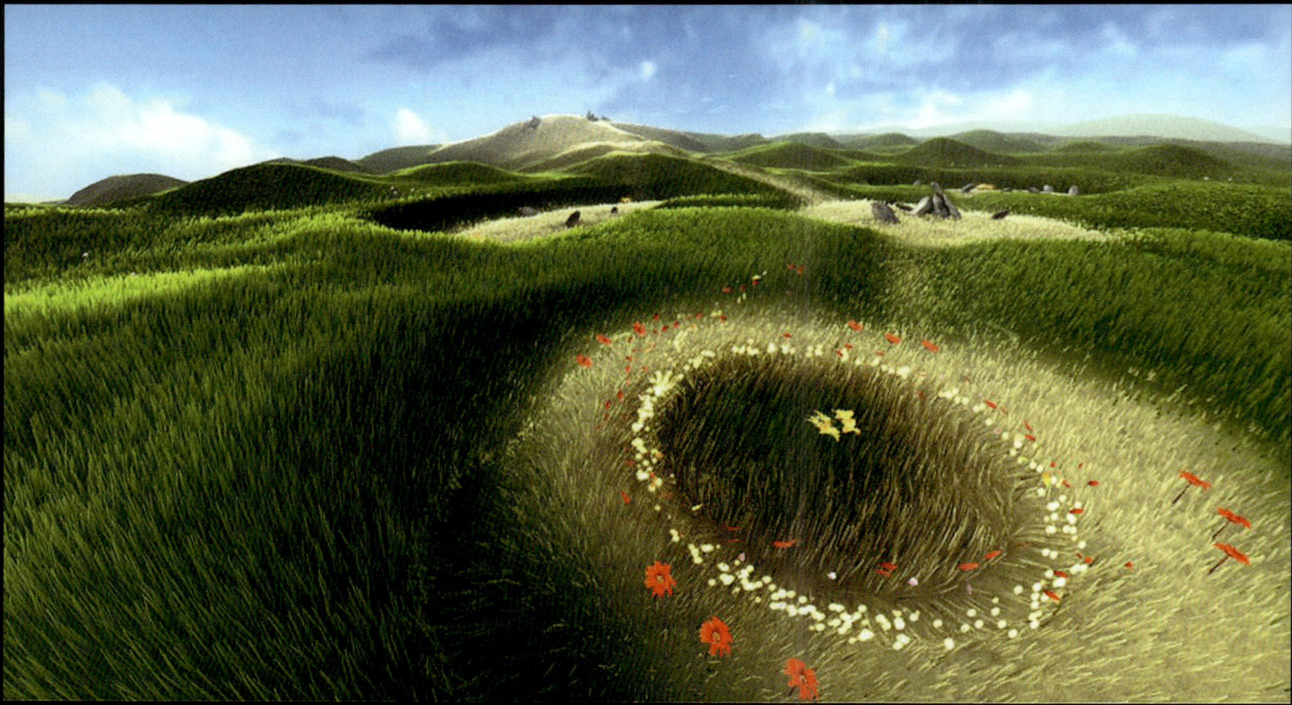

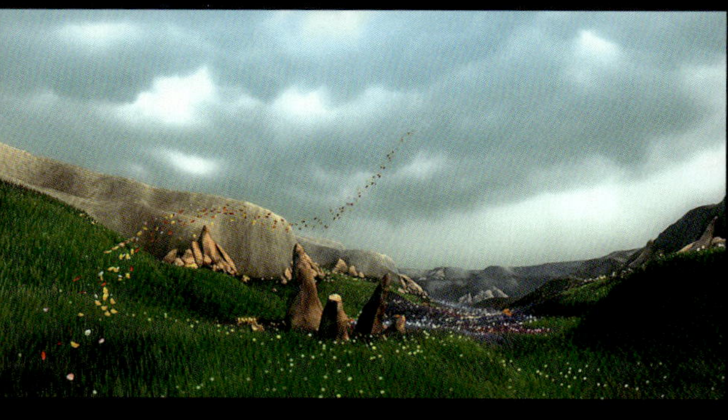

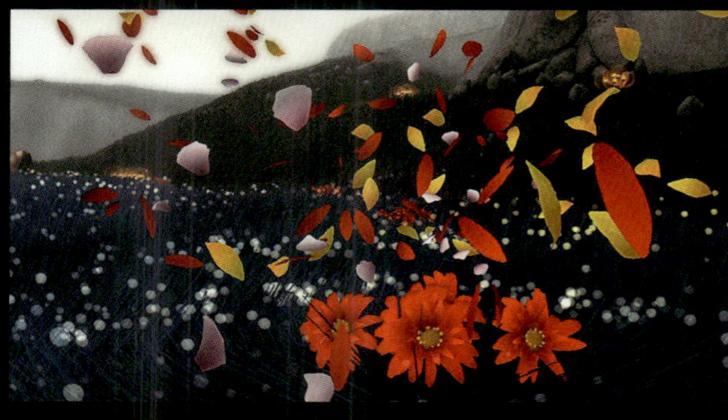

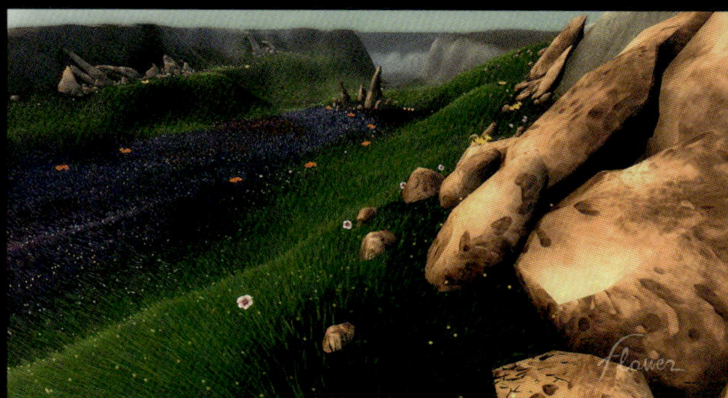

Jenova Chen describes Flower as an interactive poem exploring "the tension between urban bustle and natural serenity."[1] In reaction to his urban upbringing—he grew up in Shanghai and saw a hill for the first time when he moved to California for graduate school—he designed a game that immerses the player in the natural world. The player controls the direction of the wind in a fantastical sequence in which a flower petal, freed from a potted plant, is blown across verdant and blooming landscapes. As it blows, the wind activates windmills, gathers more petals, and makes its way into the city, and as the single petal becomes many, the languid and contemplative sensation of being carried along by the wind is transformed into something thrilling. The eventual arrival of the petals in the city brings the desolate gray landscape to life with color and movement.

Instead of following a character's story along a narrative trajectory, Flower presents the daydreams of seven flowers in a city apartment, each one imagining itself roaming freely across the hills. As in most of Chen's work, the game contains no dialogue or text prompts. As a nonnative English speaker living in the United States, Chen is aware of the ways in which language can create barriers to understanding, whereas music can evoke moods without relying on speech or written dialogue. The score, by Vincent Diamante, dynamically responds to the player's actions and amplifies the feel of gameplay, with pianos, string instruments, and woodwinds mimicking the sound of the wind and increasing in volume as the number of petals multiplies. The tranquil music, dreamlike gameplay, and wordless action, along with the simplicity of input—tilting the controller and pressing any single button—have made Flower accessible to a wide range of players of many different abilities.

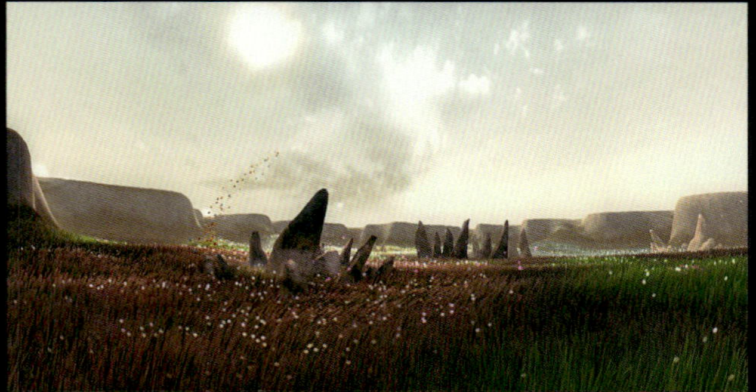

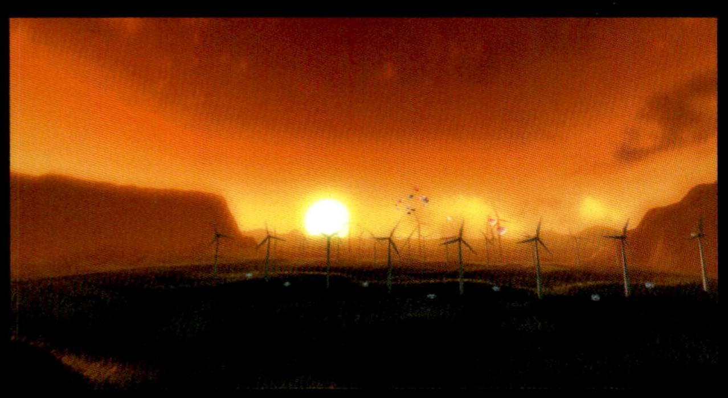

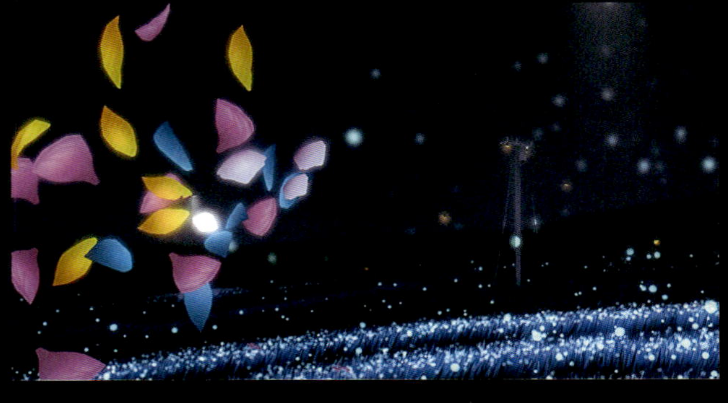

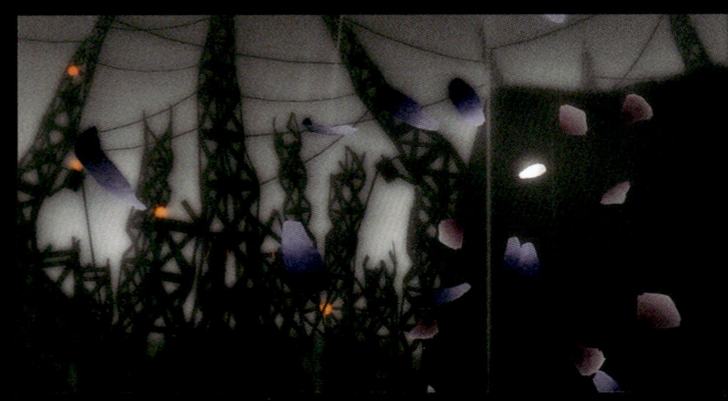

1. Jenova Chen, Flower website, jenovachen.info/flower.

Journey

Jenova (Xinghan) Chen (Chinese, born 1981)
thatgamecompany (USA, est. 2006)

Journey 2012
The Museum of Modern Art, New York.
Gift of Sony Interactive Entertainment LLC

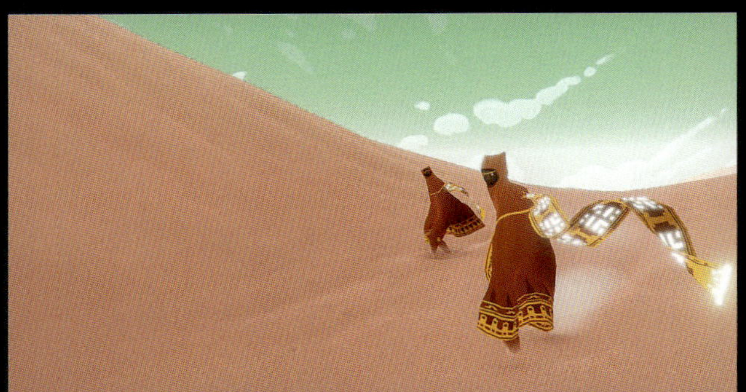

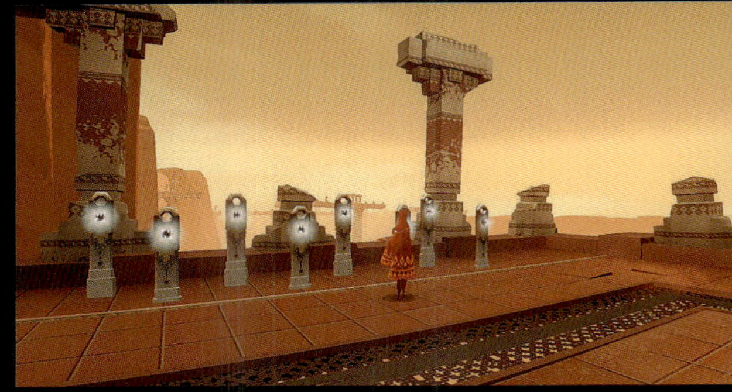

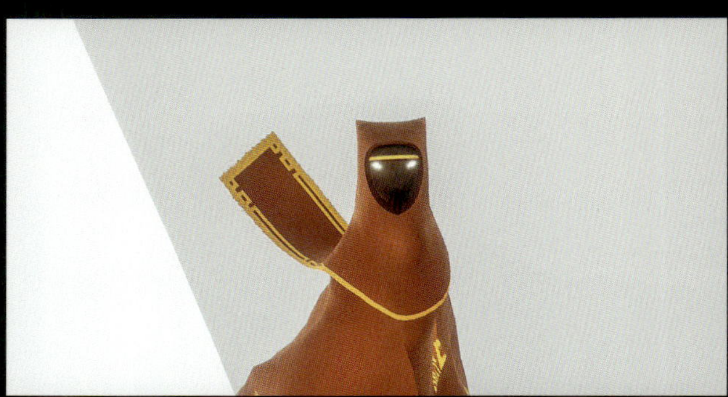

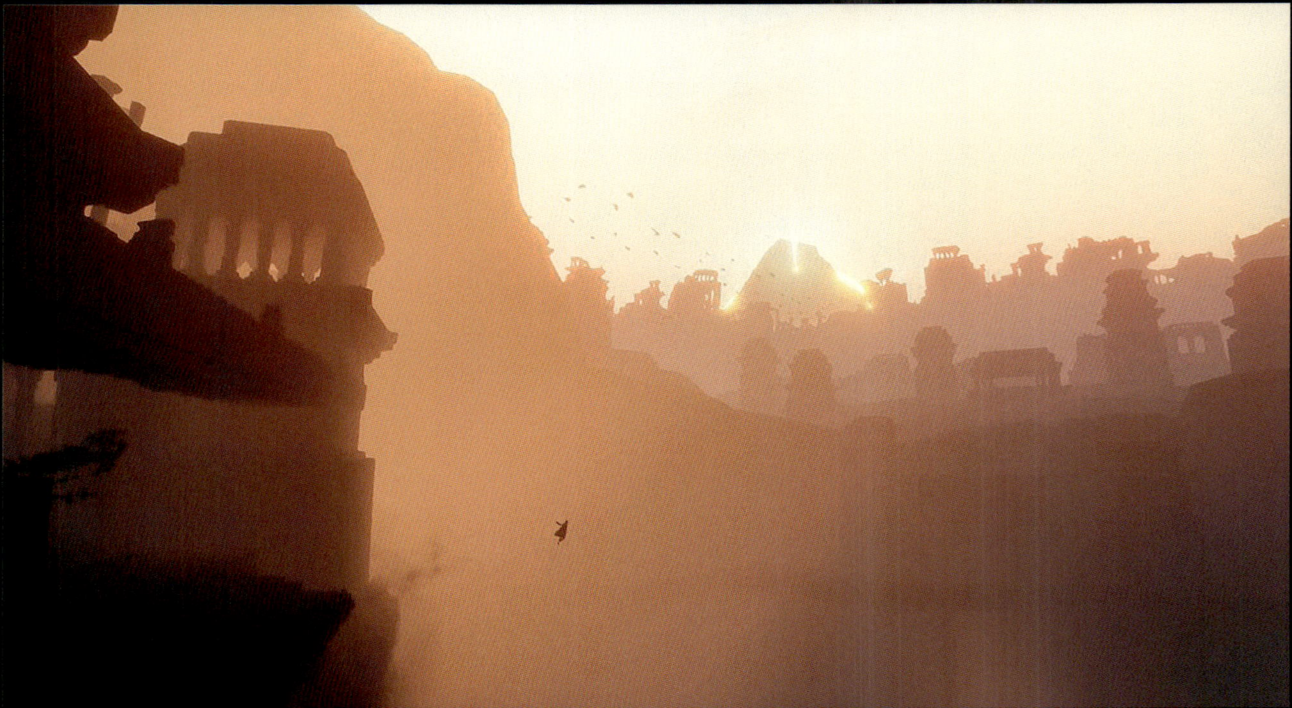

as steep snowy mountains battered by cold winds and underground lairs inhabited by large snakelike figures. But players all over the world, simultaneously connected by the Internet through the Sony PlayStation platform, can collaborate in real time as they navigate their individual journeys. Instead of encouraging competition, as most multiplayer games do, Chen and his team were interested in fostering companionship. The robed figures, who remain anonymous, can only communicate through one-note chirps and other nonverbal gestures, creating a sense of interdependence and intimacy between strangers that is rare even in real life. Two players embarking

1. "A hero ventures forth from the world of common day into a region of supernatural wonder: fabulous forces are there encountered and a decisive victory is won: the hero comes back from this mysterious adventure with the power to bestow boons on his fellow man." Joseph Campbell, *The Hero with a Thousand Faces* 3rd ed. (New York: Pantheon, 1949; Novato, CA: New World Library, 2008), 23.

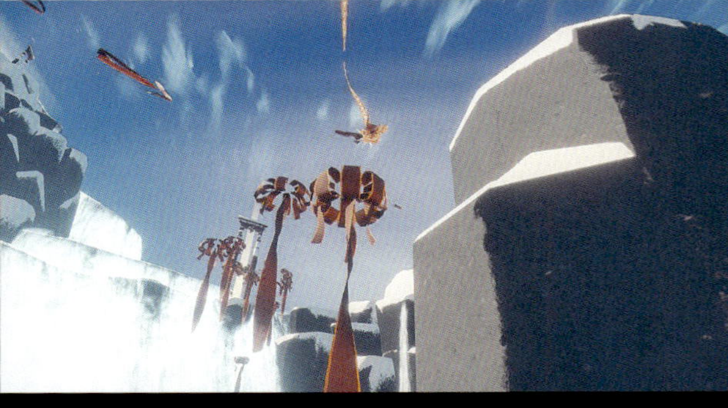

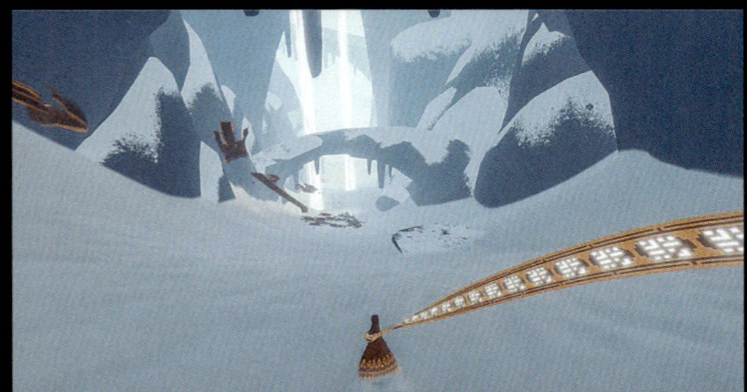

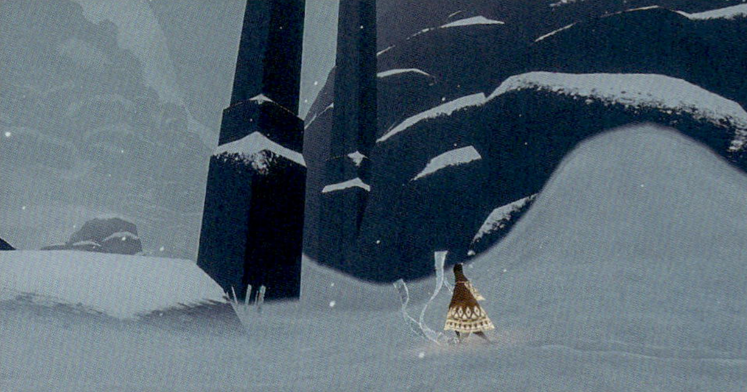

Papers, Please

Lucas Pope (American, born 1977)

Papers, Please 2013
The Museum of Modern Art, New York.
Gift of the designer

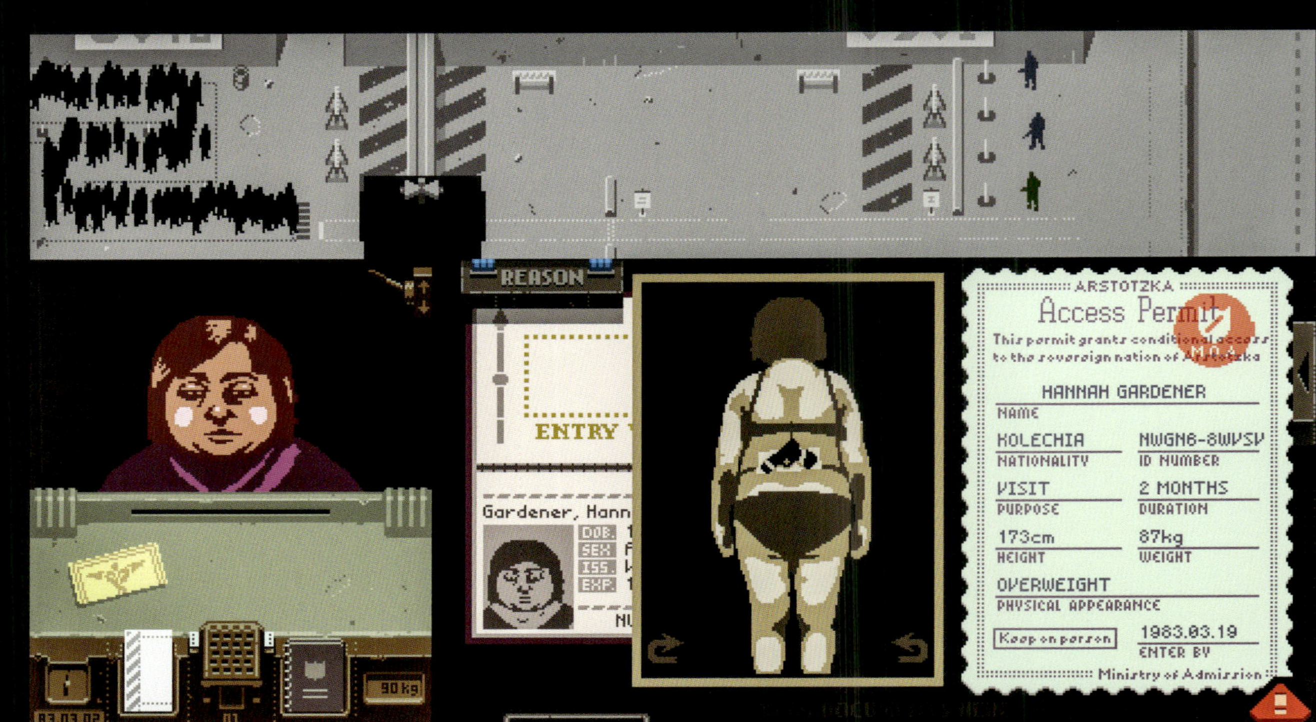

Like most white men with a US passport, Lucas Pope has never had much trouble passing through immigration. He has never had to stand in line nervously clutching his passport and other documents, hoping his encounter with an immigration officer will go smoothly. Yet he is so fascinated by the nature of the officer's work, at once tedious and consequential, that he designed an entire video game around the tense and potentially life-altering interactions routinely taking place at that small intake booth.

In Papers, Please, the player controls an unnamed government employee with the unenviable job of immigration inspector in Arstotzka, a totalitarian Eastern Bloc–like state, in 1982. The inspector screens citizens, immigrants, and asylum seekers, checking their documents for authenticity and approving or denying entry based on the (often scant) information available. After six years of war with the neighboring country of Kolechia, Arstotzka is navigating a tumultuous transition to peace, which causes an unstable work environment for this bureaucrat. His first day on the job starts simply enough: only Arstotzkan citizens are allowed into the country. But as the game

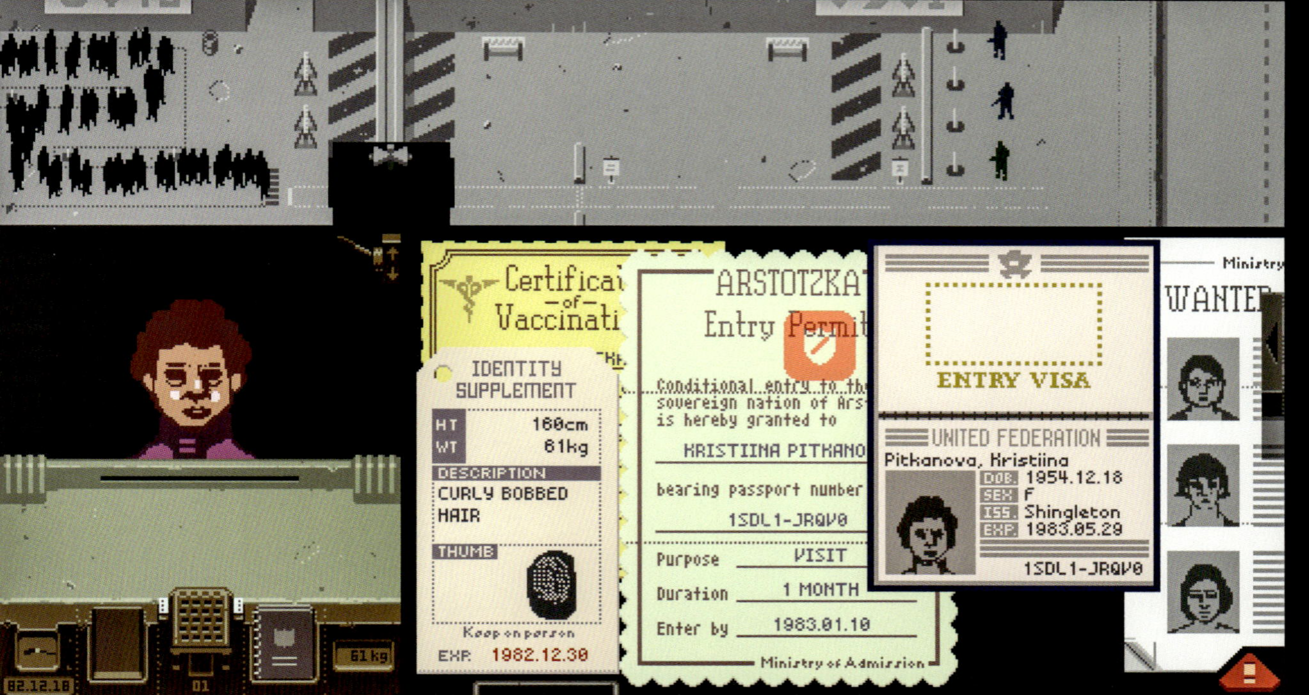

progresses, new rules and regulations are put in place, necessitating a closer look at the documents. At the end of each workday, he receives a summary of his meager earnings, based on the number of applications correctly processed that day and how diligently he has followed orders, with a report on the health and safety of his family. The player is thus forced to choose among feeding his children, buying medication, and paying his heating bill so his family does not freeze.

As a programmer and developer, Pope is interested in the parallels between user-interface interactions and bureaucratic ones. For Papers, Please, he used open-source software and programming language to design a game based on the simple idea that running a checkpoint is hard work. The inspector's seemingly straightforward interactions become more difficult with each passing day, complicated by the player's choices and the game's prompts. A larger idea also suggests itself, about the ways in which bureaucracy can be wielded to oppress. The player's moral compass is constantly challenged by decisions that might be at odds with the inspector's best interests.

Do I allow a woman with expired documents to enter the country so she will not be separated from her husband? Will I be able to afford my son's medicine if I do? Should I take a bribe from a fellow officer to pay my rent, if it means sending more migrants to detention and, most likely, death?

With twenty possible endings for the game—most of which are grim—Papers, Please prompts players to navigate a complex situation with few good options through the eyes of someone else, raising difficult questions about how empathy functions in a context of moral ambiguity. The inspector's predicament is distressing, but if the orders he has to follow to survive have a direct negative impact on other people, with whom should the player empathize?

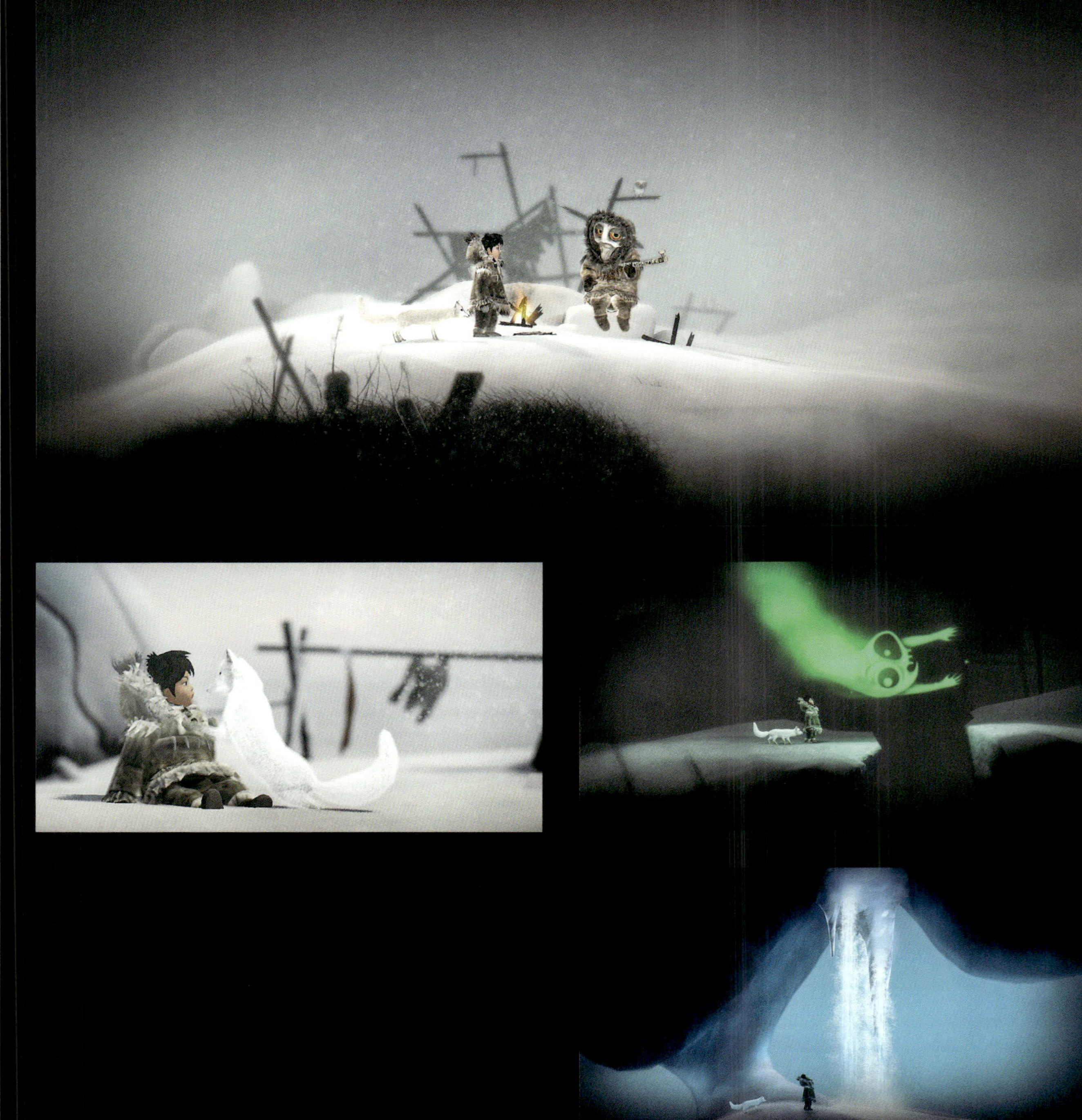

"It would be really nice to hear a story."

This common Iñupiaq saying is at the heart of the puzzle-platform adventure video game Never Alone. Stories are an essential part of Iñupiat history as well as the tribe's contemporary life. Passed down through generations, these stories strengthen their community and transfer knowledge essential for life in the harsh Alaskan climate.

The story, in this case, is a traditional Iñupiaq tale first recorded by the master storyteller Robert Nasruk Cleveland, in which a boy named Kunuuksaayuka embarks on a mission to discover the source of an endless blizzard that has ravaged his village.[1] In Never Alone (Kisima Inŋitchuŋa, or "I am not alone" in Iñupiaq), that child is Nuna, a young girl who with her Arctic fox companion must travel through extreme weather, climb frozen mountains, and explore underwater caves in order to restore balance to the ecosystem on which her community depends. The player is able to switch between playing as Nuna and playing as the fox; each has different necessary skills. Along the way, they meet spirits in the form of animals, humans, and other beings who share insights and wisdom that help them on their quest for survival.

Never Alone began with the Cook Inlet Tribal Council (CITC), a nonprofit organization that provides support services to Native tribes in the Cook Inlet region of Southcentral Alaska and elsewhere. Looking for a way to encourage Iñupiat youth to connect with their culture, the council landed on the idea of a video game and partnered with E-Line Media and the storyteller Ishmael Angaluuk Hope to create one that would record the traditions of a living people and share them with the world.[2] This undertaking required extensive research and hours of conversations with Iñupiat tribal members and scholars to ensure that the game—its characters, narrative, and animations— would be an accurate portrayal of a complex culture and the landscape it inhabits, from the colors and patterns of the northern lights to the texture of a caribou's fur to the movement of ice in a river. Created in collaboration with more than twenty elders, storytellers, and cultural ambassadors, Never Alone is rooted in the importance of intergenerational wisdom and in the principle of interdependence at the heart of Iñupiaq life. As Nuna and her fox cannot survive on the tundra without each other—if one dies, the other dies, too—the Iñupiat depend on the land, the animals, and the conditions that surround and sustain them.

1. The date of the story's first recording is unknown; it is included in Robert Nasruk Cleveland, *Unipchaanich imagluktugmiut/Stories of the Black River People* (Anchorage: National Bilingual Materials Development Center, 1980).

2. "Never Alone: The Making Of," CITC Alaska, November 16, 2016, YouTube video, youtube .com/watch?v=d9ndBVFrc2U.

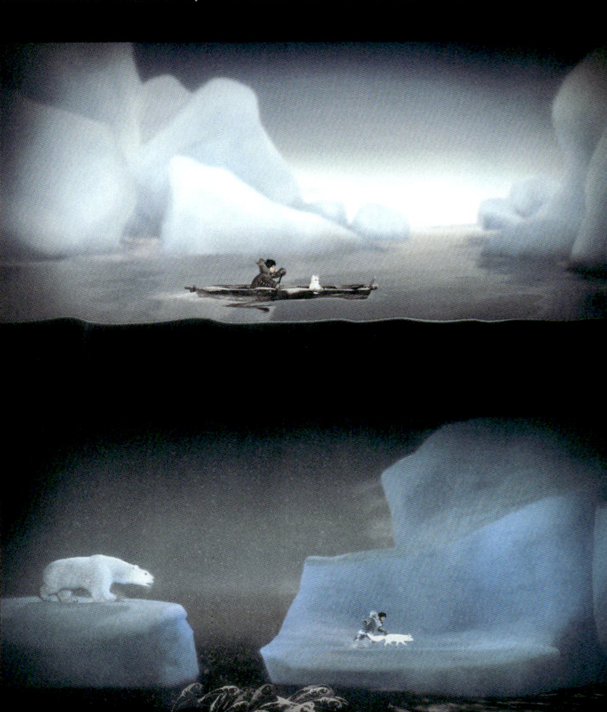

This War of Mine

11 Bit Studios (Poland, est. 2010)

This War of Mine 2014
The Museum of Modern Art, New York.
Gift of 11 Bit Studios

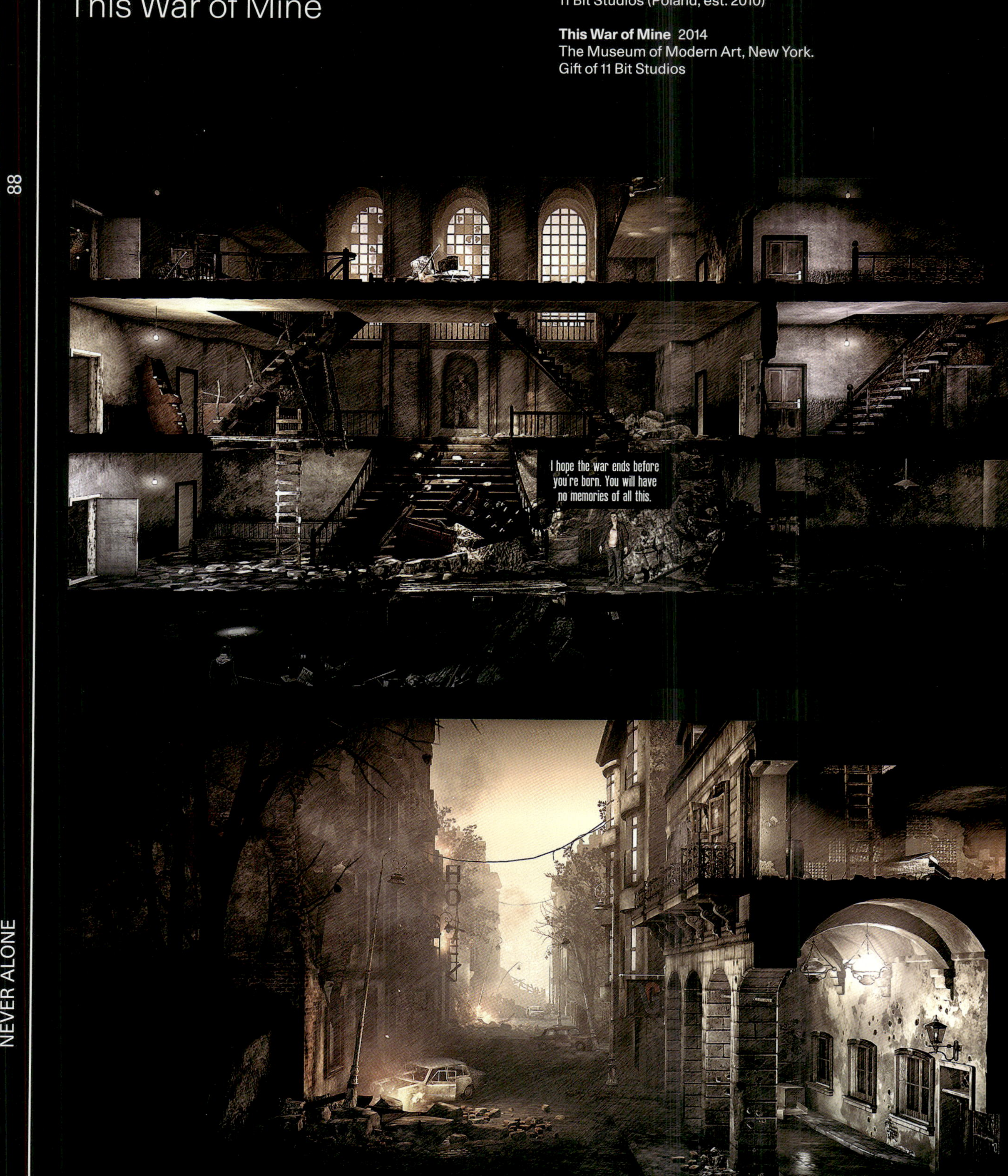

Video games about war are a dime a dozen. From Battlefield to Halo to however many versions of Call of Duty currently exist, avid gamers are familiar with the relentless violence of armed conflict. More often than not, however, these games focus on the military aspect of war in morally unequivocal tales of winners and losers. This War of Mine is not that kind of game. Set in the besieged fictional city of Pogoren, in the fictional country Graznavia—and based on the actual siege of Sarajevo of 1992–96, during the Bosnian War—this point-and-click survival game is a story of the people on war's sidelines.

The player controls a small group of civilians living in a crumbling apartment building as they attempt to secure their most basic needs—food, water, heat, and medicine. The characters spend most of the game indoors, waiting out the days while accomplishing basic but life-sustaining tasks such as building make-shift beds and heaters, eating, sleeping, and trying to hold on to what is left of their mental health. Under the cover of night, they can leave their shelter to scavenge for food, alcohol, and goods to barter with, but they risk deadly encounters with the military or other desperate civilians. The only goal of the game is to endure, until an uncertain cease-fire eventually ends the war.

With its purposefully minimal interface, 2D graphics, and muted color palette, This War of Mine provides very little context or instruction for the player who, like the characters, must figure out how to navigate a volatile situation without any training.

As conditions become more and more dangerous, the player confronts increasingly difficult questions and decisions. Am I capable of stealing or killing for food? Do I give my remaining medicine to someone who needs it more? Do I intervene in an attack if it means risking my life? At the heart of the game is the recognition that war renders most situations morally ambiguous. Regardless of the path they take, the characters (and the player) have to face the consequences of their actions, including regret, guilt, and worry.

With This War of Mine, the developers at 11 Bit Studios explore one of the ways in which a video game can be a medium for storytelling—one distinct from books, television, or movies. In those mediums, the developers argue, you are merely a spectator, whereas in video games you participate directly in the action, shaping the story and implicating yourself in the narrative.[1] This deeper involvement in the experience compels players to dwell in a character's emotional world. Like Papers, Please (2013, page 84), This War of Mine expands the traditional notion of video games beyond entertainment by transporting players into complex situations in which they must inhabit and relate to perspectives different from their own.

1. Paweł Miechowski, "How to Make a Game That Handles Complex Real-Life Problems," interview by Jonasz Rewiński, TVP World, Facebook video, June 20, 2020.

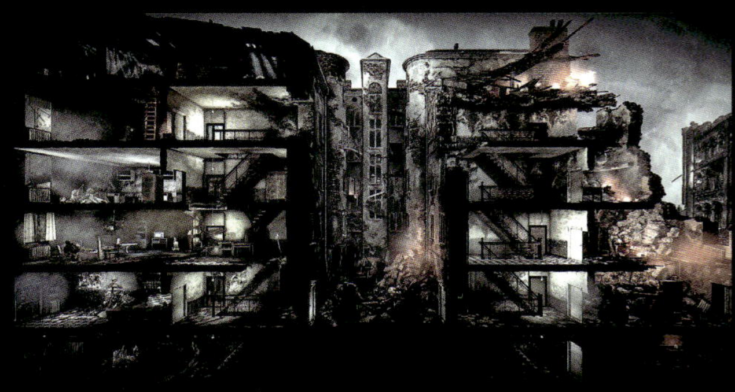

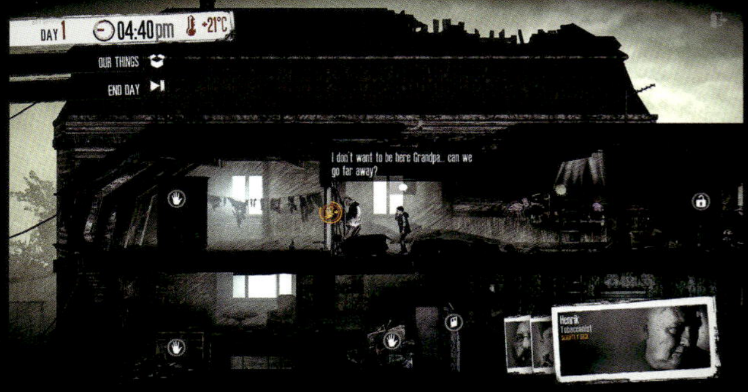

Inside

Playdead (Denmark, est. 2006)

Inside 2016
The Museum of Modern Art, New York.
Gift of Playdead

You're a small boy. You don't know what's happened or why you've been dropped into a terrifying monochromatic forest. All you know is that you have to run—you have to continue moving forward, even if it's unclear whether you're running from or toward something. As you push on through the landscape, a bleak reality sets in. Something about this eerily quiet and largely empty world is not quite right. The environment becomes increasingly unsettling and the situations increasingly dangerous: a farm where a parasite-infected pig tries to maul you, a highway checkpoint with armed guards, an underwater laboratory where you're pursued by a mysterious long-haired creature, and a city where what seem to be zombies assemble in neat rows, controlled by an unseen force.

In Inside, a puzzle-platform adventure game by the Danish studio Playdead, the player uses only two controller buttons to jump and to grab in a variety of ways, guiding the boy through challenging obstacles

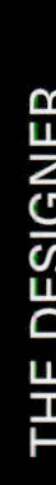

that provide further information about the world he inhabits and, eventually, his terrible destination. Some puzzles depend on the player's keen observation of distinct patterns or sequences (the behavior of the chickens inside a barn, a piece of machinery's specific action), while others require precise calculation of the boy's movements, such as jumping over a lunging pig. Each puzzle propels the game forward, invites contemplation, and heightens the feeling of ominous isolation that permeates the game.

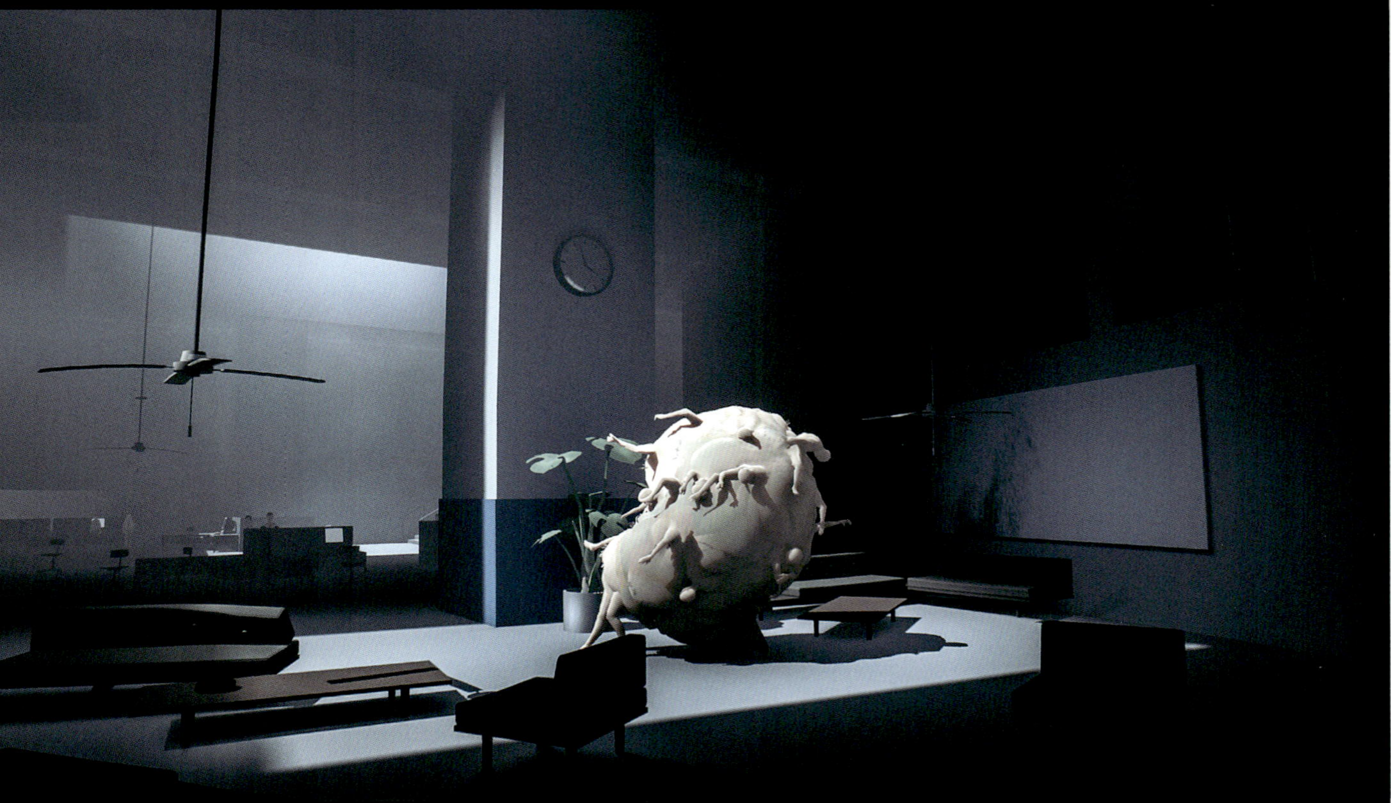

The strength of Inside is its stark and minimalist premise and its simple but sophisticated puzzle-based structure, in a singular exploration of the possibilities of the puzzle-platform format. A haunting narrative of violence and scientific experimentation is implied but never articulated, with no text or spoken audio to give context or guidance for the player. As the boy runs and jumps from scenario to scenario, a larger story, amply open to interpretation, is slowly revealed, with dark, beautiful visuals rendered

in 2.5D animation, a technique that makes 2D objects appear 3D through the use of shadows, lighting, or other textures that create an illusion of depth.

Inside's advanced animation, foreboding soundtrack (composed by Martin Stig Andersen and recorded inside a human skull), and straightforward inputs produce a game to be experienced rather than solved. In the face of darkness and menace, the player embarks on an uncertain and disquieting journey in which the only option is to keep moving.

Everything Is Going to Be OK

Nathalie Lawhead (American, born 1983)

Everything Is Going to Be OK 2017
The Museum of Modern Art, New York.
Gift of the artist

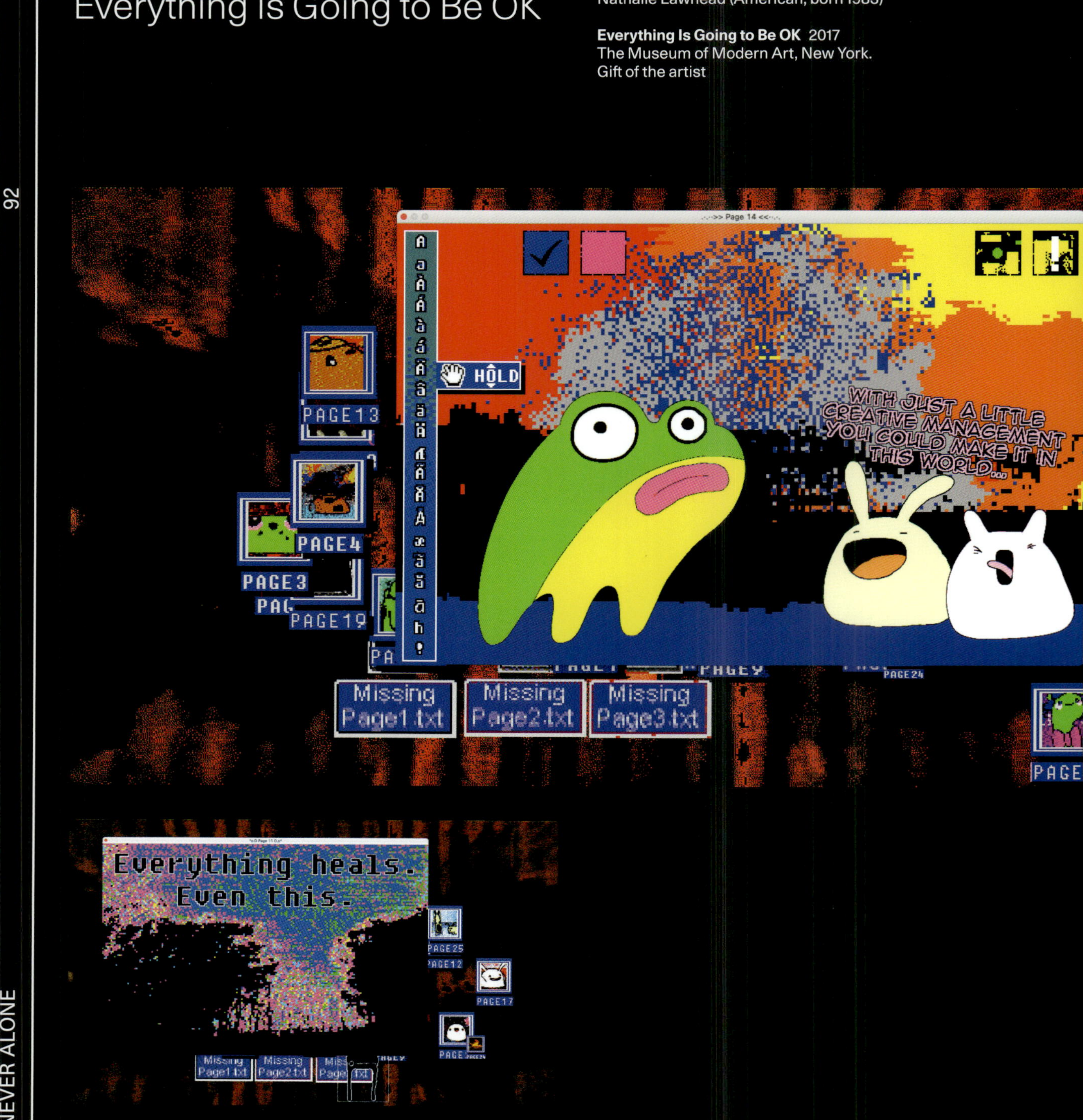

In a vignette in Nathalie Lawhead's Everything Is Going to Be OK, an adorable rabbit and what looks like a very round cat are being burned alive in a pit of lava. "I don't think I'm going to survive this," the bunny announces as they slowly submerge in the fires of hell. In response the cat offers toxic positivity: "Claim your power!" and "I have a therapist I can recommend" are two of its hilariously infuriating replies. In another scene, the player prepares a meal but must be attentive to another bunny's long list of food allergies, lest it die a painful death. In yet another, a blob-shaped beast can be comforted either by "creating a safe space to talk about its faith in the system" or by granting it a helpful handshake. Both options prove unsurprisingly hopeless; negative thoughts have already consumed the beast, in the form of a parasitic worm in its head.

In Everything Is Going to Be OK—a free or name-your-own-price desktop labyrinth program—Lawhead transformed personal experiences and writing into miniature games and animations. Through the absurdist, abrasive vignettes—loud colors and expressive graphics paired with a lot of cartoon gore and blood—the player is confronted by the artist's struggle as the target of harassment

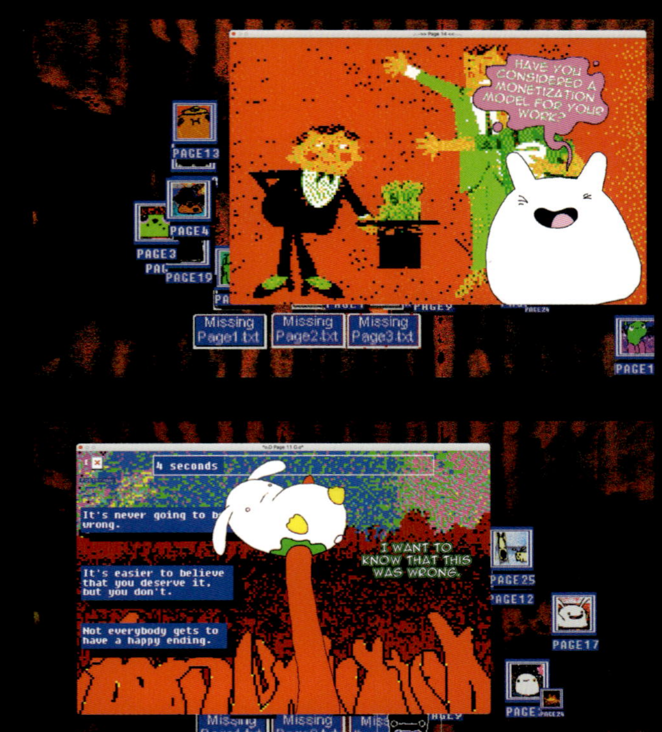

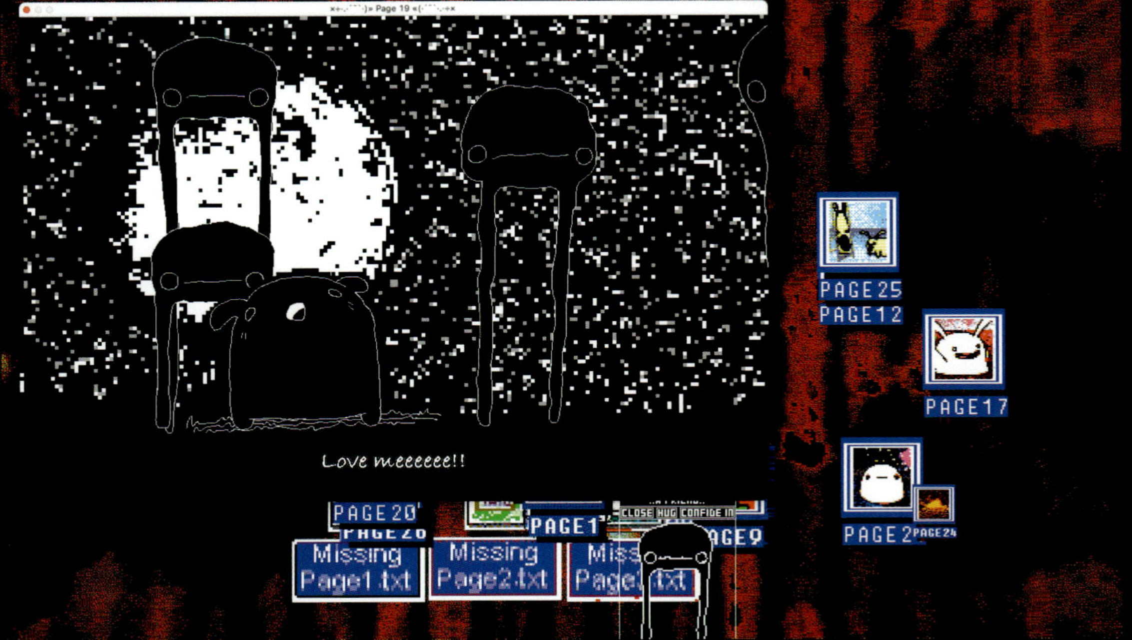

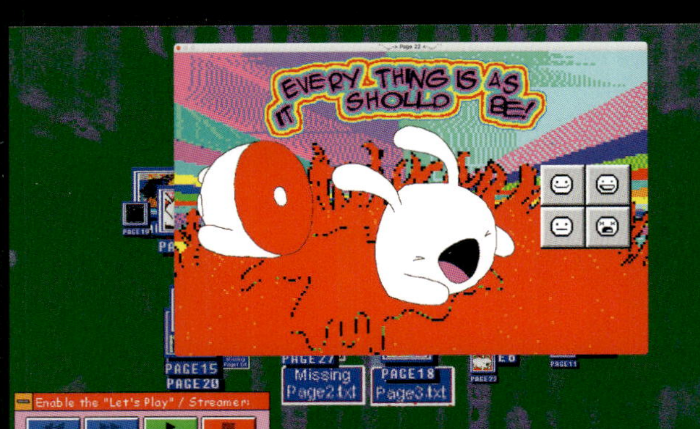

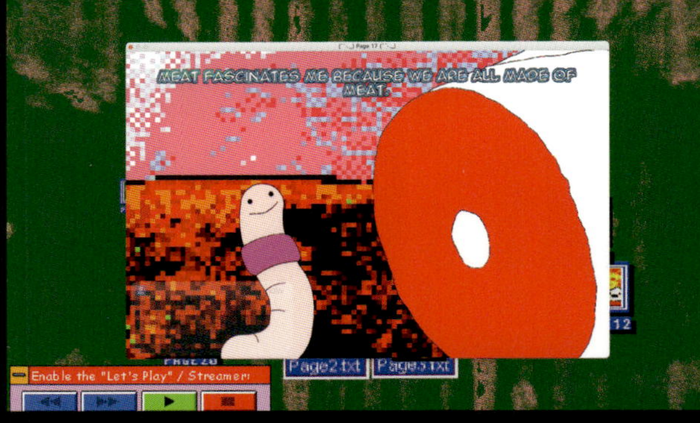

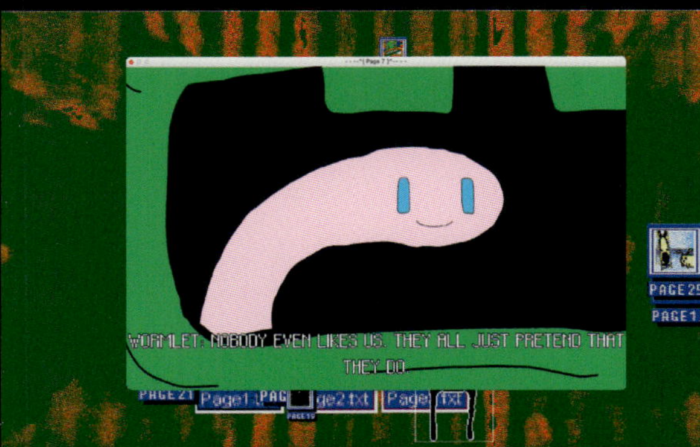

survivor's standpoint," Lawhead has said. "We don't teach people how to heal, to overcome, or to be powerful. We teach people to be perpetual survivors."[1] The game opens with an aggressively chaotic computer desktop, cluttered with files that erratically change locations as the player attempts to click on them. Each file contains a scene filled with an anxious mix of contradictions—humor and pain, the crude and the cute. In graphics recalling early Flash animations and other bygone Internet visuals, the vignettes oscillate from nihilistic meditations on suffering and insecurity to earnest attempts at emotional connection.

Lawhead, a multidisciplinary artist who was active in the net.art movement of the late 1990s and early 2000s, favors computer-based games for their versatile expressive and interactive capabilities. But the mainstream video-game world, with its limited view of what games are for, has at times been critical; Lawhead has been dismissed by players who think games should be fun and entertaining and are puzzled by those that offer unpleasant or challenging experiences.[2] The artist often rejects the label "video game" altogether—Everything Is Going to Be OK is, instead, an interactive zine.

Its interactions move a bit too quickly, the effects of the commands are never fully clear, and any click can lead to an undesired destination. There is a sense that in this game—as in life—nothing is within the player's control. By rejecting such needs and expectations, Everything Is Going to Be OK becomes an uneasy and deeply nuanced exploration of trauma, coping mechanisms, and survival.

1. Natalie Lawhead, artist's website, unicornycopia.com /ARTIST_STATEMENT.html.

2. Lawhead, "Road to the IGF: Nathalie Lawhead's Everything Is Going to Be OK," interview by Joel Couture, Game Developer, February 18, 2018, game developer.com/disciplines /road-to-the-igf-nathalie -lawhead-s-i-everything-is -going-to-be-ok-i-.

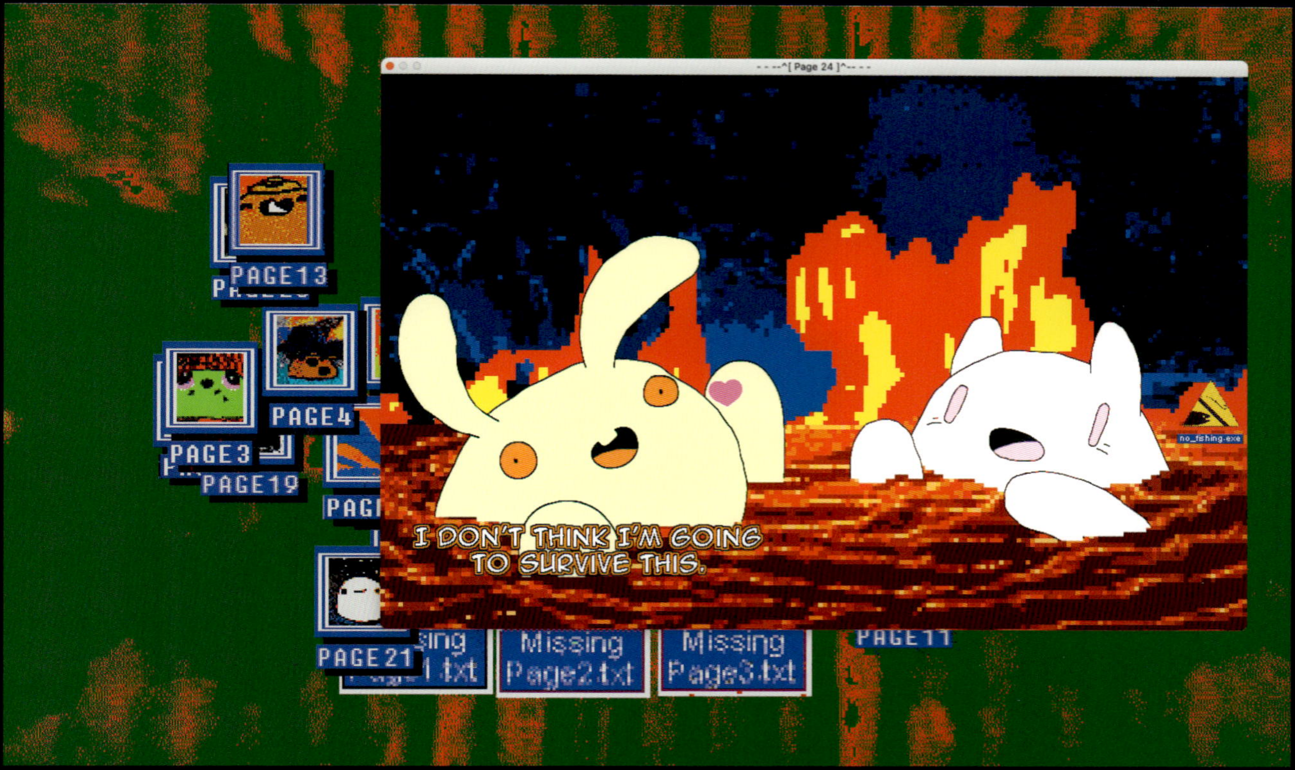

- - - ^[Page 24]^ - - -
PAGE13
PAGE3
PAGE19
PAGE4
PAGE21
I DON'T THINK I'M GOING TO SURVIVE THIS.
Missing Page2.txt
Missing Page3.txt
PAGE11
no_fishing.exe

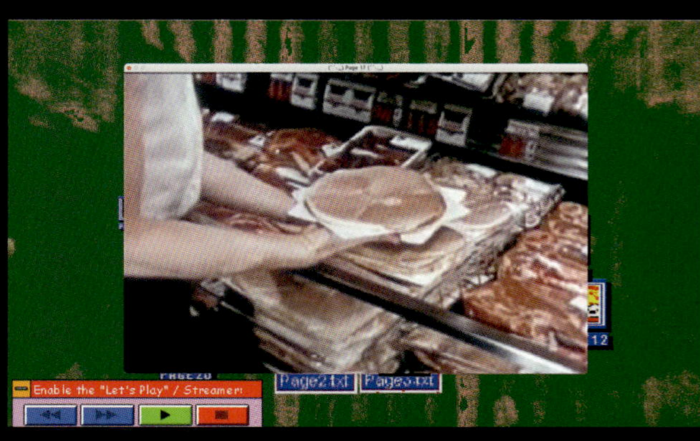
[Page 17]
Enable the "Let's Play" / Streamer:
PAGE20
Page2.txt
Page4.txt
12

Getting Over It with Bennett Foddy

Bennett Foddy (Australian, born 1978)

Getting Over It with Bennett Foddy 2017
The Museum of Modern Art, New York.
Gift of the designer

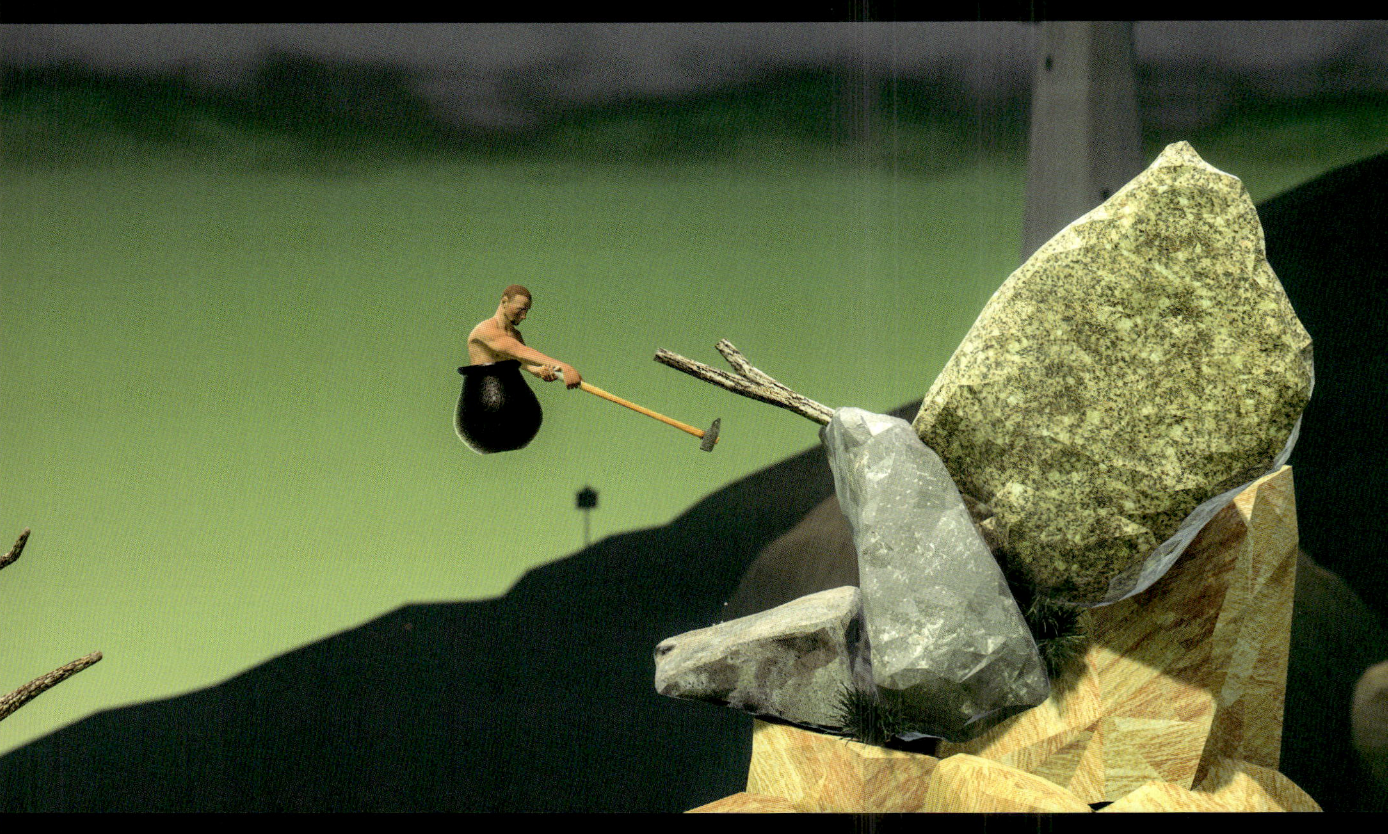

Shortly after you click Play, a narrator—the game designer Bennett Foddy himself—offers a gentle warning: "If you've already had a bad day, what you're about to go through might be too much. Feel free to go away and come back." Now that you have been cautioned, do you keep going? The computer game Getting Over It with Bennett Foddy is not about winning, nor is it about progress or growth—it is about failure and our emotional responses to it, wrapped in the guise of what many players consider to be one of the most irritating games ever conceived.

The player controls a shirtless man attempting to scale a mountain of rocks, garbage, and other objects. Because his lower half is stuck in a cauldron, and because he has only a sledgehammer to help him, his maneuvers are limited to flinging and propelling himself along. The game's commands are equally clumsy—a labored upward movement with a mouse wields the hammer—but the man's progress depends on a precise calibration of speed and angle. These commands, moreover, are often met with disobedience. And with no way to save his progress, the smallest miscalculation can send him back to the bottom of the mountain. In the soundtrack Foddy gives encouragement (with a bit of goading), philosophizes about frustration and ambition, and talks about his design process, as soft lounge music plays in the background.

As the man in the cauldron struggles over a barrel, Foddy explains that the central task of the game— like that of Sexy Hiking (2002), the free B-game that inspired it—is so difficult that forward progress is rare.[1] Because most obstacles in video games are fake, he says, players can be confident of eventually getting through. Even when their avatar dies, they can usually try again without starting from the beginning. By comparison, Getting Over It, like the physical act of climbing, relies on a player's sustained and strenuous efforts to introduce a sense of developing stakes. For this to happen, players must feel that failure is a real possibility.

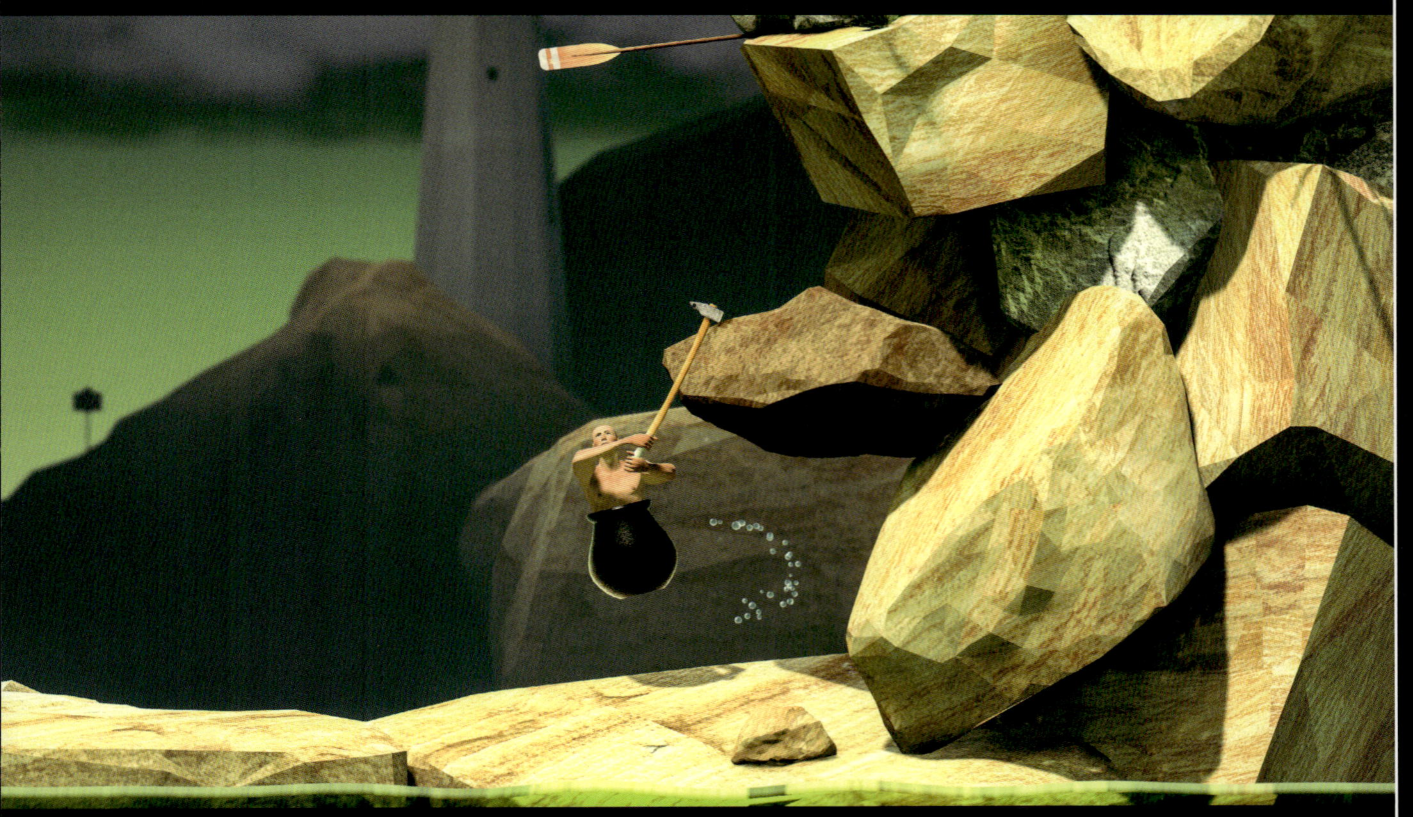

Foddy created Getting Over It for a certain kind of person and, he says in the game's trailer, for a specific reason: to hurt them. Players who crave success or demand that a game's software be designed for their comfort and ease should think twice before embarking on this one. Its main objective is to thwart its players, but for those who are open to its particular pain, it is a meaningful reflection on why we play, how we fail, and what it means to get up and try again. In the words of the film actress Mary Pickford, quoted by Foddy as the shirtless man falls hopelessly back to the game's beginning, "This thing that we call 'failure' is not the falling down but the staying down."

1. In the game's audio Foddy defines B-games as "rough assemblages of found objects. Designers slap them together very quickly and freely, and they're often … rough and unfriendly. … They're built more for the joy of building them than as polished products."

Return of the Obra Dinn

Lucas Pope (American, born 1977)

Return of the Obra Dinn 2018
The Museum of Modern Art, New York.
Gift of the designer

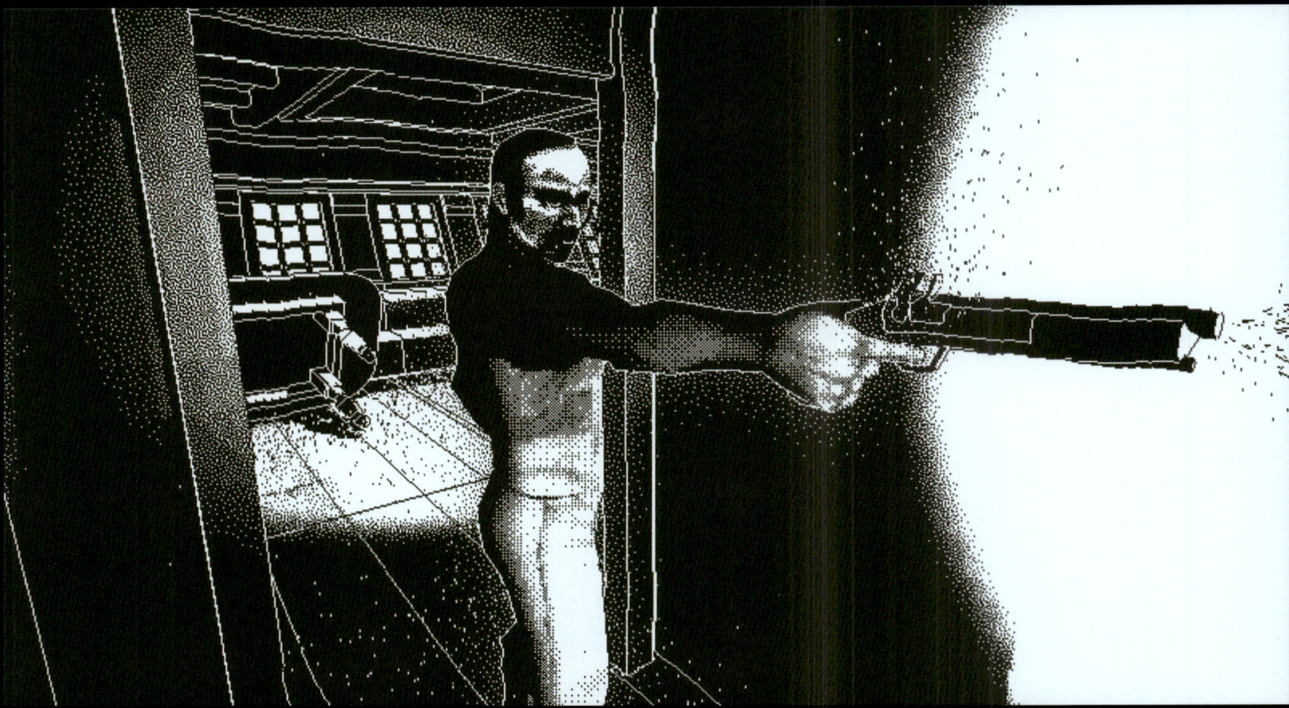

It is 1807. The *Obra Dinn*, a British merchant ship missing for five years—believed to have been lost at sea on its way to the Orient—has drifted up to the coast of England with damaged sails and no living crew. Dispatched to the ship to perform an appraisal, an insurance inspector for the East India Company must reconstruct its journey, identify more than sixty bodies found on board, and determine the cause of death for each. A set of artifacts, both ordinary and supernatural, is provided, among them a logbook containing crew lists, maps, and blueprints, as well as the Memento Mortem, a magical pocket watch.

Lucas Pope wanted to design a game with 3D animations rendered in 1-bit graphics (monochrome pixels each stored in one bit of memory), a style common in the computer games of the 1980s. He wanted to evoke the games he had played as a child, mostly on Apple's Macintosh Plus, but employing current technology. The game engine he developed, using a platform called Unity, allows the player to

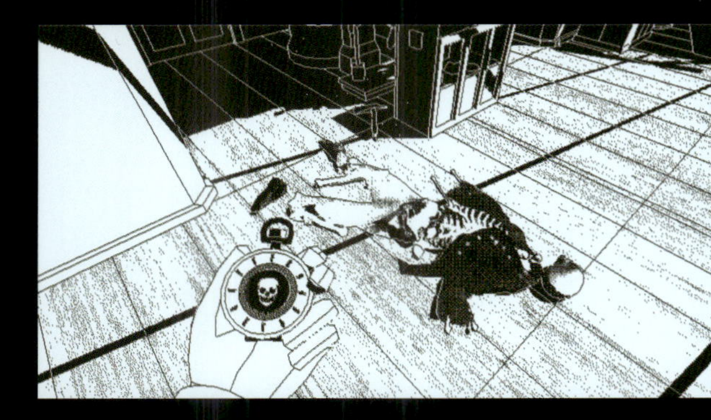

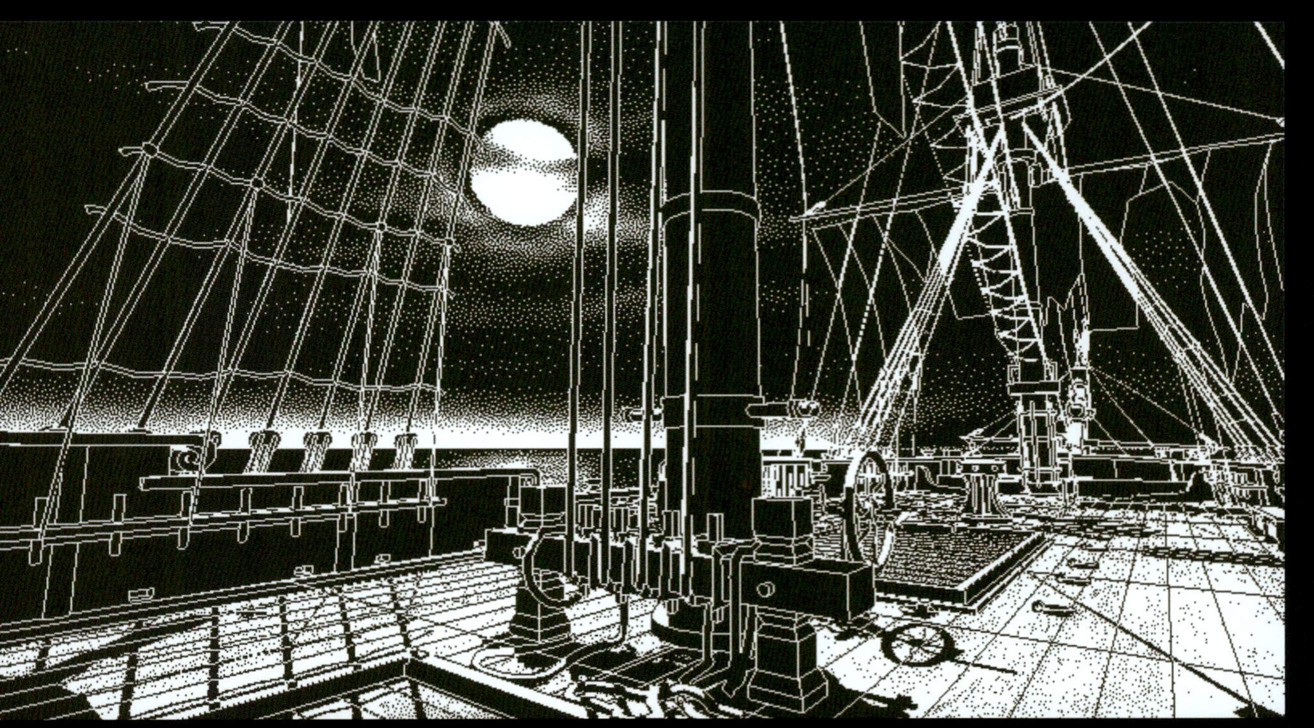

When the inspector, controlled by the player, approaches a body with the Memento Mortem, he is briefly transported back in time. He hears an audio clip of the victim's last interaction, which reveals crucial information such as names and accents, and is then shown the exact moment of their death. Although the characters and other elements in the flashback are frozen, the inspector can wander about freely and closely examine the crime scene. The dithered graphics have a vintage look but are crisp and sophisticated—fragments of gunpowder blasting from the barrel of a gun are as intricately rendered as the ship's architecture—allowing him to identify faces, clothing, and other clues. Meticulous attention to detail is critical for the inspector, whose only task is to uncover the story behind each dead body; as he moves deeper into the heart of the ship, a layered narrative unfolds, progressing backward through time. The fates of the doomed crew can be solved only through keen observation and deduction.

Pope is an exemplar of the independent designer that has defined the last decade of video-game production. Both Return of the Obra Dinn and Papers,

Please (from 2013 [page 84], also from the point of view of an administrative official with a mundane job) were released through his two-person company, in which he is the sole developer and programmer, responsible for modeling, scoring, and everything else. This has given him the liberty to turn his obsession with bureaucratic tasks and paperwork—along with a commitment to the core mechanics of interactive experience—into complex and commercially successful video games. The result of Return of the Obra Dinn's intricate graphics and elaborate narrative is, ultimately, an appreciation for the slow, at times tedious act of looking closely at details.

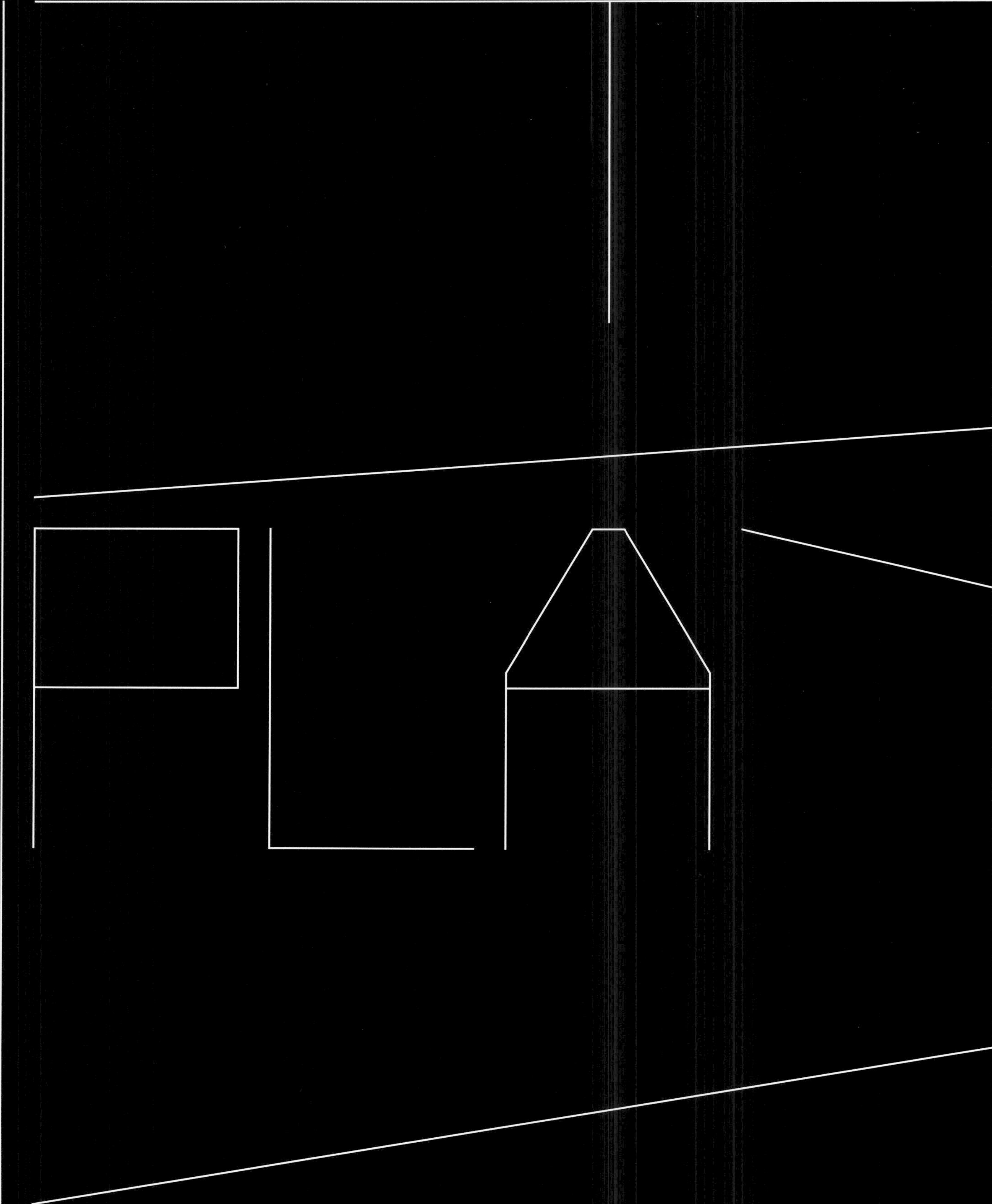

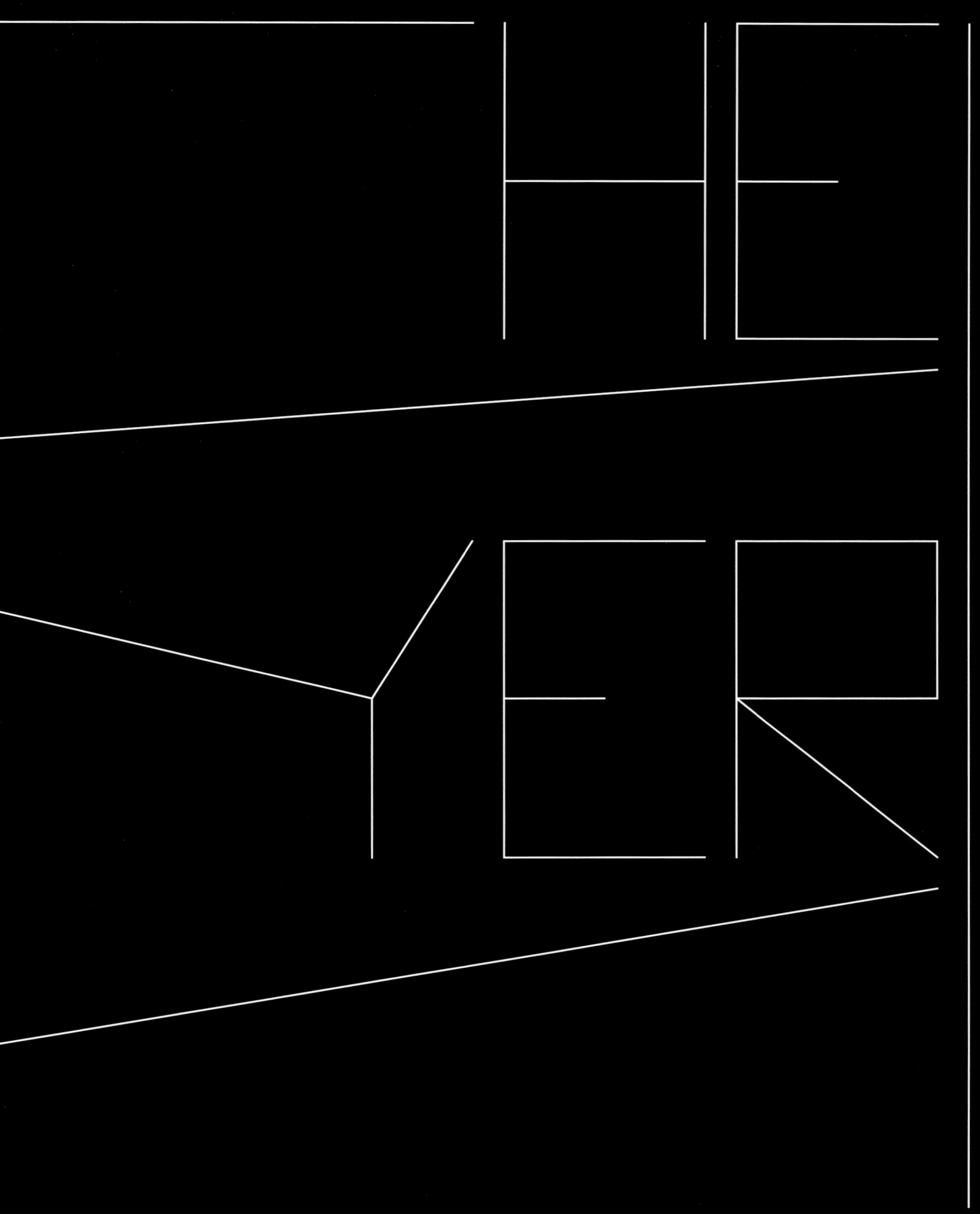
THE
FLYER

There is a certain music to well-written computer code—a rhythm, a structure, a pronounced harmony. But, much like a musical score, code is merely a set of instructions waiting to be executed. The *meaning* of music emerges when musicians take up their instruments and interpret the work, through a participatory exchange between the composer, the musician, and the listener. Video games, like music, are dependent on the player. The machinery of the input and the vision of the designer dictate the overall shape of the experience, but it is the performance of the player that brings it to life and, often, reveals its meaning. Playing transforms lines of code into works of art.

Playing a video game starts with a choice: whether to play alone or with others. From this decision branch thousands of paths to different video-game cultures, languages, and communities. Playing with others connects us historically to the video-game arcades where enthusiastic players gathered; it reflects and solidifies a critical social function. We play together for leisure, or to resolve conflicts, or to bond with our peers. But solo play, too, can be traced to early video games, in the lore of lonely computer scientists entranced by the capabilities of their magical machines. It invokes our imaginative interior worlds, the make-believe that gives film, theater, and literature the power to transport. But whether in private or in public, the act of playing a video game creates a space that collapses the real world and the game world, subsuming the player into the drama unfolding on-screen.

Video games ask us to identify with what we control. We flinch when the tank we are piloting is hit; we moan when the house we spent weeks designing and building is blown up by a random monster. In games such as The Sims (fig. 1 and page 114), this identification is taken to an extreme: players must attend to the quotidian physical and emotional needs of a character dwelling in a society generated and managed by the game's software. As in real life, competing demands must be carefully weighed and balanced. Navigating a Sim's fundamental need for home and community, and the myriad ways in which it manifests, is a challenging endeavor; the more pronounced the player's sense of responsibility for the digital character, the more emotionally affecting the result.

But The Sims is also a solo experience, played alone on a personal computer, in which players slip into different bodies—of any gender, ethnicity, or age—and inhabit lives made up of choices entirely dissimilar from their own.[1] Our Sim characters invert the spiritual meaning of

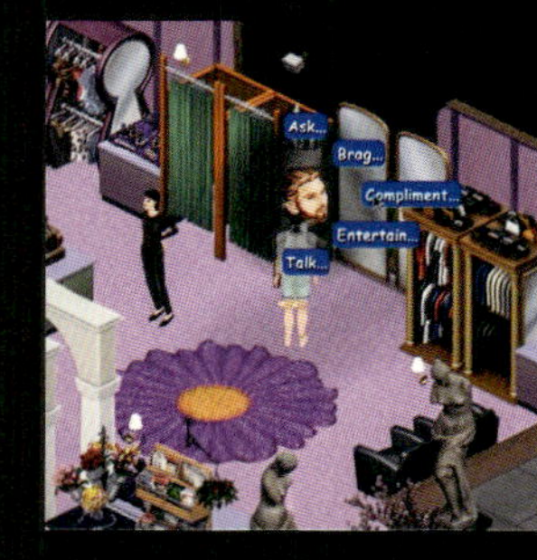

Fig. 1. The Sims. 2000 (page 114)

1. In 2002, Electronic Arts attempted to turn The Sims into an online multiplayer game, but stiff competition and high subscription costs made it unsuccessful. It was closed down in 2008.

"avatar"—a god made flesh—in transmutations from the physical plane to the digital, becoming masks behind which we perform borrowed selves. This is one of the many (not always successful) forms anonymity takes in video games, as well as all over the Internet, and through anonymity, players can be at once disconnected from reality and, possibly, display something of their true natures. We are both better and worse than we behave on-screen; the bullying, boasting, cheering, and knee-jerk reactions in livestream chats and Reddit threads do not necessarily reveal who we are off it (unless they do). The Sims performs a feat of pre-social-media digital alchemy, transforming both the player and the game, and suggesting that even when playing by ourselves we seek human contact.

For many players, fulfillment can be found by gathering, whether on a grassy field or a glassy screen. Trash is talked, frustration boils and is soothed, jokes are told, and the boundaries between us dissolve in what can be crucial, community-building exercises. From the early days of Pong arcade cabinets in California bars to the current global mania for e-sports, this need to play together and to watch others play has been shaped by video games. The rise of arcade culture through the 1980s and 1990s produced new social mores, new fashions, and new language. Many of the neologisms of past decades remain in use today: nerf, pwn, noob.[2] The intense competition in games such as Street Fighter II (1991, page 106) heightened this cultural phenomenon, with crowds of players and onlookers obeying emergent unwritten rules of propriety in the raucous, cacophonous atmosphere of the arcade (fig. 2): respectful distance between players and watchers; a place in line held by a quarter on the game's screen; defeat accepted gracefully, with a sportsmanlike "good game." For players, the game was and is a chance to perform, show off, and earn the esteem of peers. For observers, it is a chance to cheer for friends and, above all, to witness mastery—to relish the sight of a skilled video game player taking down an opponent with liquid grace.

With the advent of high-speed Internet service, the social nature of gaming migrated online, but the change of venue, from IRL to virtual, did nothing to lessen the intensity of the atmosphere—indeed, the community became supercharged. Now, rather than performing for a crowd of dozens, gamers play in livestreams for audiences in the tens of thousands (or millions, in some cases). The crowd is still trash talking, still cheering on their heroes and slinging mud at their opponents, but

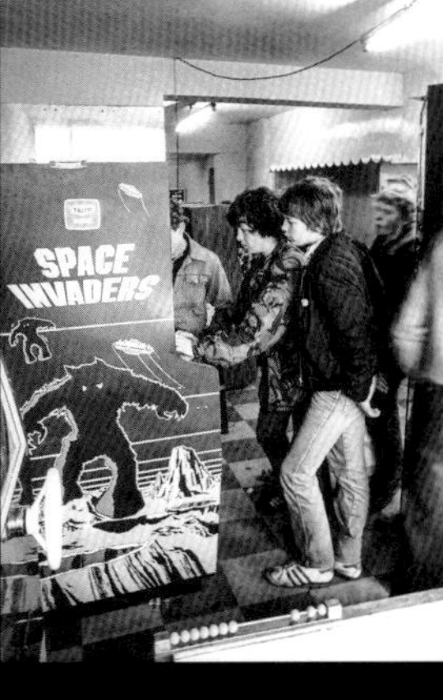

Fig. 2. Teenagers playing Space Invaders (1978, page 40), Newcastle, England, 1980

2. Nerf: to devalue game elements in order to balance gameplay, e.g., by making a weapon less powerful; pwn (pronounced "pone"): to dominate another player, derived from the slang use of "own," often used in the passive voice, as in "You just got pwned"); noob: a new, inexperienced player, derived from "newbie,"

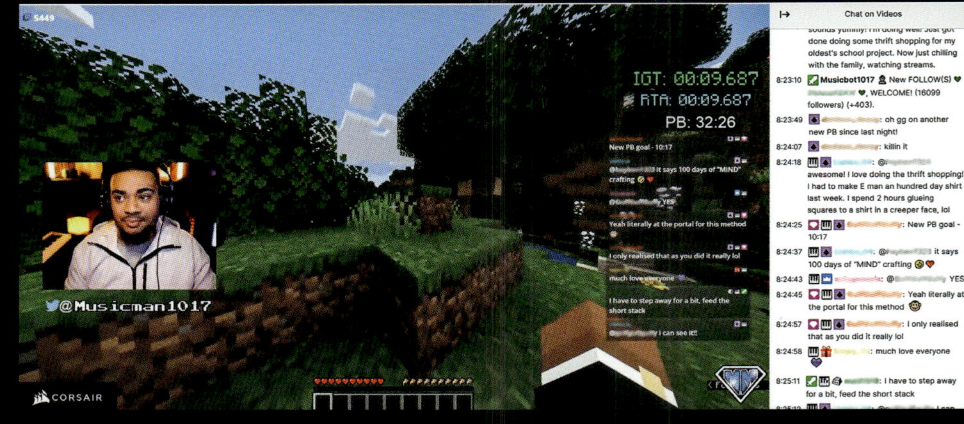

3. Twitch and YouTube, the largest streaming platforms, enable and monetize millions of hours of content and are increasingly prevalent in video-game consumption, especially by younger audiences.

4. Mob: an enemy character, derived from "mobile"; OP: overpowered; yeet: to throw, often used in the passive voice, as in "I was yeeted off a tower," but also an exclamation of excitement. Leeroy Jenkins was a 2005 World of Warcraft character who unexpectedly charged a room full of enemies, dooming his player group's meticulous plans. After footage of the attack went viral, his battle cry "LEEEEROY JENKINS" was turned into a meme that has come to mean the irrepressible urge to embrace chaos, regardless of the cost.

this now takes place in the chat windows of Twitch and YouTube (fig. 3).[3] Comments rain in as gamers watch a favorite streamer simultaneously narrate and play, using vocabularies that revel in baroque and insular slang: this mob is so OP; that noob got yeeted; some ding-dong went full Leeroy Jenkins.[4] Online gaming communities are fully as rowdy as the arcades of thirty years ago. They offer a social and global outlet for players, as well as a place to connect; in this, they proved invaluable for millions of people during the trying, isolating years of the Covid-19 pandemic.

Whether in arcades, online, or at home, players find ways to build experiences for themselves that go far beyond the visions of the games' designers. There are speed runs, in which players attempt to complete a game in as short a time as possible, often by identifying design flaws and exploiting them. There are cosplayers, who craft elaborate costumes in the style of favorite characters, bringing a game's aesthetics into the physical world. And there is modding, in which players modify a game's software or hardware (or both) in order to make it perform in ways not originally intended in the design; here the distinction between player and designer diminishes, and sometimes disappears altogether. Earlier in video-game history, modding led to games such as NetHack (1987, page 46), which shares characteristics with many other, similar titles. Since the 1990s, the development of new game engines (which simplify coding) and the support of online communities has made modding easier, leading to the profusion of options available today.

Mods are usually minor changes to an existing game, such as a feature that makes it easier to tame animals in Minecraft (2011, page 120). They can also take an existing game and redirect it entirely. The Stanley

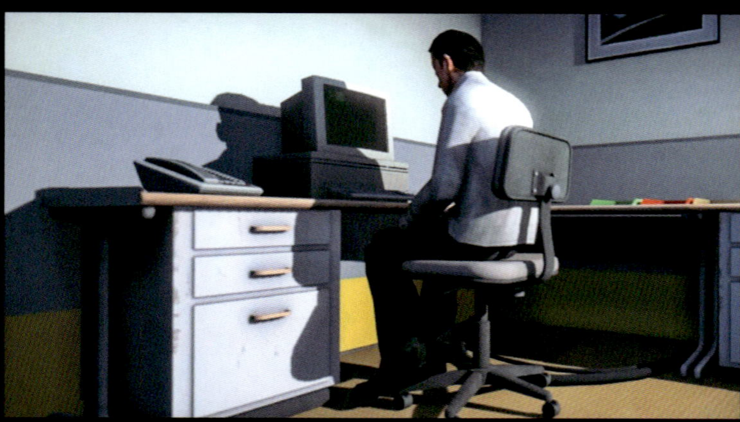

Fig. 4. The Stanley Parable. 2011
(page 126)

Parable (fig. 4 and page 126)—a beguiling narrative about isolation, freedom of choice, and, ultimately, game design itself—was adapted by the designer Davey Wreden from the game engine of an action-packed first-person shooter game. Players can ignore the game's prompts and commands, in an approach that foregrounds the illusion of agency in which we participate. In what we understand to be the designer-player dynamic, I (the designer) create variables, and you (the player) make choices that affect the outcome. But those outcomes are not infinitely variable; we certainly do not have as much agency as we think we do. In any game, the available choices are necessarily constrained by the limitations of the hardware and the imagination and skills of the designer. But we are blessed to not be restricted to the visions of those designers; if players behaved exactly as designers anticipated or desired, video games would have stagnated as a medium long ago. The richness and diversity of games today are the result of a long history of creative engagement from the community of players, who ferret out glitches, tweak code, and break every rule and stricture. Like musicians adjusting a composition's chords and rhythms, modders head for a game's edges, which are where the possibilities lie. The revelations discovered at these boundaries unite the player with the designer and remind us that when we play we are never alone.

Street Fighter II

Yoshiki Okamoto (Japanese, born 1961)
Akira Yasuda (Japanese, born 1964)
Capcom (Japan, est. 1983)

Street Fighter II 1991
The Museum of Modern Art, New York.
Gift of Capcom USA, Inc.

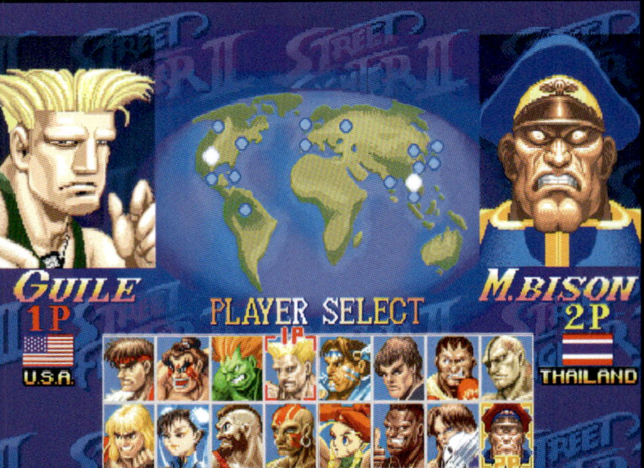

Not many people remember the original Street Fighter, from 1987. This is because it was a bad game. Or, rather, it was an arcade game ruined by an unusual—and altogether ridiculous—control system that required punching large rubber buttons. After hundreds of player injuries, Capcom, the game's publisher, changed the input mechanism to a joystick with six buttons, but at that point the game's reputation was too tarnished to recover, and it ended up being a financial disappointment. The fact that a sequel to this failure was made defied economic logic. That the sequel became one of the most influential arcade games of all time, spawning legions of imitators and creating a unique culture of competition and camaraderie, defied all expectations.

Compared with the fighting games that came before it, Street Fighter II dramatically increased the game's complexity and available moves. Two players, each steering one of eight characters, square off in timed combat, rapidly defending and attacking in order to knock out the opponent, using the joystick to control the direction and the six buttons to control the speed and power of their punches and kicks. One of the game's novel twists is a series of secret power moves that can be unlocked via different combinations of button and joystick. Executed at the correct moment, they inflict major damage (and also look supercool).

Street Fighter II's diversity of characters and fighting styles were also new in the world of fighting games. Players can learn the relative strengths and weaknesses of each character's combinations and moves, whether playing as the sumo wrestler E. Honda, the fire-breathing yoga master Dhalsim, or the American soldier Guile. Some players became so adept that Capcom was forced to make periodic adjustments to keep up with their rapidly expanding expertise, including adding characters, increasing the speed of the game, and programming new special moves and hit combinations.

An important note on the characters: Street Fighter II was far from the first (or the last) video game to render characters in crude racial, cultural, and gendered stereotypes; they were offensive when the game first came out, and in hindsight they are even worse. Our judgment of the game from today's perspective is tempered by this terrible defect, but it is

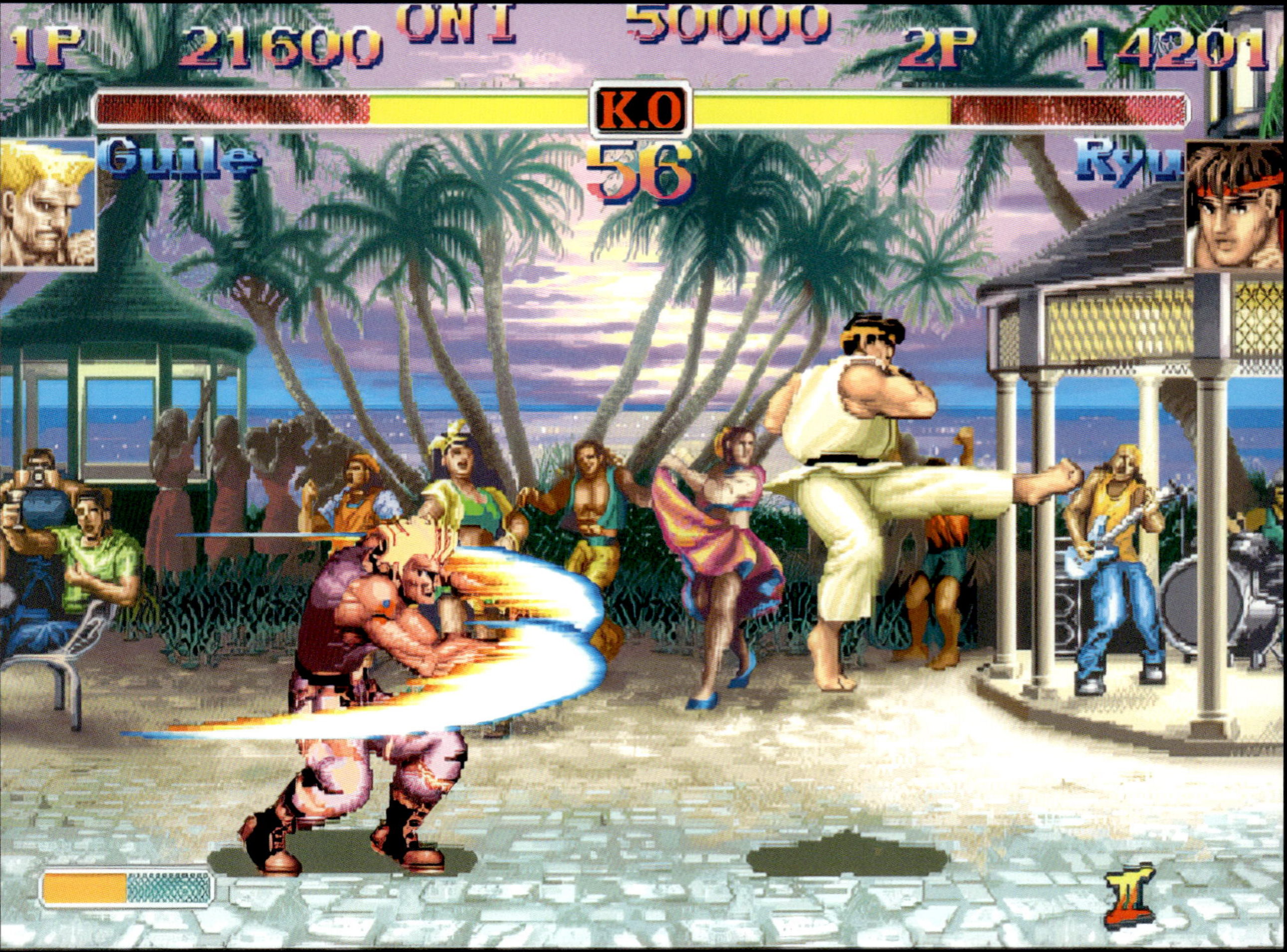

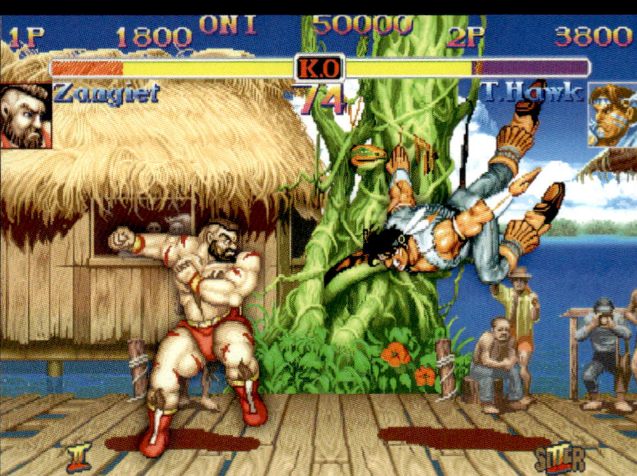

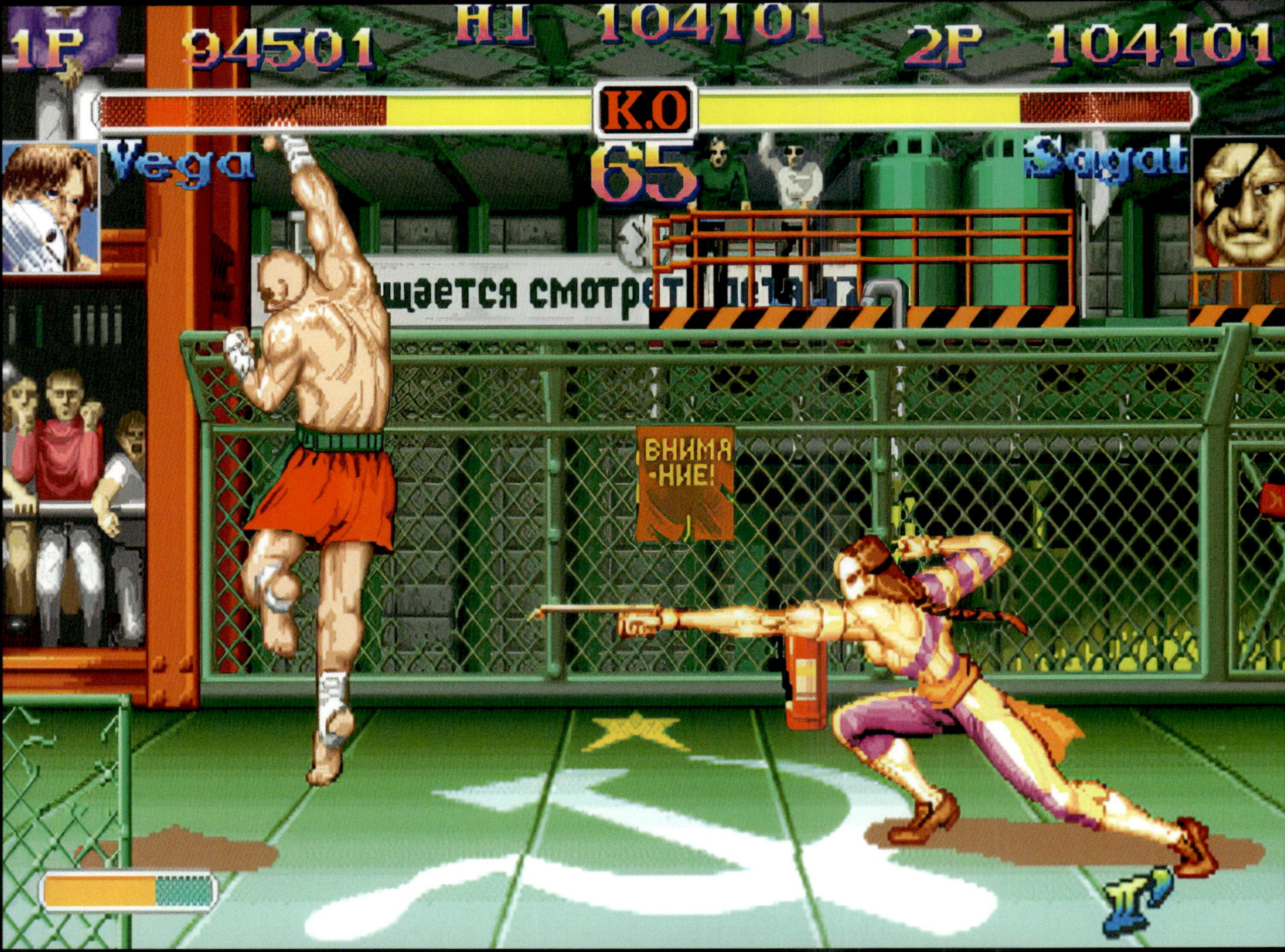

1P 94501
HI 104101
2P 104101
K.O
65
Vega
Sagat
щается смотреть
ВНИМА-НИЕ!

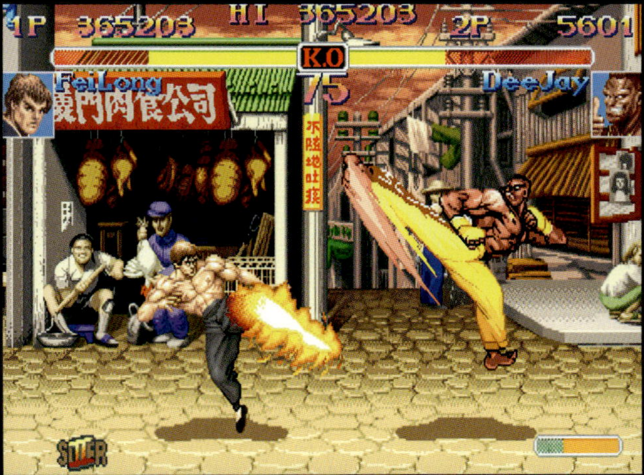

1P 365203
HI 365203
2P 5601
K.O
75
FeiLong
DeeJay
廈門肉食公司
不准隨地吐痰
SUER

also true that—by virtue of its huge popularity—Street Fighter II brought a lot of people together in arcades, in friendly, competitive, cross-cultural contact.

Indeed, arriving after years of decline in the arcade industry, Street Fighter II gave it a shot in the arm. It was enthusiastically embraced by players who queued up to try it, placing quarters on the screen to hold their place in line and then gathering around to watch and to try their luck against a dominant player. Intense matches between highly skilled contenders drew crowds of cheering onlookers. The mix of rivalry and spectatorship became a model for the competitive-gaming events of the 1990s and 2000s; Street Fighter II tournaments were organized and, often, televised, further establishing video games as a viable spectator sport. This dynamic—watching someone else play rather than actively playing—has continued into the present-day phenomenon of video-game streaming and the multibillion-dollar e-sports industry. People want to play together, and they love seeing masters at work, even when they are simply punching each other in a video game.

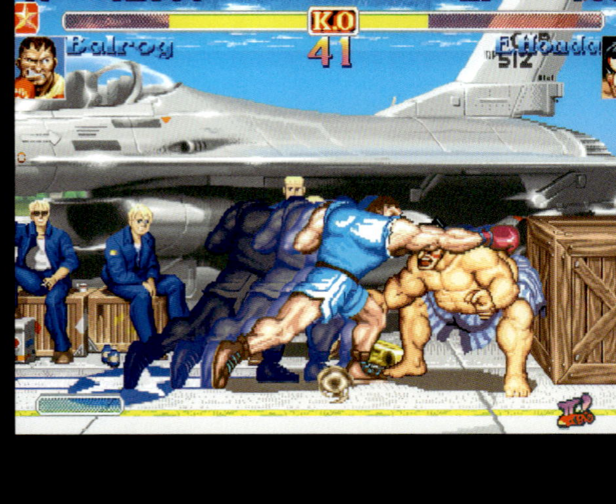

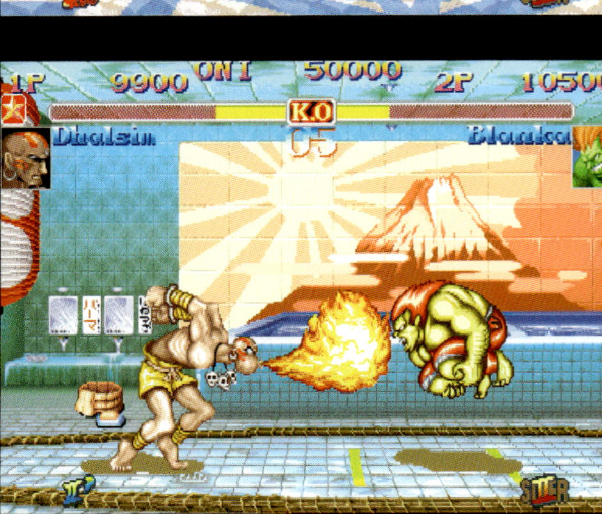

SimCity 2000

Will Wright (American, born 1960)
Maxis, Inc. (USA, est. 1987)
Electronic Arts (USA, est. 1982)

SimCity 2000 1993
The Museum of Modern Art, New York.
Gift of Electronic Arts

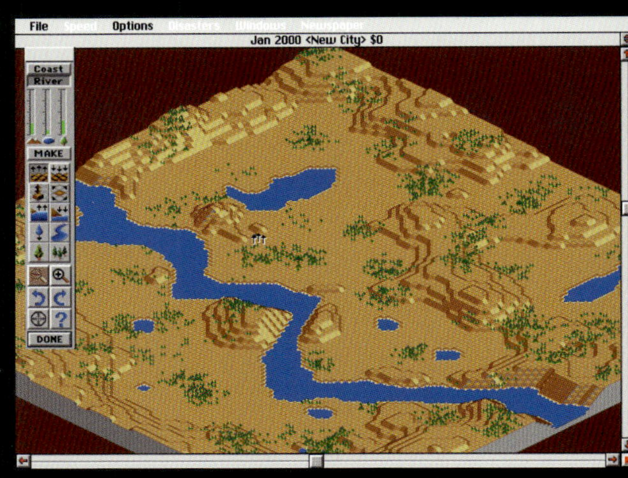

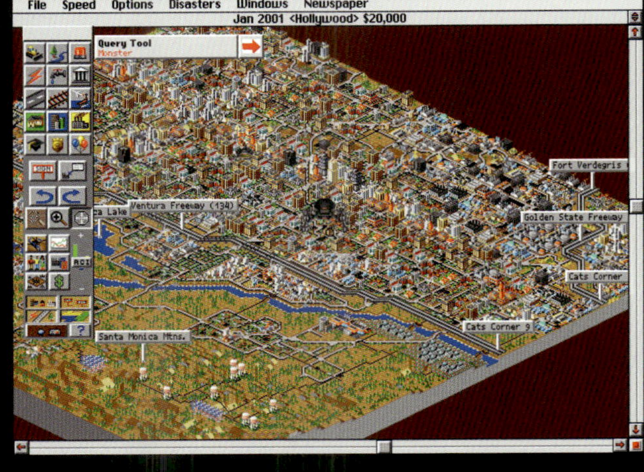

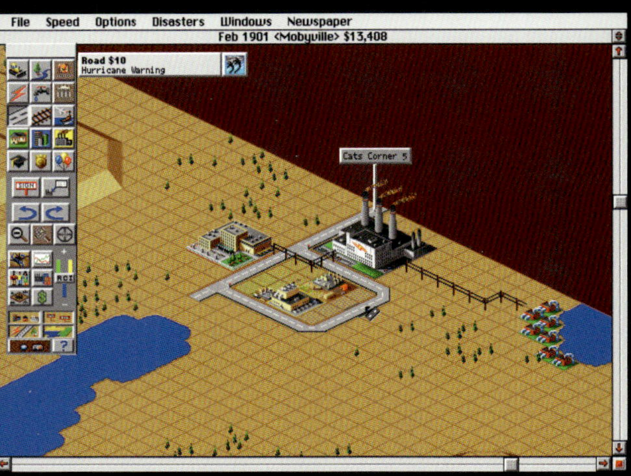

Will Wright is guided by the goal of making video games that he himself wants to play. As a result he has often found himself very much at odds with the thinking of his contemporaries. His most famous games, SimCity and The Sims, eschew the traditional systems of goals, rewards, and narrative in favor of what is known as an open-ended digital sandbox: a game in which players set up and pursue their own objectives. Sandbox games such as SimCity established a new paradigm: a story created by the player rather than imposed by the designer. Everyone wants to be the main character, and everyone loves to be in control.

SimCity grew out of Raid on Bungeling Bay (1984), Wright's first game, in which players fly military helicopters and drop bombs on various targets. During its development, Wright was drawn to the game's level editor, the tool he was using to design the environment, and found the process of building structures to be far more appealing than bombing them—creation turned out to be more fun than destruction. After the release of Raid on Bungeling Bay he continued to expand the level editor, adding functions and complexity. What eventually grew out of this tool was SimCity, a game that reflects Wright's view of urban life as an organic whole achieved by balancing its physical, political, and social demands. In SimCity the player is an all-powerful mayor-for-life who must attend to the minutiae of the city's growth: directing zoning for residential, commercial, or industrial development; laying

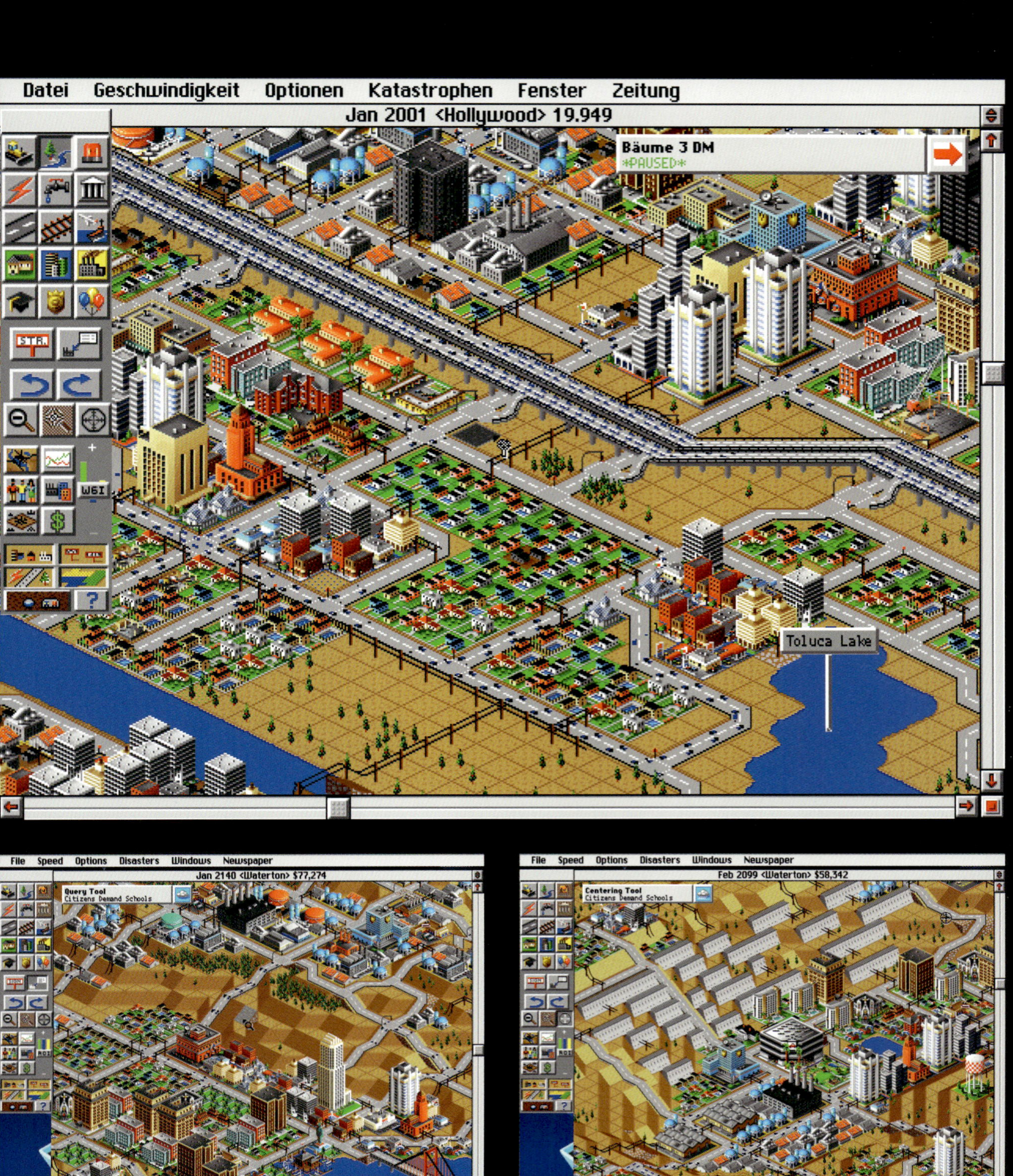
Datei   Geschwindigkeit   Optionen   Katastrophen   Fenster   Zeitung
Jan 2001 <Hollywood> 19.949
Bäume 3 DM
PAUSED
STR.
W6I
Toluca Lake
File   Speed   Options   Disasters   Windows   Newspaper
Jan 2140 <Waterton> $77,274
Query Tool
Citizens Demand Schools
File   Speed   Options   Disasters   Windows   Newspaper
Feb 2099 <Waterton> $58,342
Centering Tool
Citizens Demand Schools
©1993 MA
©1993 MAX

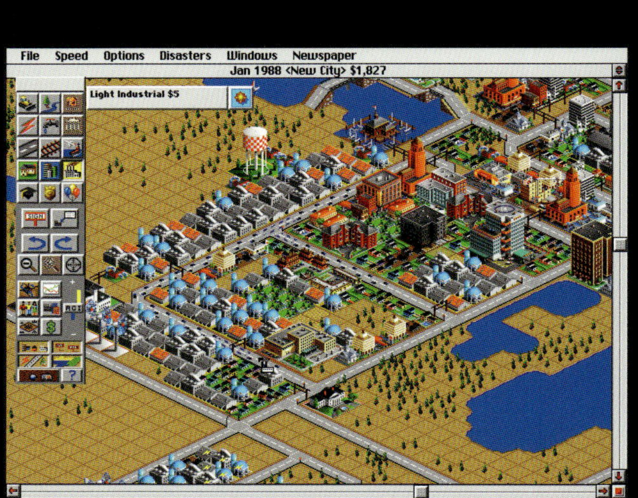

What complicates the mayor's decisions—in a feature that elevated what would have been an amusing diversion into a masterpiece—are the needs of the virtual inhabitants: the Sims (from "simulations") who live in the apartments, work in the factories, and lounge in the parks. Yes, as a virtual dictator you certainly have the power to place a school directly across the street from a smog-belching factory—but your inhabitants will flee, your tax base will shrink, and crime will bloom, eventually dragging your city into decline. Do a bad job, Madame Mayor, and your constituents will be sure to let you know. These constraints have the surprising effect of goading the player into more and more inventive solutions to the challenges of running a successful city.

SimCity and its sequel, the even more ambitious SimCity 2000, expanded the market for sandbox games, equipping players with a broad range of choices and outlets for creative expression. With these games, Wright calls on our imaginations and empowers us to direct our own stories, to envision our own most fun version of the game, while also forcing us to always, always remember the little people.

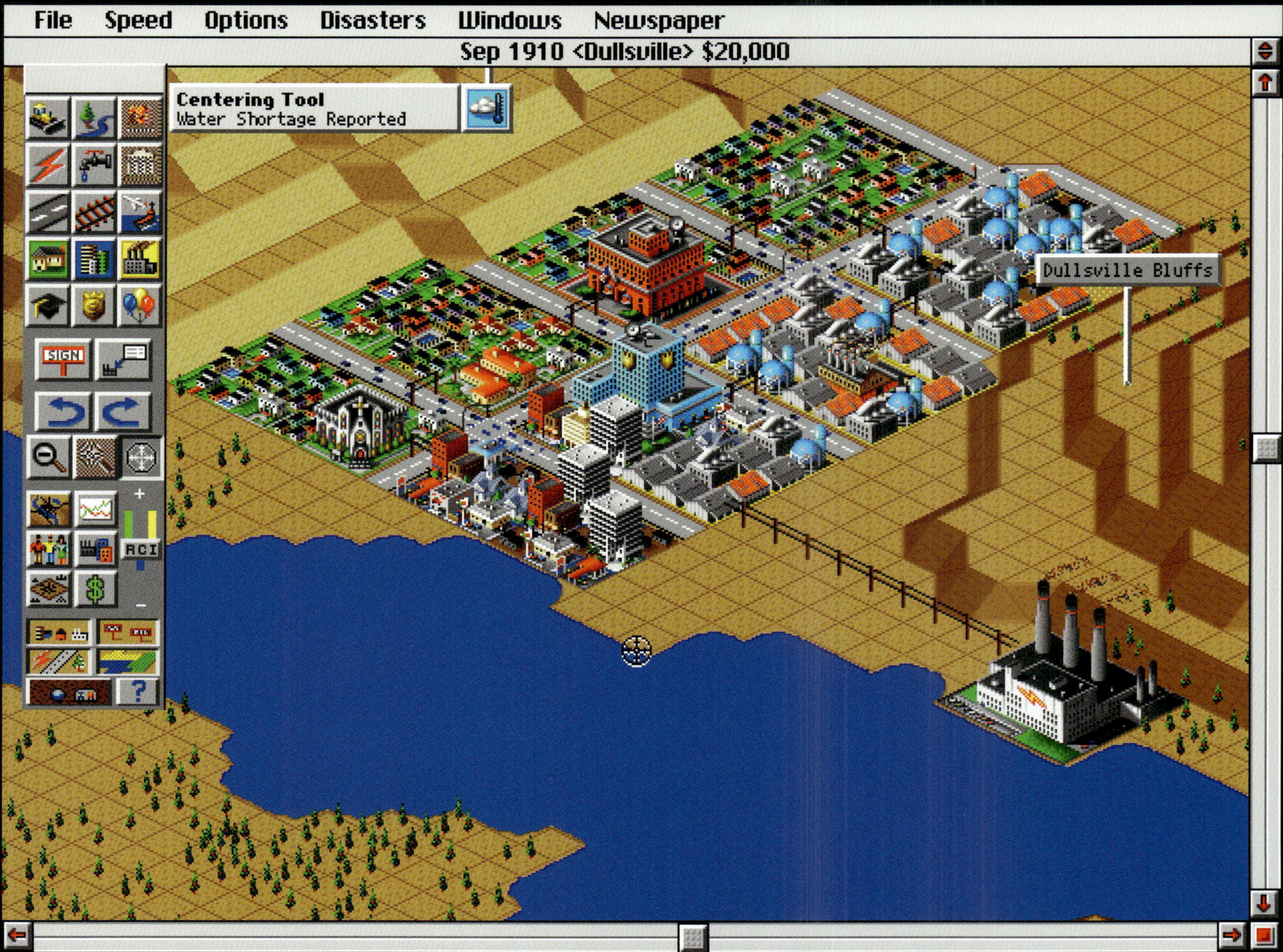

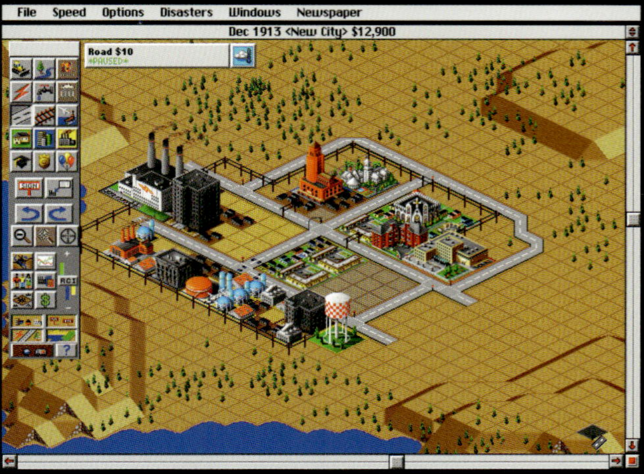

File Speed Options Disasters Windows Newspaper
Dec 1913 <New City> $12,900
Road $10
PAUSED

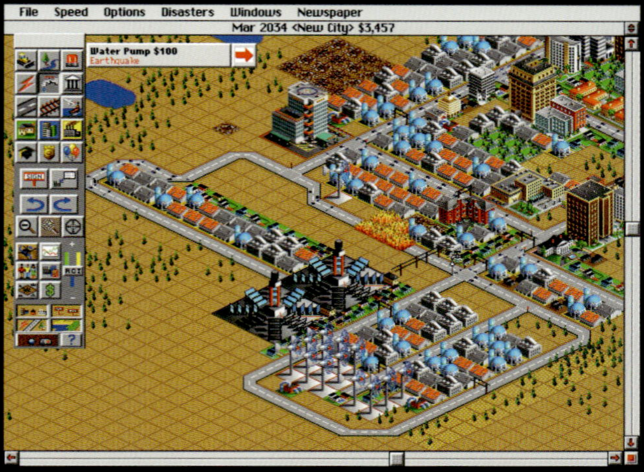

File Speed Options Disasters Windows Newspaper
Mar 2034 <New City> $3,457
Water Pump $100
Earthquake

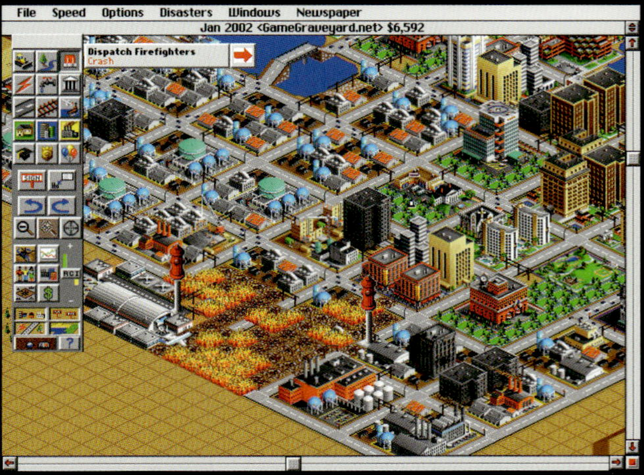

File Speed Options Disasters Windows Newspaper
Jan 2002 <GameGraveyard.net> $6,592
Dispatch Firefighters
Crash

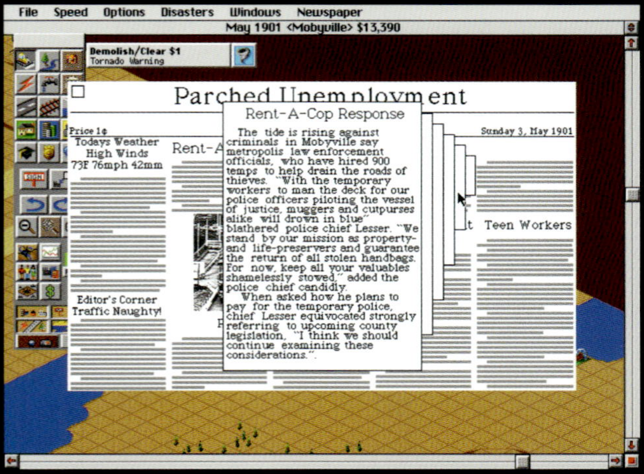

File Speed Options Disasters Windows Newspaper
May 1901 <Mobyville> $13,390
Demolish/Clear $1
Tornado Warning

Parched Unemployment
Price 1¢
Todays Weather
High Winds
73F 76mph 42mm
Rent-A-
Editor's Corner
Traffic Naughty!
Sunday 3, May 1901
Teen Workers

Rent-A-Cop Response
The tide is rising against criminals in Mobyville say metropolis law enforcement officials, who have hired 900 temps to help drain the roads of thieves. "With the temporary workers to man the deck for our police officers piloting the vessel of justice, muggers and cutpurses alike will drown in blue" blathered police chief Lesser. "We stand by our mission as property- and life-preservers and guarantee the return of all stolen handbags. For now, keep all your valuables shamelessly stowed," added the police chief candidly.
When asked how he plans to pay for the temporary police, chief Lesser equivocated strongly referring to upcoming county legislation, "I think we should continue examining these considerations.".

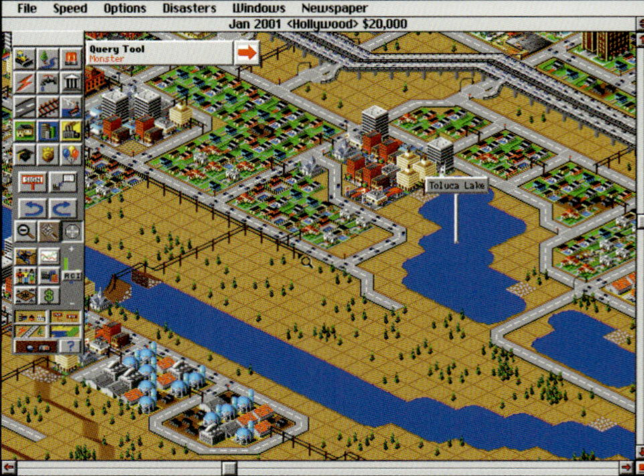

File Speed Options Disasters Windows Newspaper
Jan 2001 <Hollywood> $20,000
Query Tool
Monster
Toluca Lake

The Sims

Will Wright (American, born 1960)
Maxis, Inc., (USA, est. 1987)
Electronic Arts (USA, est. 1982)

The Sims 2000
The Museum of Modern Art, New York.
Gift of Electronic Arts

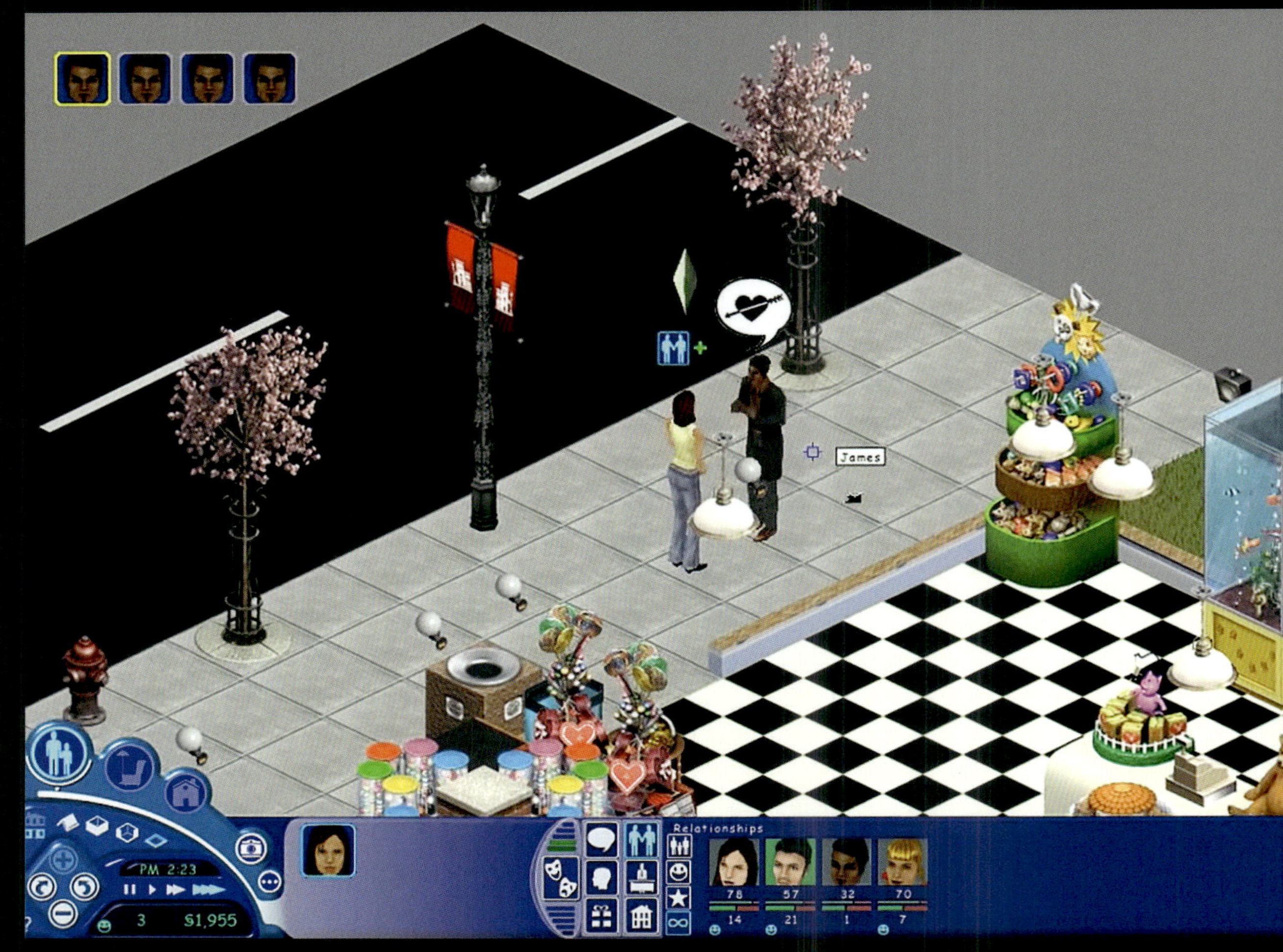

The global success of SimCity and its sequels
spawned all manner of Sim games, including
SimEarth, SimFarm, SimCoaster, SimCopter, SimGolf,
and SimAnt, in which players shape the destiny of a
colony of ants. At the core of all these simulations lies
the fascination of perceiving the world from a position
of ultimate authority. In SimEarth players step into the
shoes of a god, overseeing the layout of continents
and seas, affecting the lives of Earth's inhabitants on
the grandest scale. But whether creating at the plan-
etary scale of the Book of Genesis or the miniscule
dimensions of an insect metropolis, players are drawn
in by a feeling of control. Omnipotence is powerfully
intoxicating.

The Sims reverses the perspective of SimCity,
zooming from the godlike macro view of the masses
down to the level of the individual. The player guides
one or more Sims and must attend to their various
emotional and physical needs: sleeping, dressing,
eating, eliminating, working, maintaining friendships,
flirting—all daily activities that require the player's
constant attention in order to ensure a healthy and
happy Sim. As in other Sim games, a careful balance
of variables is necessary, but within those limitations
the player is free to create a life of their own design.
The individual Sim's point of view makes the game
compelling; answering to the plight of a faceless
population is one thing, but watching your carefully
cultivated Sim wither from a lack of friendship is
an altogether different, more emotionally affecting
experience.

The care of a Sim becomes an exercise in digital
empathy, a real-time diary in which the costs and
benefits of daily choices are readily quantified. Your
Sim is an extension of you, the player, a fantasy of a
life different from your own. Dress how you've always
wanted. Flirt with people you'd never have the nerve
to approach in real life. Change genders. Dance in
public. Tell off your boss. Act out a version of yourself
that you've always wished you were brave enough to
try. The Sims offers a private fantasy world in which all
of this is possible and all of this is safe. Like its many
Sim cousins, The Sims empowers players to make
their own stories, to direct their own destinies. And,
unlike real life, if all else fails they can always quit and
start again.

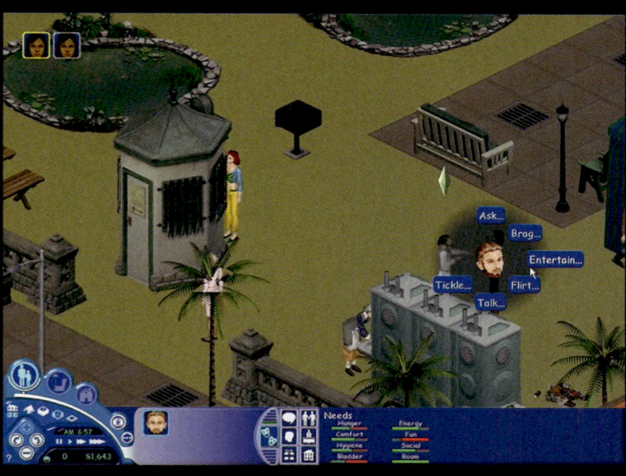

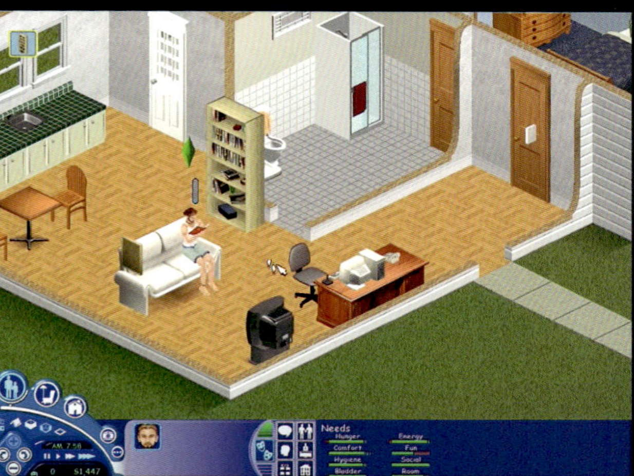

Vib-Ribbon

Masaya Matsuura (Japanese, born 1961)
NanaOn-Sha Co., Ltd. (Japan, est. 1993)
Sony Computer Entertainment, Inc. (Japan, est. 1993)

Vib-Ribbon 1997–99
The Museum of Modern Art, New York.
Gift of Sony Computer Entertainment, Inc.

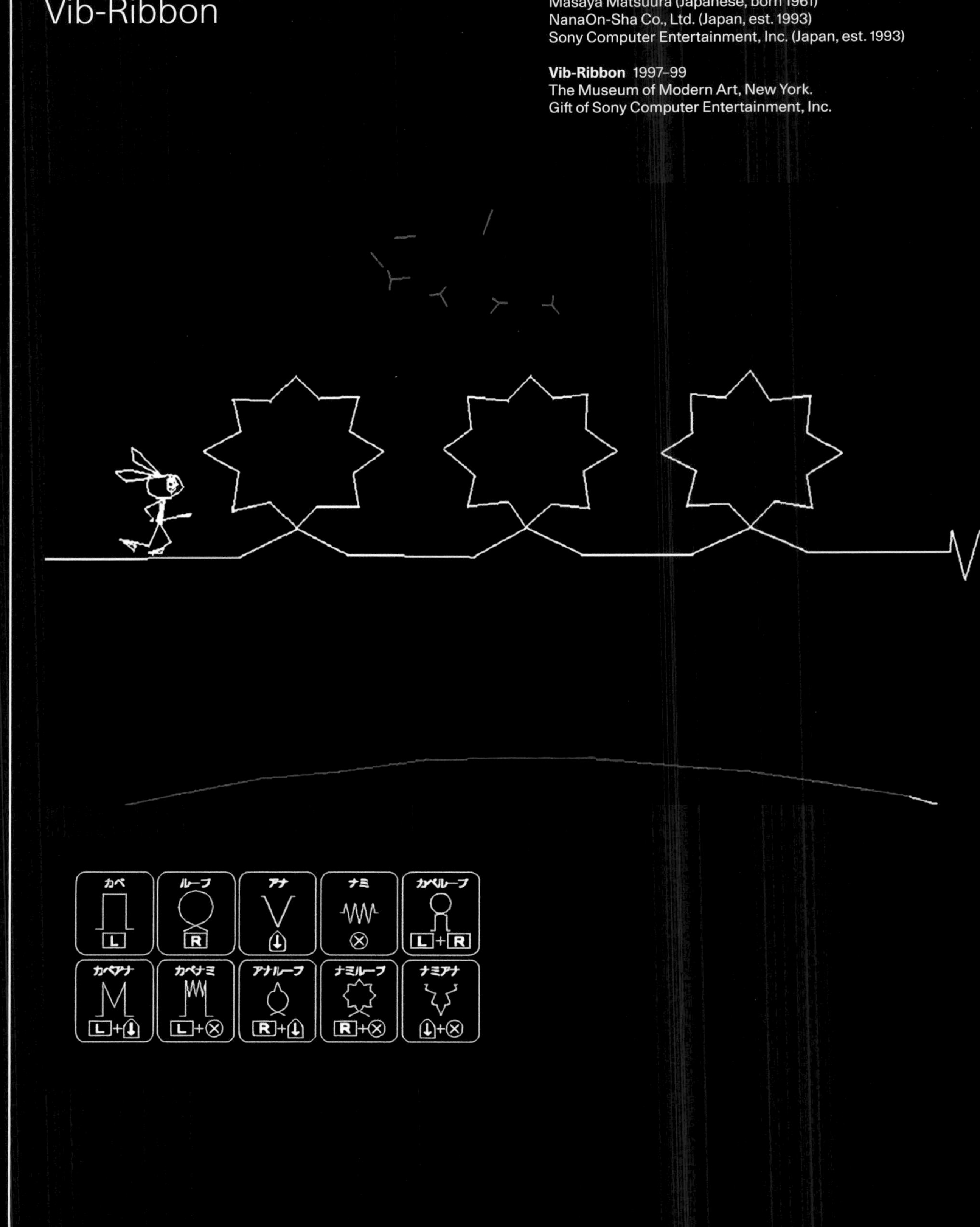

From the menacing electronic boops and beeps of Space Invaders to the soft orchestral movements accompanying a Minecraft sunrise, designers have employed musical compositions to augment the sensorial experience of video games. As it does in films, music sets the game's rhythm, creates levels of tension and serenity, and deepens our perception of nuances in characters and situations. Programmers began experimenting with ways to create computer-generated music in the early 1970s; by the 1980s and '90s, player-directed musical games were flourishing. Not everyone, however, wanted to compose their own music, regardless of how easy a computer made the process. Masaya Matsuura's Vib-Ribbon emphasizes a simpler joy, with a game that allows players to be immersed in music they love while also dictating gameplay through their personal preferences. In this video game, players are also DJs.

Vib-Ribbon is a rhythm game—a genre in which players must match a game's soundtrack by pressing buttons in precise sequences. The electronic memory game Simon, created in 1978 by Ralph Baer, was an early example;[1] later came the arcade hit Dance Dance Revolution (1998), which requires a sweat-inducing full-body performance. In this lineage, Vib-Ribbon stands out for its spareness and simplicity. In it, a stick-figure rabbit named Vibri walks along a ribbonlike line that is bent and curled into differently shaped obstacles generated by the music's varying frequencies. When the player presses the controller buttons in the right sequence, in time with the music, Vibri passes unharmed over and around the shapes in her path; the faster the beat, the quicker the player's reactions have to be. With each unsuccessful attempt, Vibri devolves into progressively lower life-forms, from rabbit to frog and then to worm, but with each success, she recovers and is eventually elevated to the status of fairy princess. At the end of the level, Vibri sings a congratulatory song that gets longer as the player's score gets higher.

But what truly sets Vib-Ribbon apart is the option of playing it with any music the player desires. The game is loaded onto the Sony PlayStation system's RAM, leaving the CD-ROM drive available for the player's choice of music, which the game's software renders as visual obstacles. Nothing distracts the player from focusing on the music: the black-and-white vector graphics are simple, and gameplay is straightforward. In Vib-Ribbon, as in the many music visualizers that appeared in the late 1990s, the translation of one sensorial experience into another offers opportunities for fresh appreciation.[2] Matsuura's game invites players to sit back, relax, and watch their music.

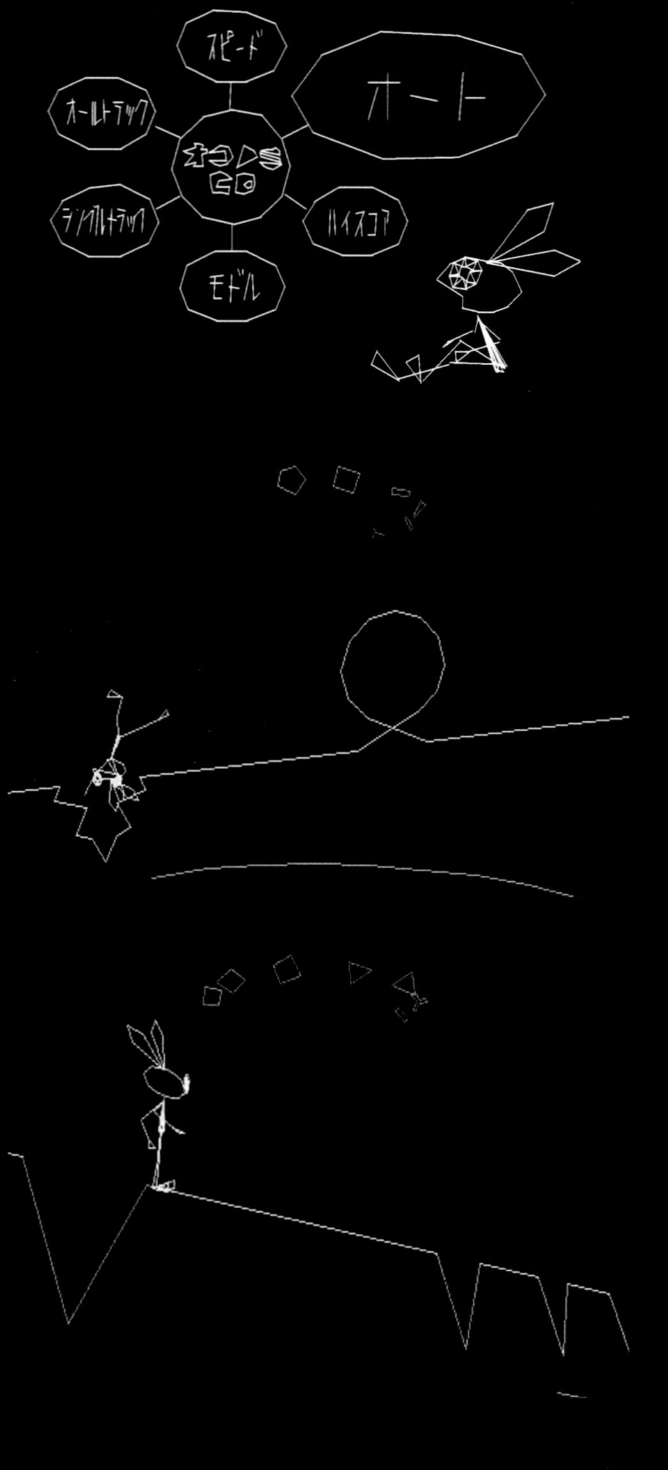

1. Ralph Baer also designed the Magnavox Odyssey (page 36).

2. A music visualizer renders sound in animated graphical forms.

Eve Online

CCP Games (Iceland, est. 1997)

Eve Online 2003
The Museum of Modern Art, New York.
Gift of CCP hf.

Few games demonstrate the power of the player community as clearly as Eve Online, which from the beginning has been shaped by the behavior and preferences of its players as much as by the choices of its designers. This bottom-up model of game design had been tried before, but never with as much player influence. As Eve Online approaches twenty years of continual use, the unique and ever-changing communities it has engendered have proven as durable, irascible, and diverse in perspective as any in real life.

Eve Online is a massively multiplayer online role-playing game (MMORPG), in which thousands of people play in the same online space. Unlike other MMOs of the early 2000s, the entire Eve universe is hosted on a single server, rather than the more typical practice of splitting players into multiple identical universes on separate servers. This has cultivated a rich shared experience in which every player's actions have an impact on a huge collective population. The game's structure is relatively straightforward, with features common to role-playing games. The player

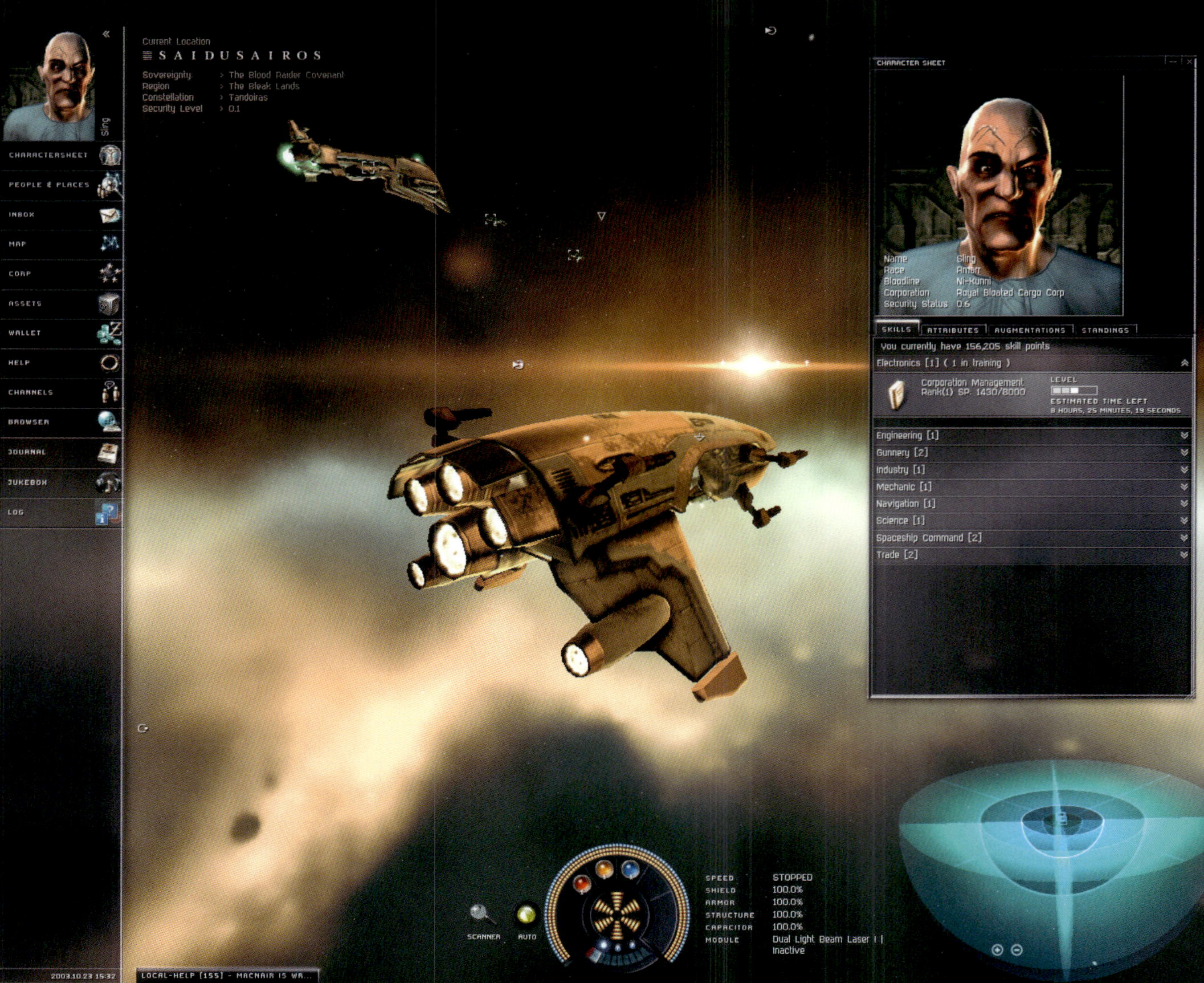

controls a spaceship, explores the stars, earns currency, engages in battles, and joins with other players to set and accomplish goals such as mining resources, attacking enemies, or purchasing new ships. Players quickly discover the importance of working with others for both survival and success, which reinforces the social nature at the heart of all MMOs. This dynamic extends to the rich dialogue that takes place in thousands of discussion forums and communication channels, which the developers monitor in order to respond to the community's demands and preferences in game updates. In the unruly world of Eve's communities, players gossip, complain, forge alliances, and plot betrayals. They have produced immense battles joined by thousands of players; in-game economies of such complexity that CCP, the game's developer, was forced to keep an economist on staff; and unexpected rebellions and behaviors deemed so unfair that the programmers had to intervene.

Jokingly referred to as "spreadsheets in space" by both aficionados and critics, Eve Online is notoriously difficult for new players thanks to its challenging gameplay, its epic and continuously evolving story, and the baroque social codes of its diverse communities. Like immigrants newly arrived in a strange country, players must find their place in a bewildering and unfamiliar culture. But new players continue to come, drawn into a universe in which the story is of their own design.

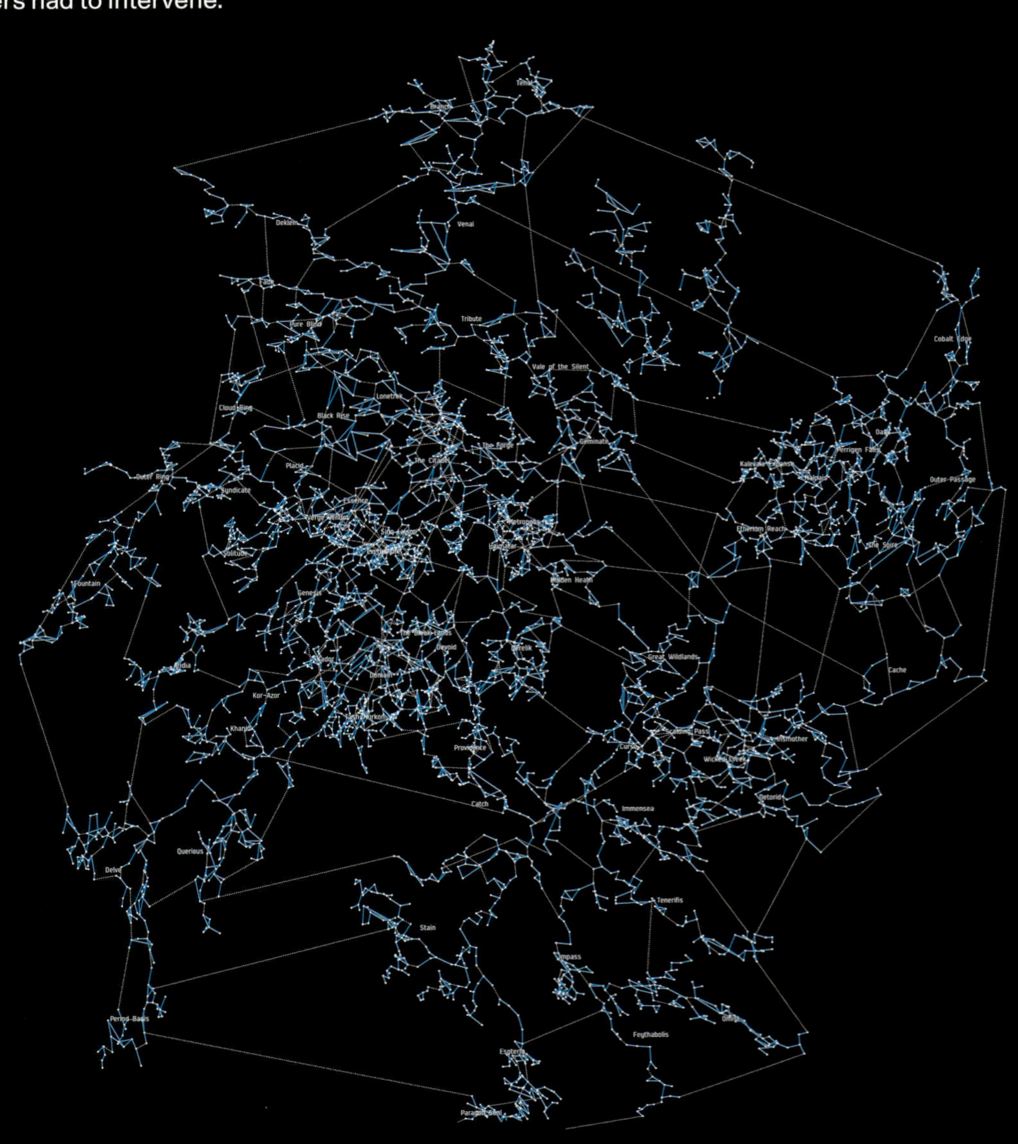

Minecraft

Markus "Notch" Persson (Swedish, born 1979)
Mojang (Sweden, est. 2009)

Minecraft 2011
The Museum of Modern Art, New York.
Gift of Mojang

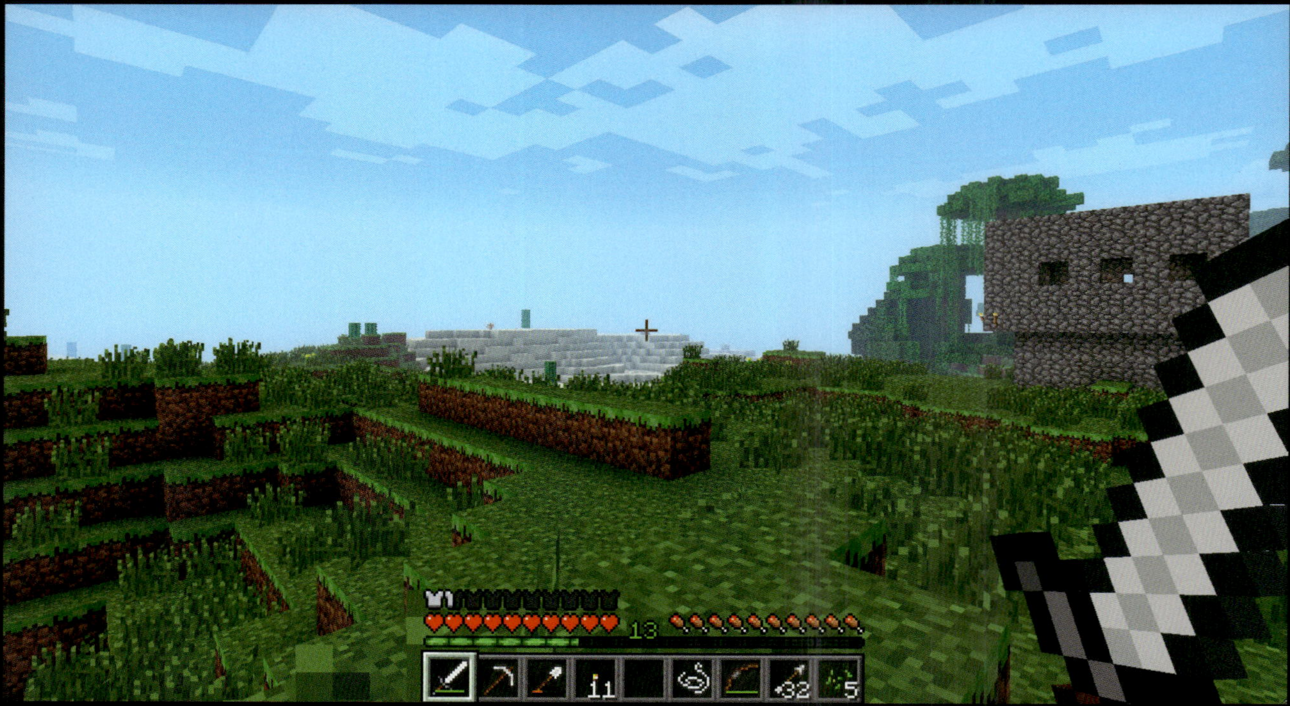

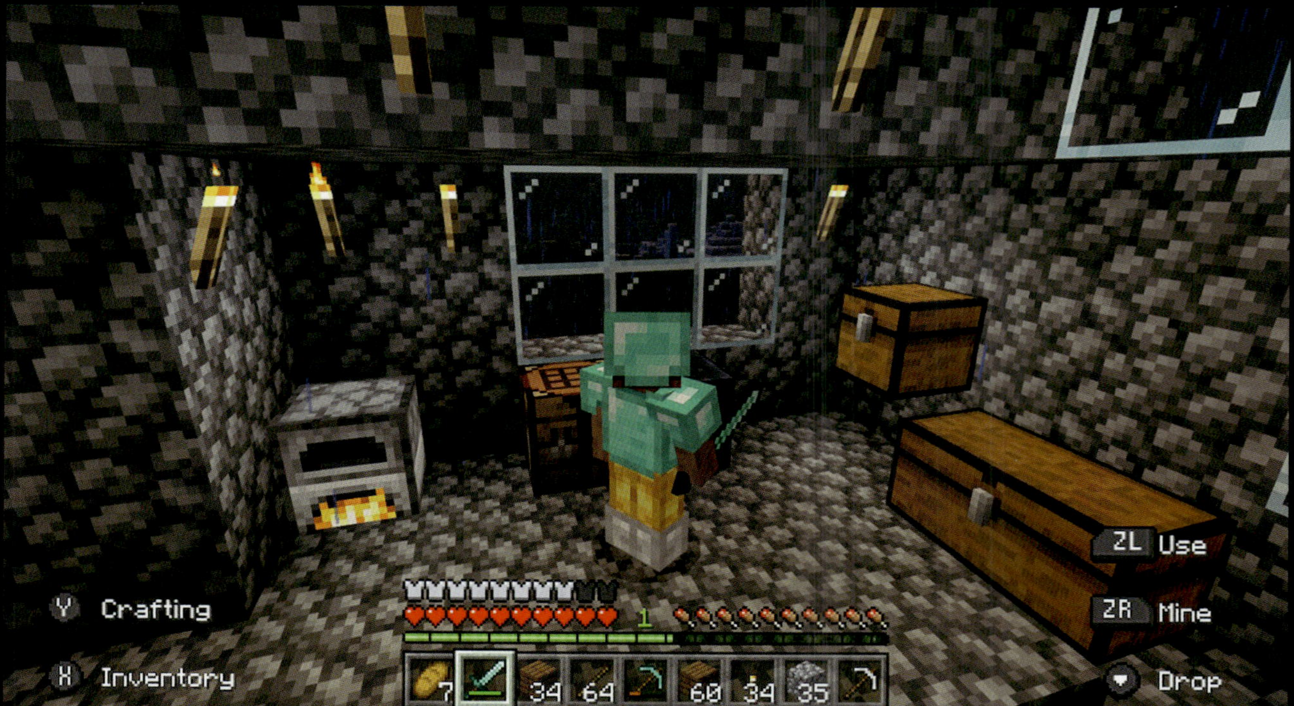

Crafting

Inventory

ZL Use

ZR Mine

Drop

In the galaxy of video games, Minecraft is a celestial body of stupefying proportions. More than 238 million copies have been sold (the most of any video game to date), it has 140 million active monthly players, Minecraft-related videos on YouTube surpassed one trillion views at the end of 2021, and an endless line of Minecraft merchandise is available, including books, furniture, clothing, and toys. Eleven years after its initial release, it remains as popular as ever, offering opportunities for play, education, and social exchange on a scale never before achieved in gaming.

The genius of Minecraft lies in its embrace of emergent gameplay, a design concept whereby complex behaviors and situations grow out of simple structures and mechanics. There is no right way to play a sandbox game like Minecraft; it has been clear from its earliest releases that the focus is on self-directed play and exploration within a loosely defined set of parameters. These include the basic actions of mining, crafting, and surviving in a procedurally generated 3D world made of cubes, each representing a square meter. Players choose either creative or survival modes; the former provides the freedom and resources to build whatever the player desires, the latter adds imperatives—avoiding monsters, satisfying hunger, gathering resources—that complicate the player's progress and keep the game under constant tension.

Starting with this basic premise, players have been endlessly innovative in coming up with ways to shape experiences within the game. They have constructed extensive one-to-one versions of real-world environments, including the entirety of midtown Manhattan, the Grand Canyon, and The Museum of Modern Art. With redstone, a resource that transmits electricity, they have created working computers within the game. Countless updates and mods have added options for player-versus-player combat, the ability to assemble rockets and fly them, and enhanced decorating functions for budding interior designers. Educators have leveraged their students' enthusiasm for the game into new pedagogical models for mathematics, history, and coding. Independent filmmakers have used Minecraft characters and settings in original video content, further embedding the game in popular culture. And in a particularly artistic project, the gamer and commentator KurtJMac has been streaming, for the last eleven years, his ongoing journey through the endlessly generated Minecraft landscape in *Far Lands or Bust*, a travelogue of his Lewis and Clark–style trek to the mathematical limits of this virtual world.

None of these outcomes were envisioned by Markus Persson when he created the first version of the game. Minecraft, perhaps more so than any game ever made, has proven the player's central role in bringing a video game to life. A sandbox, however artfully designed, is but a contained volume of dirt, awaiting activation, waiting for someone to come in and start digging.

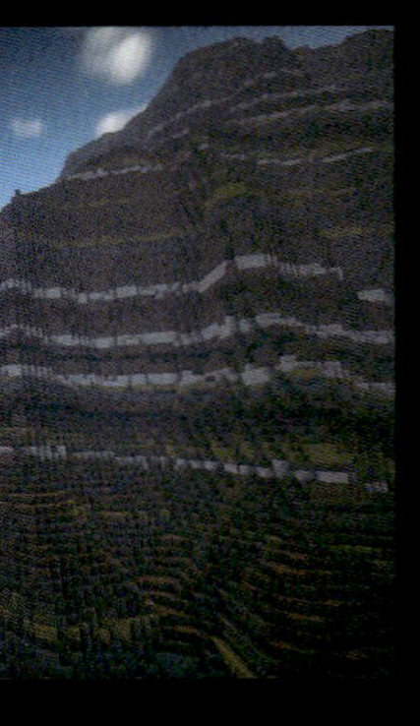

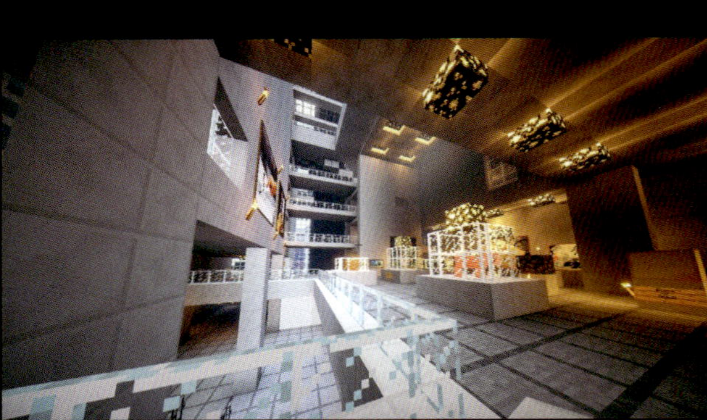

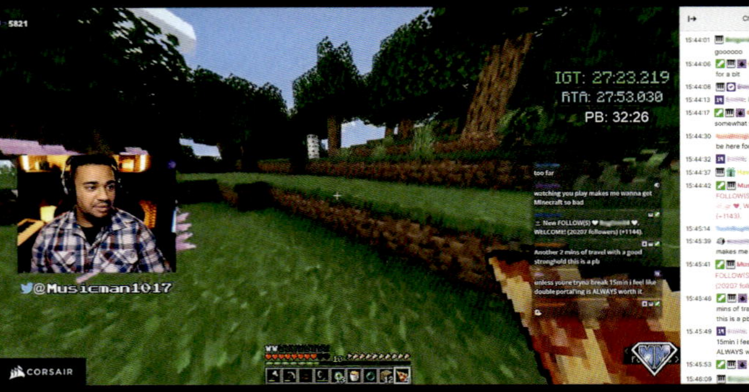

The streamer Musicman1017 playing Minecraft on Twitch, 2022

Biophilia

Björk (Icelandic, born 1965)
Mathias Augustyniak (French, born 1967) and
Michael Amzalag (French, born 1968) of
    M/M Paris (France, est. 1992)
Sjón (Sigurjón Birgir Sigurðsson) (Icelandic, born 1962)
Scott Snibbe (American, born 1969)
Max Weisel (American, born 1991) of
    RelativeWave (USA, est. 2009)
Sarah Stocker (American, born 1965) and
Mark Danks (American, born 1972) of
    Kodama Studios (USA, est. 2011)
Touch Press (UK, est. 2010)
Nikki Dibben (British, born 1969)
Stephen Malinowski (American, born 1953)
John F. Simon Jr. (American, born 1963)

Biophilia 2011
The Museum of Modern Art, New York.
Gift of Björk and One Little Indian

Cosmogeny and home screen

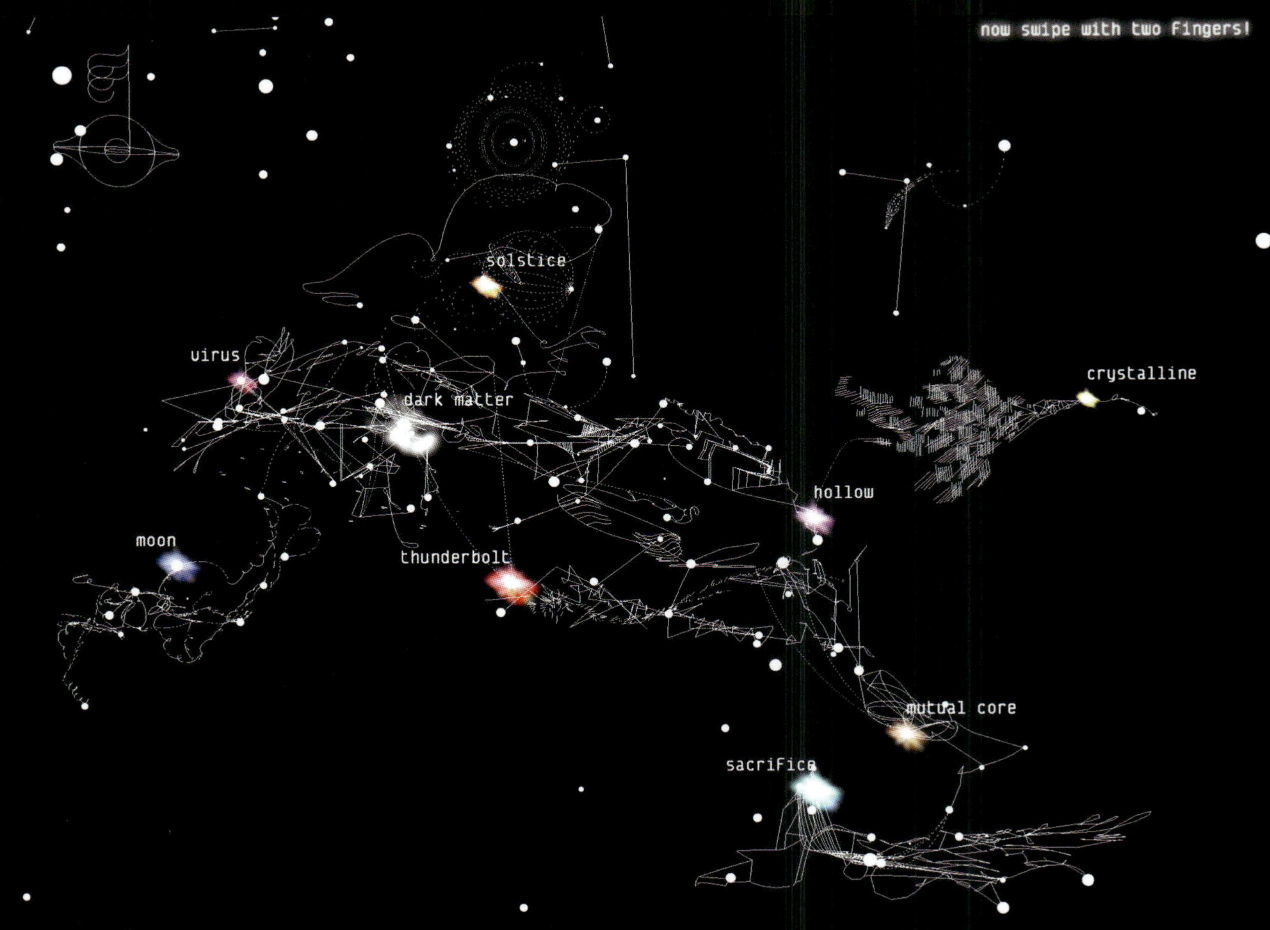

In 1984 the biologist Edward O. Wilson posited that humans are biologically driven to seek connections with other forms of life, and he called this compulsion "biophilia." The Icelandic musician Björk took this idea as a point of departure for a series of songs-cum-games that connects musician, designer, and player. Just as a human being is both a singular animal *and* a vast ecosystem, Biophilia is both a music album *and* a video game. Such classifications are merely words attempting to define the contours of the myriad biological, emotional, and artistic expressions that result when life seeks life—or when music seeks performers. We sing together, we play together, and—considering the billions of lives we carry within us—we are never truly alone. In Hollow, Björk sings of humanity's connection to our ancestors as well, and through them, to all living creatures:

> *Now come forth*
> *All species*
> *Hollow*
> *Like a bead in [a] necklace*
> *Thread me upon this chain*
> *I'm part of it*
> *The everlasting necklace*
> *Jewels after jewels after jewels after jewels*
> *after jewels after jewels.*

Biophilia opens with a definition of the term, voiced by the revered biologist and television host David Attenborough; as he speaks, the view swoops across the heavens to a constellation of galaxies. Each one represents a song and, when clicked, draws players into a game in which their actions affect the musical composition. In Solstice, players send planets into orbit around the sun; each orbit is rendered as a simple colored circle that adds a melodic line, played by a gravity harp and modulated by the user. In Moon, a song about life cycles, shifting the moon's phase changes the tones and sequence of the harp's accompaniment. The decisions of the player, the designers, and the musician are thus combined in a participatory musical experience in which endless variations are possible, from the spare to the highly layered and complex. Björk, who frequently works with other artists, invites players into an elegant collaboration whose relative ease fluctuates from song to song. In

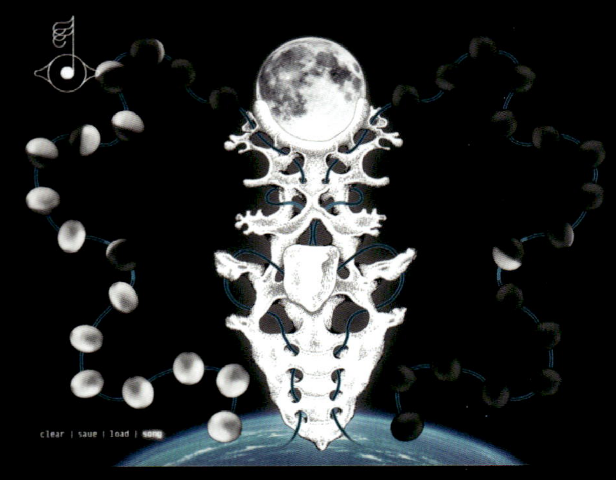

Moon

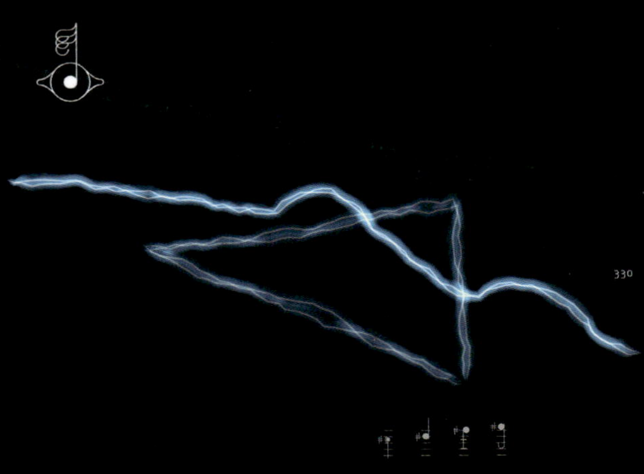

Thunderbolt

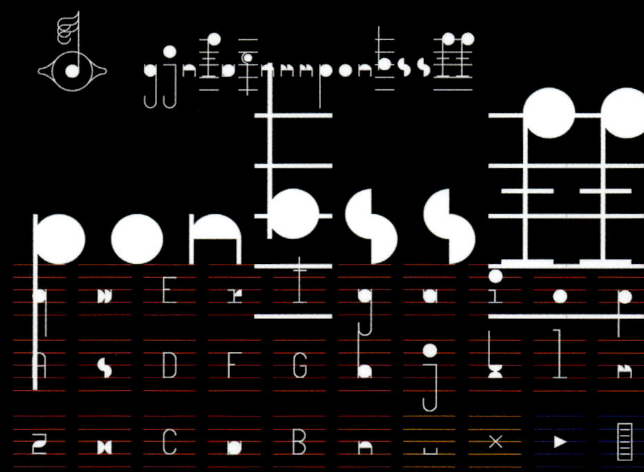

Sacrifice

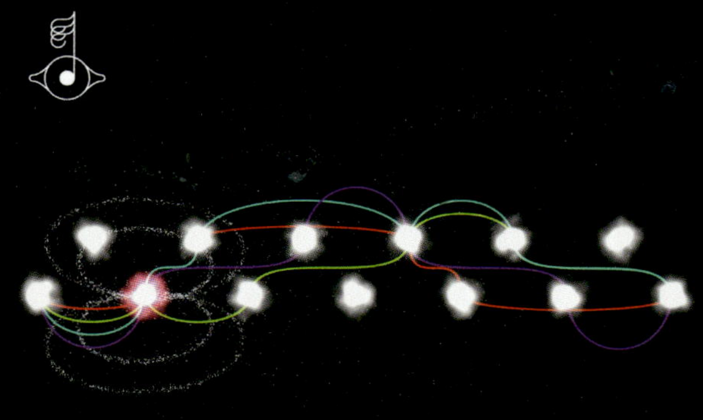

Dark Matter

Mutual Core, for example, the task of pulling together tectonic plates to produce chords is purposefully difficult and unwieldy, matching the song's weighty lyrics.

Biophilia is the result of a collaboration among many artists, musicians, designers, programmers, and poets. Players add their own perspective into the mix, and in doing so they, too, become performers. By bringing her listeners into the process, Björk emphasizes one of the biophilia hypothesis's central tenets: that desiring connection with others is natural and expected, even when it is difficult

To match our continents
To change seasonal shift
To form a mutual core.

Crystalline

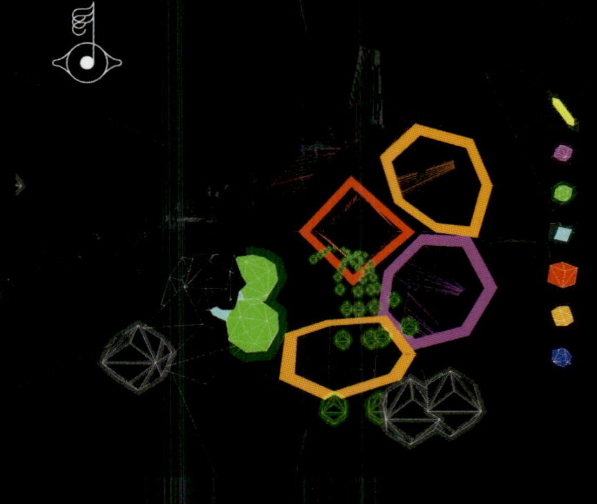

Mutual Core

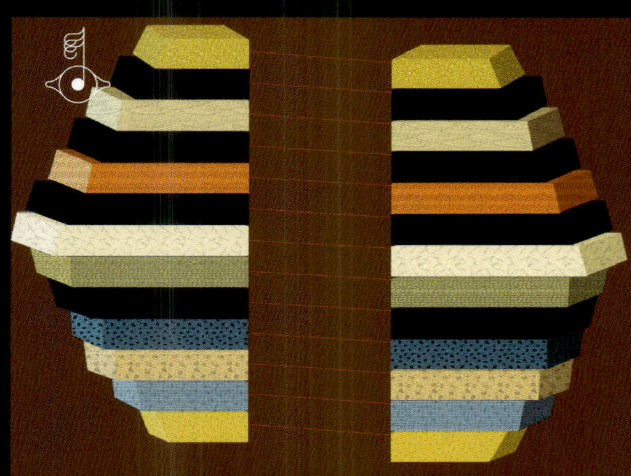

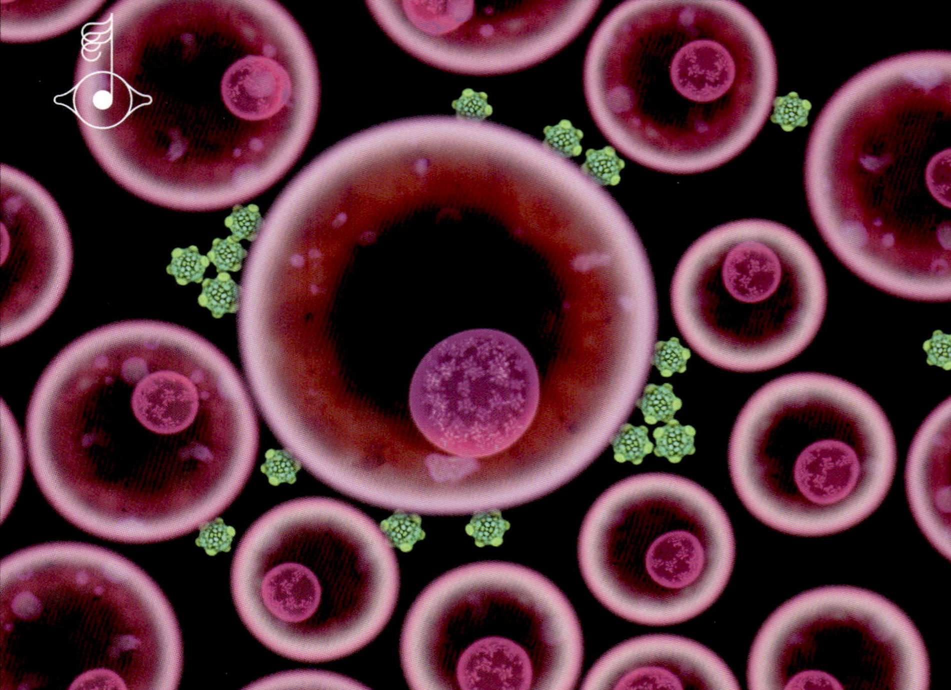

Virus

Solstice

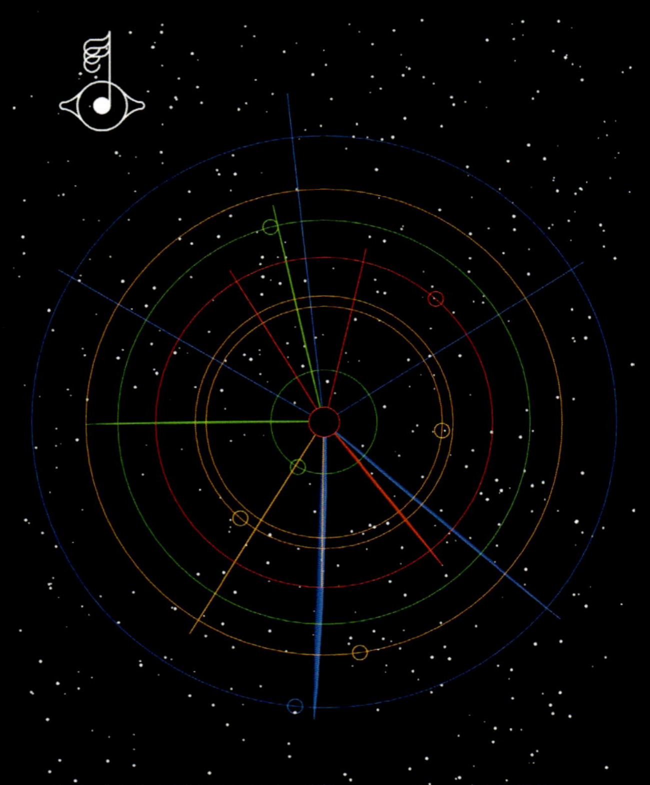

Hollow

The Stanley Parable

Davey Wreden (American, born 1988)

The Stanley Parable 2011
The Museum of Modern Art, New York.
Gift of the designer

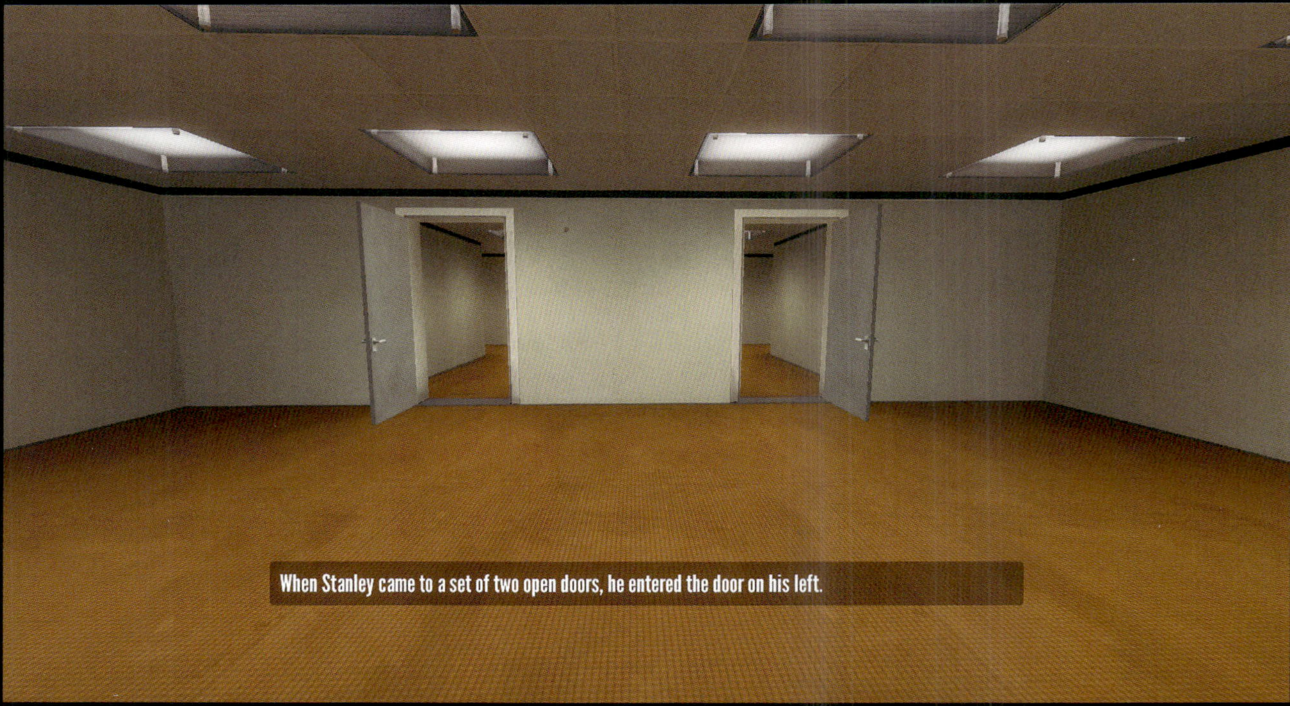

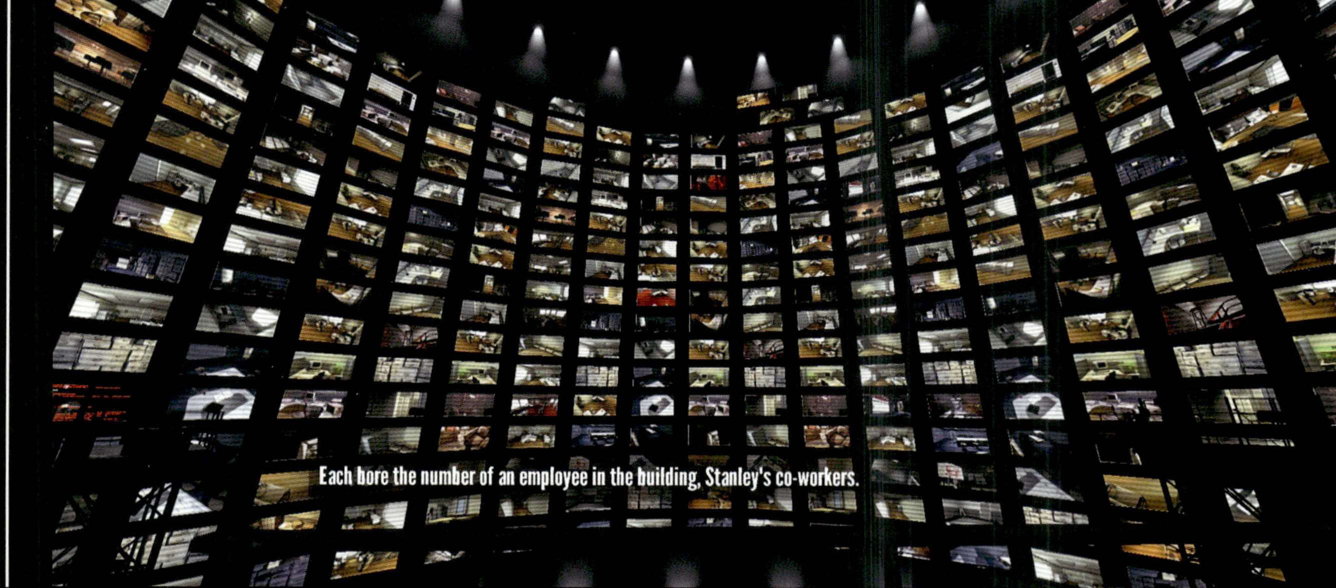

Early in The Stanley Parable, the game's title character, directed around a deserted office by the player, encounters two doors. The narrator informs us that Stanley "entered the door on his left." But Stanley is not obliged to go through the door on the left; Stanley can disobey the authoritative voice and choose the door on the right. This rebellious disregard for the dictates of the narrator (who is a stand-in for the designer) represents the ethos of the game: Stanley doesn't have to do what he's told. In this video game, it is the player who decides.

Stanley is presented with multiple opportunities for defiance. Like a choose-your-own-adventure novel, each option forces the narrative in a new direction. As Stanley deviates further from the prescribed path, the narrator grows increasingly exasperated and desperate to return to the original story, a rote dystopian tale. The branching storylines lead to nineteen possible endings, some hewing close to the ostensible "real" conclusion and others diverging from it in resolutions of pronounced absurdity (in one, the narrator drags Stanley into simulations of other video games — Minecraft [2011, page 120] and Portal [2005–07, page 72] — in a hopeless attempt to discern what this capricious, obstinate player wants). The player soon discovers that there is no larger — or more satisfying — objective than sticking a thumb in the narrator's eye; rebellion and the pursuit of freedom become the goal.

The game is a modification (or mod) of Valve Software's popular first-person-shooter game Half-Life 2 (2004) designed by Davey Wreden, using Source, Valve's game engine. The practice of modding has existed since the beginning of video-game history; computer programmers frequently tweak each other's code in pursuit of new functions and design directions. Such alterations are usually minor and iterative, but Wreden dismantled an entire action-packed, dramatic game and produced a completely different, altogether more humorous experience from its bones. (Two years after The Stanley Parable's release, Wreden collaborated with the game designer William Pugh on an ambitiously expanded remake.) Like Stanley, Wreden charted his own journey, and in doing so he demonstrated the ultimate power of the player: choice. Choosing is a creative act; from every small decision a cascade of consequences and possibilities blooms. Some choices are anticipated by the designer, who must account for an array of variables, including player behavior. But the last word always belongs to the player, who, when all else fails, has the power to quit. Or to make a new game. Or to pick the door on the right.

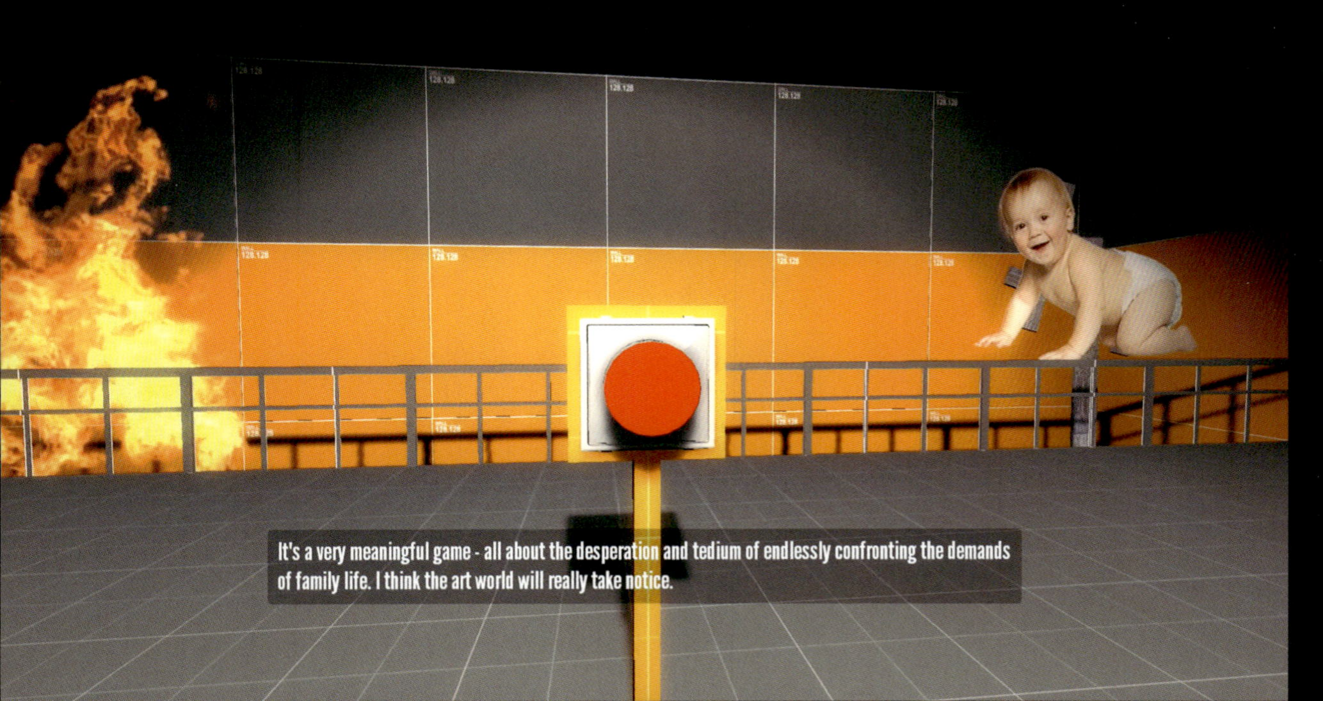

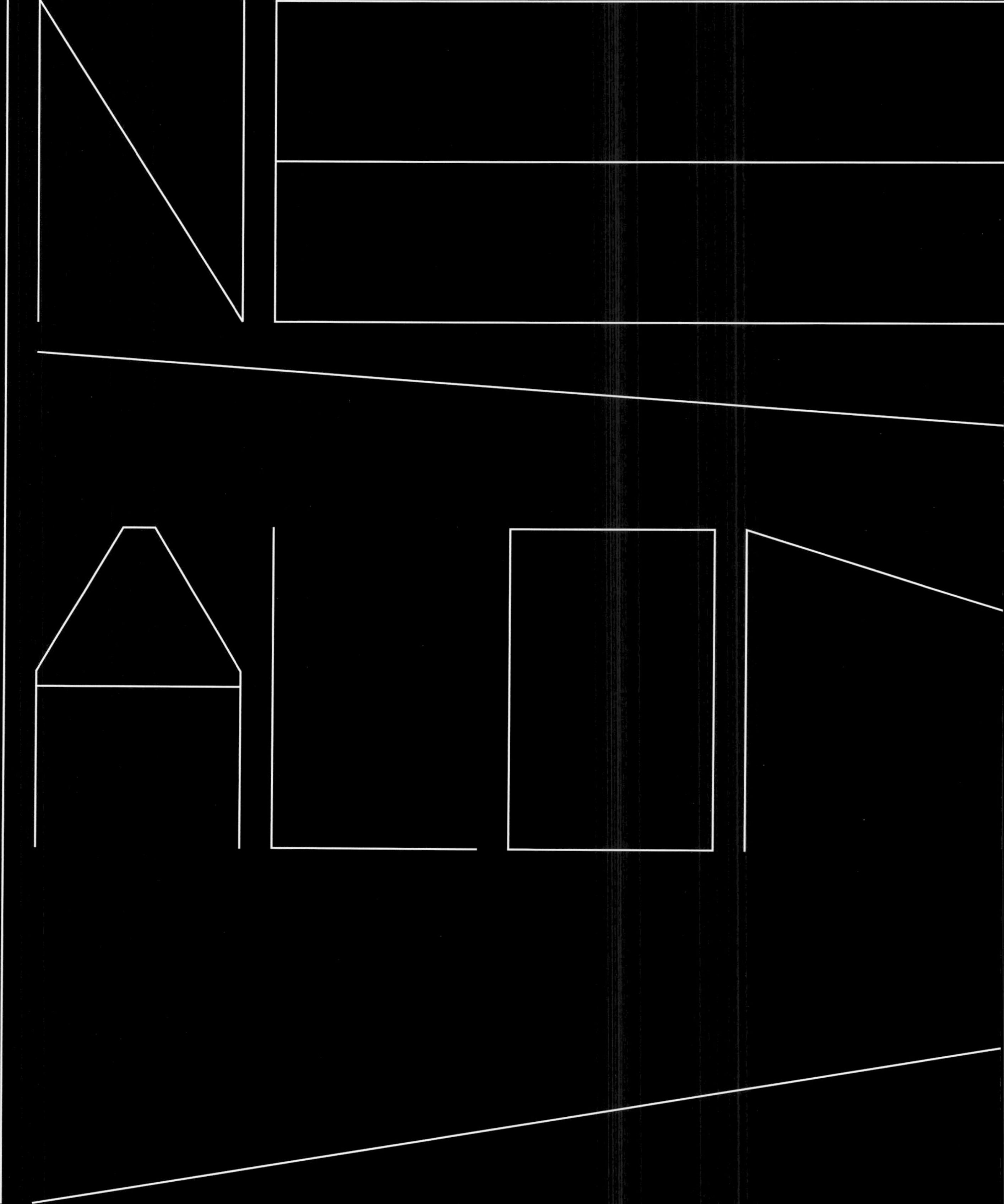

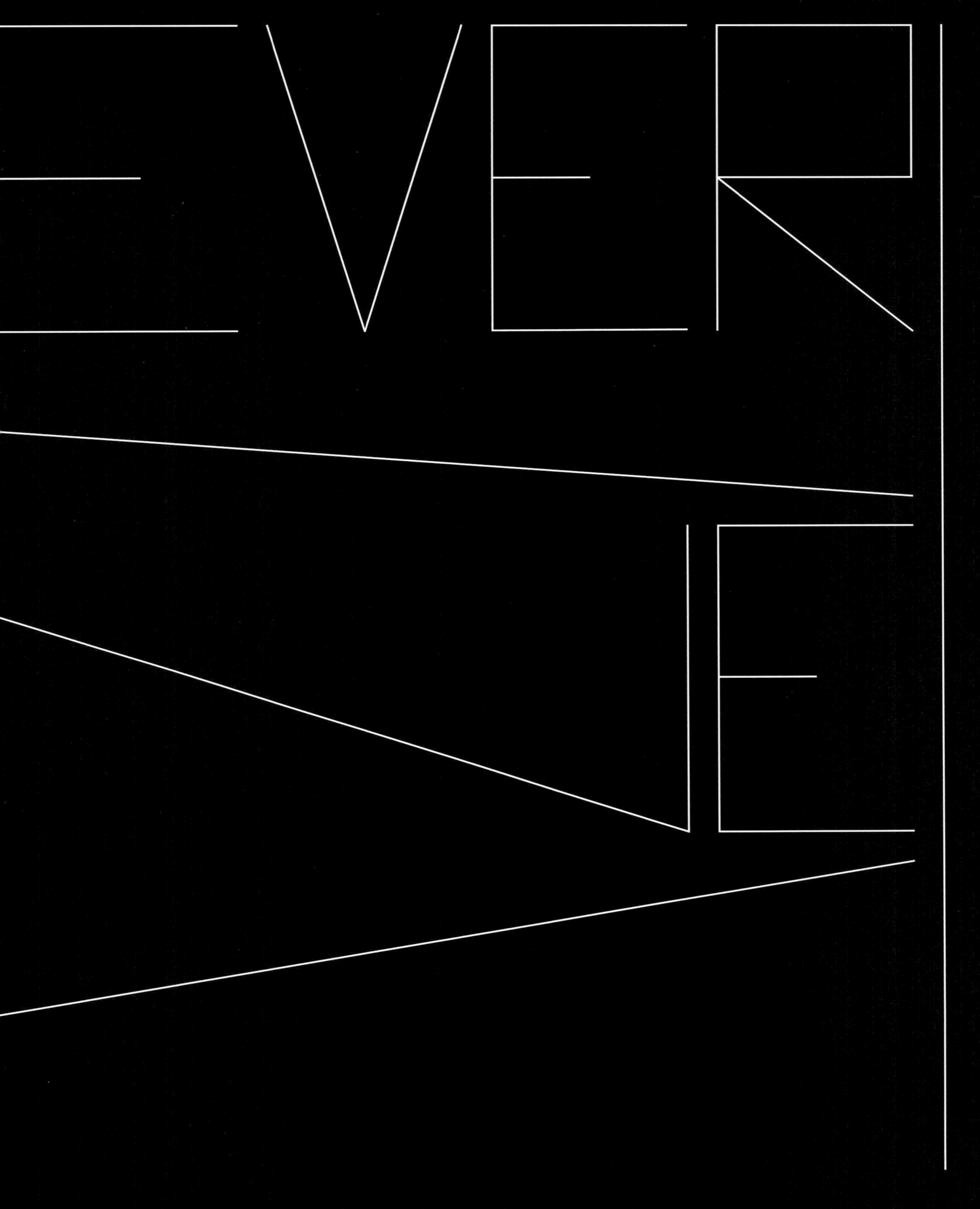

Glossary

adventure game an interactive story in which characters explore, gather resources, and solve puzzles.
→ Colossal Cave Adventure (1976), King's Quest (1980), Myst (1993, page 70), Zork (1977)

ASCII (American Standard Code for Information Interchange) a set of 7-bit characters, including the digits 0 to 9, the twenty-six letters of the English alphabet, and some special characters, designed in the early 1960s. The character-encoding standard allows computers and other electronic devices to communicate with each other in formats that can also be read by humans.

avatar the visual representation of the player in a game. These can be graphical renderings of a person (Inside [2016, page 90]), a creature, a simple icon, or even a single letter (NetHack [1987, page 46]).

B-game an obscure indie game, often notable for bizarre or clumsy controls and intentionally pulpy art. While B-games are rarely commercially successful, their emphasis on experimentation is highly influential.
→ Enviro-Bear 2000 (2010), Sexy Hiking (2002)

bit abbreviation of "binary digit." The smallest unit of computer data, representing one of two possible values, such as 1 or 0, true or false, on or off, yes or no. A computer's processing power is indicated by how many bits it can process at once; this capability dictates, among other things, the resolution of a video game's graphics: 8-bit games have fewer colors and pixels, for example, than 64-bit games.

CD-ROM (compact disc read-only memory) a pre-pressed disk for storing digital optical data that can be read by a personal computer. The high memory capacity of CD-ROMs (from 194 MB to 900 MB) allowed video-game software in the 1980s and '90s to include longer narratives and more complex graphics and audio.

coding the process of writing instructions for a computer to execute, often using one or more varieties of compilers, which translate code into various programming languages. In video games, code dictates every

feature of a game; the more complex the game, the more complex the code. In some games, the coder, artist, writer, and designer are the same person; in MMORPGs such as Eve Online (2003, page 118) hundreds of coders are necessary to keep the game functioning, often with multiple independent teams assigned to the upkeep of various technical aspects.

console a dedicated device for playing video games, usually with the capability of changing games via cartridges or game libraries stored in the device's memory.
→ Atari 2600, Microsoft Xbox, Nintendo Entertainment System, Sony PlayStation

construction and management simulation (CMS) a game in which players direct the allocation of resources for building and managing complex projects or communities. *See also* simulation game
→ Civilization (1991), Dwarf Fortress (2006, page 74), SimCity 2000 (1993, page 110)

display an output device for digital text and graphics, including televisions, computer monitors, and tablet and smartphone screens.

downloadable content (DLC)/expansions scenarios, items, and characters beyond those offered in a game's original format. Video-game publishers market these features as a way to continue player engagement and generate revenue, which in some cases ends up exceeding that of the original game's sales.

dungeon crawler a role-playing game in which characters explore underground mazes while battling monsters, gathering items, and avoiding traps.
→ Diablo (1997), Gauntlet (1985), NetHack (1987, page 46)

dynamic difficulty adjustment (DDA; *also* dynamic game balancing) programming that allows a game's level of challenge to respond in real time to player behavior. As an alternative to the traditional linear increase in difficulty and complexity, DDA can be used to balance competition (Super Mario Kart [1992]) or encourage a state of immersion (flOw [2007, page 78]

Easter egg a message, feature, item, or image hidden in a game's software. Easter eggs are often an inside joke, and they are difficult to find: usually it is only a game's dedicated fans that are able to locate and appreciate them.

emergent gameplay the player-devised situations and strategies that arise from a game that provides only basic rules and structure. It is related to emergent narrative—a story that develops through a player's interaction with a game's simple, nonlinear elements. *See also* sandbox game
→ Eve Online (2003, page 118), Minecraft (2011, page 120), The Sims (2000, page 114)

empathy game a game in which players direct characters in challenging or morally ambiguous situations and make choices based on emotional identification with them.
→ Papers, Please (2013, page 84), This War of Mine (2014, page 88)

endless runner a game in which a figure runs and avoids obstacles. These games typically feature fast-paced movement in one direction.
→ Canabalt (2009, page 54), Crossy Road (2014), Temple Run (2011)

e-sports short for electronic sports, which are competitive video games that often take place online and with multiple players.
→ Fortnite (2017), League of Legends (2009), Minecraft (2011, page 120)

fantasy game a narrative influenced by mythology, folklore, and legends, usually incorporating magic, monsters, and the supernatural. Other game genres often feature fantasy elements, including role-playing games, puzzle games, and simulations. *See also* RPG, roguelike
→ Elden Ring (2022), NetHack (1987, page 46), World of Warcraft (2004)

Flash game a browser game created with Adobe Flash software. In the early 2000s, when both Internet use and download speeds were rapidly increasing, they were a source of rich experiments with different kinds of gameplay. Thousands of independent Flash games reached the public, which laid the groundwork for the rise of indie games in the 2010s.
→ Canabalt (2009, page 54), flOw (2007, page 78), QWOP (2008)

freeware/shareware alternative models for software distribution, used extensively in the 1980s and '90s: freeware (such as Dwarf Fortress [2006, page 74]) is distributed at no cost to anyone who wishes to use it, and shareware (such as Doom [1993]) is free for trial periods or without access to the full functionality available for purchase.

game engine an efficient software-programming development tool. Before game engines, code for individual games had to be written from scratch. Prominent game engines such as Unreal Engine and Unity have been used as the foundation of thousands of games including Monument Valley (2014, page 56) and Inside (2016, page 90). Valve's Source engine was used to create Half-Life 2 (2004), Portal (2005–07, page 72), and other titles.

gameplay the user's actions (input) and the computer's responses (display, sound, haptic feedback).

gamer a person who plays video games, although the term can also be used to describe someone whose entire life revolves around them.

heightmap a memory-efficient way to create landscapes in video games.

indie game a video game produced by a smaller studio or individual. Like the films produced by independent studios, indie games are often notable for their emphasis on art and creative gameplay, in contrast to the advanced graphics and long, complex narratives favored by large corporate studios and enabled by their deep pockets.
→ Everything Is Going to Be OK (2017, page 92), flOw (2007, page 78), Flower (2009, page 80), Getting Over It with Bennett Foddy (2017, page 96), Journey (2012, page 82), Never Alone (2014, page 86), Papers, Please (2013, page 84), Return of the Obra Dinn (2018, page 98), Monument Valley (2014, page 56)

input device hardware that conveys information from user to a computer, either via the physical manipulation of a mouse, keyboard, controller, or touchscreen, or through motion sensors or speech and audio input.

interactive design (*also* **interaction design**) the design of the relationship between humans and electronic machines, or between humans via electronic machines—a field that includes interfaces, input and output devices, graphics, and audio. Thoughtful interactive design is vital for devices as everyday as ATM machines and smartphones and as critical as medical equipment and spacecraft.

iterative design a process that arrives at a design solution through repeated experimentation.

massively multiplayer online (MMO)/massively multiplayer online role-playing game (MMORPG) an online game in which players interact with others who are signed into the server at the same time. MMO games include first-person shooters, sports, and simulation games. MMORPGs are online role-playing games. *See also* role-playing game
→ Eve Online (2003, page 118), Fortnite (2017), Rocket League (2015), World of Warcraft (2004)

modding the practice of altering a video game to produce features not originally intended by the game's creator. Some mods are simple changes to a game, and others, such as The Stanley Parable (2011, page 126), repurpose a game's code to create a wholly different experience.

platform game (*also* platformer) an action game in which players move one or more characters across terrain and platforms by running, jumping, and climbing. In early platform games, such as Donkey Kong (1981), characters literally jump from platform to platform; in later games, such as Super Mario Bros. (1985), the character moves through a side-scrolling landscape, jumping on platforms, blocks, and other structures. Games in the puzzle-platform subgenre orient this dynamic around structural or narrative puzzles that the player must solve in order to progress.
→ Another World, (1991, page 90), Never Alone (2014, page 86), Portal (2005–07, page 72)

point-and-click game a style of game control in which actions are brought about via mouse click for a computer or finger tap on a touchscreen.
→ Monument Valley (2014, page 56), SimCity 2000 (1993, page 110)

procedural generation algorithmically created content—such as landscapes, music, and creatures—primarily employed to create randomness and a sense of surprise from level to level, or from game to game.
→ Minecraft (2011, page 120), NetHack (1987, page 46)

publisher the company that designs, markets, and releases a video game to the public, from small studios such as E-Line Media to corporate behemoths such as Sony and Microsoft.

roguelike a genre of role-playing adventure games descended from Rogue (1980), typically featuring a Dungeons & Dragons–style exploration of underground mazes in which the player gathers items, battles monsters, and fulfills a quest. *See also* role-playing game, fantasy game
→ Dwarf Fortress (2006, page 74), NetHack (1987, page 46)

role-playing game (RPG) an interactive storytelling game in which players assume the role of characters in a fictional setting and make choices that affect both the direction of the narrative and the growth of their character.
→ Eve Online (2003, page 118), NetHack (1987, page 46), Papers, Please (2013, page 84)

rotoscoping an animation technique in which film footage is traced or otherwise adapted to create correspondingly lifelike actions in another form such as a cartoon or a video game.

sandbox game an open-ended game in which players are given only a limited set of parameters, leaving them free to behave as they like without prompting or guidance. *See also* emergent gameplay
→ Minecraft (2011, page 120), SimCity 2000 (1993, page 110), The Sims (2000, page 114)

simulation game a game that mimics real-world activities or settings. *See also* construction and management simulation
→ SimCity 2000 (1993, page 110), The Sims (2000, page 114), This War of Mine (2014, page 88)

skin a downloadable feature that alters the appearance or abilities (or both) of avatars. Recent games such as Fortnite (2017) have heavily promoted the use of skins and other features for customizing the game's content, the sales of which make up the bulk of their revenue.

speed run an attempt to complete a game in as short a time as possible, often by identifying and exploiting its glitches and/or design flaws. Gamers often share videos documenting their record-breaking runs on Twitch and YouTube to showcase their techniques and inspire competition.

Usenet newsgroups the decentralized bulletin boards for sharing information that were the precursors to Internet forums. Usenet emerged from academia in the 1990s, when communication over the Internet was defined by smaller-scale collectives. NetHack (1987, page 46) grew out of a collaboration among coders via a Usenet group.

Index

Video games in MoMA's collection

Another World, 68–69
Asteroids, 19, 42–43, 46
Biophilia, 122–25
Canabalt, 54–55
Dwarf Fortress, 21, 24–25, 48, 63, 74–75
Eve Online, 22, 24, 24n19, 118–19
Everything Is Going to Be OK, 28, 62, 63, 92–95
flOw, 78–79
Flower, 80–81
Getting Over It with Bennett Foddy, 62–63, 96–97
Inside, 21, 90–91
Journey, 19, 28, 82–83
Katamari Damacy, 52–53
Magnavox Odyssey, 36–37, 39
Minecraft, 21, 26, 63n7, 104, 120–21
Monument Valley, 34, 56–57
Myst, 70–72
NetHack, 46–47, 48, 74, 104
Never Alone, 28, 29, 86–87
Pac-Man, 16, 23, 24n19, 33, 44–45
Papers, Please, 61–62, 84–85, 89, 97
Passage, 22, 76–77
Pong, 21, 33, 34, 37, 38–39, 103
Portal, 18, 24n19, 72–73
Return of the Obra Dinn, 22, 98–99
Sims, The, 24n19, 102–3, 114–15
SimCity 2000, 20–21, 110–13
Snake, 50–51, 55
Space Invaders, 40–41, 43, 65, 103
Stanley Parable, The, 19, 104–5, 126–27
Street Fighter II, 103, 106–9
Tempest, 64
Tetris, 48–49
This War of Mine, 88–89
Vib-Ribbon, 116–17
Yars' Revenge, 60, 66–67

Designers, artists, and producers

11 bit studios, 88–89
Adams, Tarn, 63n8, 74
Adams, Zach, 74
Alcorn, Allan, 42–43
Amzalag, Michael, 122
Armanto, Taneli, 50–51
Atari, 16, 28n28, 33, 37, 38–39, 42–43
    66–67
Augustyniak, Mathias, 122
Baer, Ralph, 36–37, 117
BANDAI NAMCO, 23, 44, 52
Bay 12 Games, 74
Björk, 122–24
Bushnell, Nolan, 28n28, 37, 39
Capcom, 106
CCP Games, 118–19
Chahi, Éric, 68–69
Chen, Jenova (Xinghan), 28, 61, 78–8
Clark, Nicholas, 61, 78–79
Cook Inlet Tribal Council, 86–87
Cyan, 70
Danks, Mark, 122
Dibben, Nikki, 122
Electronic Arts, 110, 114
E-Line Media, 86–87
Foddy, Bennett, 62, 63, 96–97
Hope, Ishmael Angaluuk, 86–87
Iwatani, Toru, 44
Kodama Studios, 122
Lawhead, Nathalie, 23 (fig. 13), 28, 62
Logg, George "Ed," 42–43
Magnavox, 36–37, 39
Malinowski, Stephen, 122
Matsuura, Masaya, 116–17
Maxis, 110, 114
Miller, Rand, 70
Miller, Robyn, 70
M/M Paris, 122
Mojang, 120
NanaOn-Sha, 116
NetHack DevTeam, 46–47
Nishikado, Tomohiro, 40–41
Nokia Corporation, 50–51, 55
Okamoto, Yoshiki, 106
Pajitnov, Alexey, 48

Persson, Markus "Notch," 120–21
Playdead, 90
Pope, Lucas, 61–62, 84, 98–99
Rains, Lyle, 42–43
RelativeWave, 122
Rohrer, Jason, 76–77
Saltsman, Adam, 54–55
Simon, John F., Jr., 122
Sjón (Sigurjón Birgir Sigurðsson), 122
Snibbe, Scott, 122
Sony, 53, 79, 83, 116, 117
Stephenson, Mike, 46
Stocker, Sarah, 122
Swift, Kim, 73
Taito Corporation, 40–41
Takahashi, Keita, 52–53
thatgamecompany, 61, 78–83
Theurer, Dave, 64–65
Touch Press, 122
ustwo games, 56
Valve, 72, 127
Warshaw, Howard Scott, 60, 66–67
Weisel, Max, 122
Wong, Ken, 56
Wreden, Davey, 105, 126–27
Wright, Will, 110, 114
Yasuda, Akira, 106

Acknowledgments

Like the creation of a video game, the development of an exhibition and a publication is a complex endeavor with multiple moving parts—and ample opportunities for problems to arise. *Never Alone* came to fruition thanks to the invaluable support of so many colleagues and partners who offered advice, lent support, and, in a sense, debugged our program. We express our heartfelt gratitude to the many people without whom our efforts never would have seen the light of day.

For their vital support, we thank Glenn D. Lowry, The David Rockefeller Director of The Museum of Modern Art, and MoMA's Board of Trustees.

We are deeply grateful for the leaders of the MoMA departments that helped make *Never Alone* happen, including Lana Hum, Director, Exhibition Design and Production; Kate Lewis, The Agnes Gund Chief Conservator, Conservation; Sarah Suzuki, Associate Director; and Christy Thompson, Senior Deputy Director, Exhibitions and Collections. Our special thanks go to Martino Stierli, The Philip Johnson Chief Curator, Department of Architecture and Design, for his continued support and advocacy on our behalf.

The members of our core team have been stellar. Among them, we celebrate Hiroko Ishikawa, Exhibition Designer, Exhibition Design and Production, whose patience and creativity ensured a beautiful presentation for the public; Chloe Capewell, Exhibition Manager, Exhibition Planning and Administration, whose nimble organization and keen attention to detail kept us on track and on schedule; and Steven Wheeler, Associate Registrar, Collection Management and Exhibition Registration, who managed the shipping, logistics, and care of objects with good humor and aplomb. We thank Rob Jung, Manager, and Tom Krueger, Assistant Manager, Art Handling and Preparation, along with their dedicated team.

We are hugely indebted to the many members of the Department of Conservation, past and present, who guided us toward the realization of our cockamamie dream of bringing video games to MoMA. Glenn Wharton, former Media Conservator, Ben Fino-Radin, former Assistant Media Conservator, and Lynda Zycherman, Sculpture Conservator, were there from the beginning, later joined by Annie Wilker, Associate Paper Conservator. We especially thank Peter Oleksik, Media Conservator, whose collaborative spirit and brilliance has ensured that MoMA can share these important works with the public, now and into the future.

We are grateful to our colleagues in our own department, including Kate Carmody, former Curatorial Assistant; Michelle Millar Fisher, former Curatorial Assistant; Shayna Gentiluomo, former Department Assistant; and Pamela Popeson, former Preparator.

We owe special thanks to the many external partners who helped us with our research and acquisition, especially the designers, publishers, and companies who donated video games to the collection. Without their generosity, enthusiastic participation, and creative wrangling of legal issues, this project would never have happened. From the very beginning we were guided by the crucial input of a design panel, convened in 2006, with Tarek Atrissi, Michael Bierut, Matthew Carter, Hillman Curtis, Peter Girardi, Emily King, Rick Poynor, Mikon van Gastel, and Khoi Vinh, and with organizational help from Christian Larsen. Later, we benefitted from advice offered by Jamin Warren, Ryan Kuo, Kevin Slavin, and Chris Romero. In 2012, as part of a forum on games in contemporary art and design, an esteemed group of artists and scholars significantly expanded our thinking: our thanks to Coco Fusco, Frank Lantz, James Paul Gee, Hannah Higgins, Pippin Barr, Scott Snibbe, Daphne Dragona, Susan Laxton, Pekko Koskinen, Pedro Reyes, Mary Flanagan, and Erica Gangsei.

To the many colleagues who have been working with video games at other museums: we stand on your shoulders and walk the path with you. Thank you to Natalie D. Kane, Curator, Victoria and Albert Museum, London; Alex Handy and all the inspiring staff at Museum of Art and Digital Entertainment, Oakland, California; and Jason Eppink, former Curator, Museum of the Moving Image, Queens, New York, as well as to our colleagues at the Computer History Museum, Mountain View, California; the Smithsonian American Art Museum, Washington, DC; Computerspielemuseum, Berlin; and the Strong National Museum of Play, Rochester, New York. And our profound thanks go to the curator and games doyenne Marie Foulston for her irrepressible wit and wisdom and for helping us think about players as creative voices in their own right.

Our deep gratitude goes to MoMA's indefatigable Department of Publications, without whose expert guidance this tome would not be in your hands. The book was edited by Emily Hall, Editor, with the support of Don McMahon, Editorial Director. We also owe many thanks to Curtis Scott, Associate Publisher, and Hannah Kim, Business and Marketing Director, for their help in making this book a reality, and to Marc Sapir, Production Director, and Matthew Pimm, Production Manager, for bringing it to life. Every page was skillfully proofread by Lynn Scrabis, Rebecca Roberts, Editor, and Jackie Neudorf, Assistant Editor. Choi Sulki and Choi Sung Min of Sulki and Min channeled the spirit and aesthetics of video games to create this book's singular design.

We extend wholehearted thanks to the people who made the exhibition's physical manifestation possible, including Elle Kim, former Director of Design, Claire Corey, Production Manager, Damien Saatdjian, former Associate Director of Design, Prin Limphongpand, Senior Graphic Designer, and Christie Zhong, Graphic Designer, Creative Team; Chay Costello, Associate Director, Retail Merchandising, Karen Hernandez, Senior Product Manager, and Michelle Campo, Licensing Manager, Retail; and Anna Luisa Vallifuoco, Manager of Institutional Giving, Global Partnerships. In Exhibition Design and Production we thank Peter Perez, Foreman, Frame Shop, and his team of brilliant framers; Paul Errico, James Allgeier, and their steadfast and hardworking team of painters; Sean Brown, Foreman, Lighting Studio, and his team, including Ray Martin and Andrew Tedeschi, Mechanics; Allan Smith, Foreman, Carpenter Shop, Jason Fry, Lead Carpenter, and their dedicated team of carpenters, including Craig Anderson, Chris DaSilva, Graham Stockmayer, and John Wood. We are particularly indebted to Mike Gibbons, AV Exhibitions Foreperson, Aaron Harrow, AV Design Manager, Travis Kray, AV Tech, and the rest of the stellar Audio Visual department; and to our colleagues in Information Technology, in particular to Matias Pacheco, Senior Manager, Client Services, Luis Pascual, Client Service Specialist, and Jean Paul Guerrero, Helpdesk and Desktop Support.

In the Museum's Creative Team, we thank Michelle Pae, Director of Digital Product; Rebecca Stokes, Director, Marketing Campaigns and Audience Development; Prudence Peiffer, Managing Editor; Jason Persse, Editorial Manager; Sarah Cowan, Senior Video Producer; Allison Knoll, Digital Marketing Manager; Alex Halberstadt, Senior Writer; and Francesca Lo Galbo, Administrative Assistant. Special thanks to Elizabeth Margulies, Director, Family Programs and Resources, in the Department of Learning and Engagement, whose early commitment to the exhibition helped ensure its reach beyond the Museum's galleries.

We also wish to recognize the contributions of MoMA colleagues past and present, including Alexis Sandler, Nancy Adelson, Henry Lanman, Ava Childers, and James Grooms, in the General Counsel's office; Sara Bodinson, Director, and Oriana Gonzales, Associate Educator, Interpretation, Research, and Digital Learning, in the Department of Learning and Engagement; Sara Beth Walsh, Manager, and Olivia Oramas, Publicist, in Communications and Public Affairs.

Finally, from each of us, a sustained thanks to our partners Larry Carty, Erin Manning, and Kimi Weart, without whose support none of this would have been possible.

Paola Antonelli
Anna Burckhardt
Paul Galloway

Allianz ⑪

The exhibition is made possible by Allianz, MoMA's
partner for design and innovation, and supporter of
programs that look to a more sustainable future.

Major support is provided by UNIQLO, MoMA's proud
partner of #ArtForAll.

Leadership contributions to the Annual Exhibition
Fund, in support of the Museum's collection and
collection exhibitions, are generously provided by
Sue and Edgar Wachenheim III, Jerry I. Speyer and
Katherine G. Farley, the Sandra and Tony Tamer
Exhibition Fund, The Contemporary Arts Council of
The Museum of Modern Art, Eva and Glenn Dubin,
the Kate W. Cassidy Foundation, Alice and Tom
Tisch, Mimi Haas, the Noel and Harriette Levine
Endowment, The David Rockefeller Council, the
William Randolph Hearst Endowment Fund, the
Marella and Giovanni Agnelli Fund for Exhibitions,
Anne Dias, Kathy and Richard S. Fuld, Jr., Kenneth C.
Griffin, The International Council of The Museum of
Modern Art, Marie-Josée and Henry R. Kravis, and Jo
Carole and Ronald S. Lauder.

Major contributions to the Annual Exhibition Fund are
provided by The Junior Associates of The Museum
of Modern Art, Emily Rauh Pulitzer, Brett and Daniel
Sundheim, Karen and Gary Winnick, and Anna Marie
and Robert F. Shapiro.

Additional funding is provided by the Dale S. and
Norman Mills Leff Publication Fund.

Published in conjunction with the exhibition
Never Alone: Video Games and Other Interactive Design,
at The Museum of Modern Art, New York,
September 10, 2022–July 16, 2023.
Organized by Paola Antonelli, Senior Curator,
Paul Galloway, Collection Specialist, and
Anna Burckhardt, Curatorial Assistant, Department of
Architecture and Design

The exhibition is made possible by Allianz, MoMA's
partner for design and innovation, and supporter of
programs that look to a more sustainable future.

Major support is provided by UNIQLO, MoMA's proud
partner of #ArtForAll.

Leadership contributions to the Annual Exhibition Fund,
in support of the Museum's collection and collection
exhibitions, are generously provided by Sue and
Edgar Wachenheim III, Jerry I. Speyer and Katherine G.
Farley, the Sandra and Tony Tamer Exhibition Fund,
The Contemporary Arts Council of The Museum of
Modern Art, Eva and Glenn Dubin, the Kate W. Cassidy
Foundation, Alice and Tom Tisch, Mimi Haas, the Noel
and Harriette Levine Endowment, The David Rockefeller
Council, the William Randolph Hearst Endowment Fund,
the Marella and Giovanni Agnelli Fund for Exhibitions,
Anne Dias, Kathy and Richard S. Fuld, Jr., Kenneth C.
Griffin, The International Council of The Museum of
Modern Art, Marie-Josée and Henry R. Kravis, and Jo
Carole and Ronald S. Lauder.

Major contributions to the Annual Exhibition Fund are
provided by The Junior Associates of The Museum
of Modern Art, Emily Rauh Pulitzer, Brett and Daniel
Sundheim, Karen and Gary Winnick, and Anna Marie and
Robert F. Shapiro.

Additional funding is provided by the Dale S. and
Norman Mills Leff Publication Fund.

Produced by the Department of Publications
The Museum of Modern Art, New York

Hannah Kim, Business and Marketing Director
Don McMahon, Editorial Director
Marc Sapir, Production Director
Curtis R. Scott, Associate Publisher

Edited by Emily Hall
Designed by Sulki and Min, Seoul
Production by Matthew Pimm
Proofread by Lynn Scrabis, with Rebecca Roberts and Jackie Neudorf
Color separations by t'Ink, Brussels
Printed and bound by Graphius, Belgium

This book is typeset in Unica77 LL.
The paper is 150 gsm Magno Satin.

Published by The Museum of Modern Art
11 West 53 Street
New York, NY 10019-5497
www.moma.org

Library of Congress Control Number: 2022939990
ISBN: 978-1-63345-141-4

Distributed in the United States and Canada by
ARTBOOK I D.A.P.
75 Broad Street, Suite 630
New York, NY 10004
www.artbook.com

Distributed outside the United States and Canada by
Thames & Hudson
181A High Holborn
London WC1V 7QX
www.thamesandhudson.com

Printed in Belgium